NorthStar

Focus on Reading and Writing

Advanced

Judy L. Miller

Robert F. Cohen

SERIES EDITORS
Frances Boyd
Carol Numrich

 LONGMAN

NorthStar: Focus on Reading and Writing, Advanced

Pearson Education, 10 Bank Street, White Plains, NY 10606

Senior acquisitions editor: Allen Ascher
Director of design and production: Rhea Banker
Development editor: Carolyn Viola-John
Production manager: Marie McNamara
Managing editor: Halley Gatenby
Production editor: Linda Moser
Manufacturing supervisor: Edith Pullman
Photo research: Aerin Csigay
Cover design: Rhea Banker
Cover illustration: Robert Delaunay's *Circular Forms, Sun No. 2*,
     1912–1913. Giraudon/Art Resources, NY. L&M Services B.V.
     Amsterdam 970902
Text design and composition: Delgado Design, Inc.
Text credits: see page xiii
Photo and art credits: see page xiv

Library of Congress Cataloging-in-Publication Data

Miller, Judy L.
     NorthStar.   Focus on reading and writing, advanced / Judy L.
     Miller, Robert F. Cohen
               p.   cm.
          ISBN 0-201-69421-2 (pbk.)
      1. English Language—Textbooks for foreign speakers. 2. English
     language—Problems, exercises, etc. 3. Reading comprehension—
     Problems, exercises etc. 4. Report writing—Problems, exercises, etc.
     I. Cohen, Robert F.   II. Title
     PE1128.M57 1998   97-41539
     428.2'4—dc21   CIP

4 5 6 7 8 9 10-RTN-02 01 00 99

To my parents, Sylvia Sondak and Ben Miller, and to my
daughter, Ariana Jessica Miller

JLM

To my mother, Lillian Kumock Cohen

RFC

CONTENTS

INTRODUCTION

NorthStar is an innovative four-level, integrated skills series for learners of English as a Second or Foreign Language. The series is divided into two strands: listening/speaking and reading/writing. There are four books in each strand, taking students from the Basic to the Advanced level. The two books at each level explore different aspects of the same contemporary themes, which allows for reinforcement of both vocabulary and grammatical structures. Each strand and each book can also function independently as a skills course built on high-interest thematic content.

NorthStar is designed to work alongside Addison Wesley Longman's *Focus on Grammar* series, and students are referred directly to *Focus on Grammar* for further practice and detailed grammatical explanations.

NorthStar is written for students with academic as well as personal language goals, for those who want to learn English while exploring enjoyable, intellectually challenging themes.

NORTHSTAR'S PURPOSE

The *NorthStar* series grows out of our experience as teachers and curriculum designers, current research in second-language acquisition and pedagogy, as well as our beliefs about language teaching. It is based on five principles.

Principle One: In language learning, making meaning is all-important. The more profoundly students are stimulated intellectually and emotionally by what goes on in class, the more language they will use and retain. One way that classroom teachers can engage students in making meaning is by organizing language study thematically.

We have tried to identify themes that are up-to-date, sophisticated, and varied in tone— some lighter, some more serious—on ideas and issues of wide concern. The forty themes in *NorthStar* provide stimulating topics for the readings and the listening selections, including why people like dangerous sports, the effect of food on mood, an Olympic swimmer's fight against AIDS, experimental punishments for juvenile offenders, people's relationships with their cars, philanthropy, emotional intelligence, privacy in the workplace, and the influence of arts education on brain development.

Each corresponding unit of the integrated skills books explores two distinct topics related to a single theme as the chart below illustrates.

Theme	Listening/Speaking Topic	Reading/Writing Topic
Insects	Offbeat professor fails at breeding pests, then reflects on experience	Extract adapted Kafka's "The Metamorphosis"
Personality	Shyness, a personal and cultural view	Definition of, criteria for, success

Principle Two: Second-language learners, particularly adults, need and want to learn both the form and content of the language. To accomplish this, it is useful to integrate language skills with the study of grammar, vocabulary, and American culture.

In *NorthStar*, we have integrated the skills in two strands: listening/speaking and reading/writing. Further, each thematic unit integrates the study of a grammatical point with related vocabulary and cultural information. When skills are integrated, language use inside of the classroom more closely mimics language use outside of the classroom. This motivates students. At the same time, the focus can shift back and forth from what is said to how it is said to the relationship between the two. Students are apt to use more of their senses, more of themselves. What goes on in the class-room can also appeal to a greater variety of learning styles. Gradually, the integrated-skills approach narrows the gap between the ideas and feelings students want to express in speaking and writing and their present level of English proficiency.

The link between the listening/speaking and reading/writing strands is close enough to allow students to explore the themes and review grammar and reinforce vocabulary, yet it is distinct enough to sustain their interest. Also, language levels and grammar points in *NorthStar* are keyed to Addison Wesley Longman's *Focus on Grammar* series.

Principle Three: Both teachers and students need to be active learners. Teachers must encourage students to go beyond whatever level they have reached.

With this principle in mind, we have tried to make the exercises creative, active, and varied. Several activities call for considered opinion and critical thinking. Also, the exercises offer students many opportunities for individual reflection, pair- and small-group learning, as well as out-of-class assignments for review and research. An answer key is printed on perfo-

rated pages in the back of each book so the teacher or students can remove it. A teacher's manual, which accompanies each book, features ideas and tips for tailoring the material to individual groups of students, planning the lessons, managing the class, and assessing students' progress.

Principle Four: Feedback is essential for language learners and teachers. If students are to become better able to express themselves in English, they need a response to both what they are expressing and how they are expressing it.

NorthStar's exercises offer multiple opportunities for oral and written feedback from fellow students and from the teacher. A number of open-ended opinion and inference exercises invite students to share and discuss their answers. In Information Gap, Fieldwork, and Presentation activities, students must present and solicit information and opinions from their peers as well as members of their communities. Throughout these activities, teachers may offer feedback on the form and content of students' language, sometimes on the spot and sometimes via audio/video recordings or notes.

Principle Five: The quality of relationships among the students and between the students and teacher is important, particularly in a language class where students are asked to express themselves on issues and ideas.

The information and activities in *NorthStar* promote genuine interaction, acceptance of differences, and authentic communication. By building skills and exploring ideas, the exercises help students participate in discussions and write essays of an increasingly more complex and sophisticated nature.

DESIGN OF THE UNITS

For clarity and ease of use, the listening/speaking and reading/writing strands follow the same unit outline given below. Each unit contains from 5 to 8 hours of classroom material. Teachers can customize the units by assigning some exercises for homework and/or skipping others. Exercises in sections 1–4 are essential for comprehension of the topic, while teachers may want to select among the activities in sections 5–7.

1. Approaching the Topic

A warm-up, these activities introduce students to the general context for listening or reading and get them personally connected to the topic. Typically, students might react to a visual image, describe a personal experience, or give an opinion orally or in writing.

2. Preparing to Listen/Preparing to Read

In this section, students are introduced to information and language to help them comprehend the specific tape or text they will study. They might read and react to a paragraph framing the topic, prioritize factors, or take a general-knowledge quiz and share information. In the vocabulary section, students work with words and expressions selected to help them with comprehension.

3. Listening One/Reading One

This sequence of four exercises guides students to listen or read with understanding and enjoyment by practicing the skills of (a) prediction, (b) comprehension of main ideas, (c) comprehension of details, and (d) inference. In activities of increasing detail and complexity, students learn to grasp and interpret meaning. The sequence culminates in an inference exercise that gets students to listen and read between the lines.

4. Listening Two/Reading Two

Here students work with a tape or text that builds on ideas from the first listening/reading. This second tape or text contrasts with the first in viewpoint, genre, and/or tone.

Activities ask students to explicitly relate the two pieces, consider consequences, distinguish and express points of view. In these exercises, students can attain a deeper understanding of the topic.

5. Reviewing Language

These exercises help students explore, review, and play with language from both of the selections. Using the thematic context, students focus on language: pronunciation, word forms, prefixes and suffixes, word domains, idiomatic expressions, analogies. The listening/speaking strand stresses oral exercises, while the reading/writing strand focuses on written responses.

6. Skills for Expression

Here students practice related grammar points across the theme in both topics. The grammar is practiced orally in the listening/speaking strand, and in writing in the reading/writing strand. For additional practice, teachers can turn to Addison Wesley Longman's *Focus on Grammar*, to which *NorthStar* is keyed by level and grammar points. In the Style section, students practice functions (listening/speaking) or rhetorical styles (reading/writing) that prepare them to express ideas on a higher level. Within each unit, students are led from controlled to freer practice of productive skills.

7. On Your Own

These activities ask students to apply the content, language, grammar, and style they have practiced in the unit. The exercises elicit a higher level of speaking or writing than students were capable of at the start of the unit. Speaking topics include role plays, surveys, presentations and experiments. Writing topics include paragraphs, letters, summaries and academic essays.

In Fieldwork, the second part of On Your Own, students go outside of the classroom, using their knowledge and skills to gather data from personal interviews, library research, and telephone or Internet research. They report and reflect on the data in oral or written presentations to the class.

AN INVITATION

We think of a good textbook as a musical score or a movie script: It tells you the moves and roughly how quickly and in what sequence to make them. But until you and your students bring it to life, a book is silent and static, a mere possibility. We hope that *NorthStar* orients, guides, and interests you as teachers.

It is our hope that the *NorthStar* series stimulates your students' thinking, which in turn stimulates their language learning, and that they will have many opportunities to reflect on the viewpoints of journalists, commentators, researchers, other students, and people in the community. Further, we hope that *NorthStar* guides them to develop their own viewpoint on the many and varied themes encompassed by this series.

We welcome your comments and questions. Please send them to us at the publisher:

Frances Boyd and Carol Numrich, Editors
NorthStar
Addison Wesley Longman
10 Bank Street
White Plains, NY 10606-1951
or, by e-mail at:
aw/elt@awl.com

ACKNOWLEDGMENTS

This project would have never come to fruition without the kind support and sincere dedication of many people.

Our greatest debt is to Carol Numrich, whose expertise, optimism, and creative insight nurtured the growth of this book at every stage of its development. We are also grateful to Frances Boyd, whose expression of confidence in our work was a constant source of encouragement.

In addition, we would like to thank the staff at Longman for all their help: Carolyn Viola-John, whose sensitivity and artistry as an editor was our good fortune, and Linda Moser, whose support and patience got this project through the last round of production. We thank Allen Ascher for giving us the opportunity to participate in this project, Penny Laporte for her advice and support, and Aerin Csigay for helping us to negotiate the labyrinthine process of securing permissions.

Finally, our heartfelt thanks go to our colleagues at the American Language Program, Columbia University, and to our students, who are our inspiration.

JLM and RFC

Text Credits

Photo and Art Credits

MY TIME IN A BOTTLE

1 APPROACHING THE TOPIC

A. PREDICTING

Look at the title of this unit and the photo of Mickey Mantle when he was elected to the Baseball Hall of Fame in 1974. What do you think "My Time in a Bottle" refers to? Write some notes about what you expect to read in this unit. Talk about your notes with a partner, and discuss what you already know about Mickey Mantle.

B. SHARING INFORMATION

Mickey Mantle credited his skill as a baseball player to the influence of one person. Think of all the people who have influenced your development as a person. What did they contribute to your personality? Was their influence always positive? How old were you when their influence was felt? Fill in the following chart. Then share your answers with a small group.

WHO INFLUENCED YOU?	HOW DID THIS PERSON INFLUENCE YOU?	HOW OLD WERE YOU?
Family member		
Friend		
Teacher or religious leader		
National celebrity (athlete, politician, movie star, performer)		
Other		

PREPARING TO READ

A. BACKGROUND

Read this information and do the exercise that follows.

Mickey Mantle was one of the greatest baseball players of all time. He played for the New York Yankees in their years of glory. From the time Mantle began to play in 1951 to his last year in 1968, baseball was the most popular game in the United States. For many people, Mantle symbolized the hope, prosperity, and confidence of America at that time.

Mantle was a fast and powerful player, a "switch-hitter" who could bat both right-handed and left-handed. He won game after game, one World Series championship after another, for his team. He was a wonderful athlete, but this alone cannot explain America's fascination with him.

Perhaps it was because he was a handsome, red-haired country boy, the son of a poor miner from Oklahoma. His career, from the lead mines of the West to the heights of success and fame, was a fairy-tale version of the American dream. Or perhaps it was because America always loves a "natural": a person who wins without seeming to try, whose talent appears to come from an inner grace. That was Mickey Mantle.

But like many celebrities, Mickey Mantle had a private life that was full of problems. He played without complaint despite constant pain from injuries. He lived to fulfill his father's dreams and drank to forget his father's early death. Alcohol was part of his friendships, his family life, his retirement distractions.

It was alcoholism that finally destroyed his body. It gave him cirrhosis of the liver and accelerated the advance of liver cancer. Even when Mickey Mantle had turned away from his old life and warned young people not to follow his example, the destructive process could not be stopped. Despite a liver transplant operation that had all those who loved and admired him hoping for a recovery, Mickey Mantle died of cancer at the age of sixty-three.

We all have a public life and a private life, but people who are much in the public eye like Mickey Mantle are forced to pay a price for fame. Many sports players, fashion models, and others become celebrities but do not necessarily have happy lives. Complete the following sentences and compare your answers with a partner.

1. Many people want to become famous because _____

_____

2. Some celebrities become famous because _____

_____

3. People want to know everything about celebrities because _____

_____

4. We admire sports heroes because _____

_____

B. VOCABULARY FOR COMPREHENSION

Work in a small group and help each other to guess the meaning of the highlighted words based on your knowledge of English. In each set of words, underline the two words that have similar meanings to the word in bold letters on the left. Use your dictionaries if necessary. The first one has been done for you.

1. **hereditary**	<u>genetic</u>	<u>inherited</u>	environmental
2. **tough**	delicate	demanding	strong
3. **devastated**	cynical	crushed	desolate
4. **depression**	dejection	gloom	thrill
5. **controversial**	debatable	agreeable	disputable
6. **choked up**	filled with tears	unable to speak	unable to breathe
7. **sober**	dry	intoxicated	abstinent
8. **donor**	supplier	receiver	giver

3 READING ONE: My Time in a Bottle

A. INTRODUCING THE TOPIC

Before you read, discuss this question with a partner.

What effect can a parent's addiction have on a child?

Mickey Mantle with his parents and family.

By Mickey Mantle (from *Sports Illustrated*)

My Time in a Bottle

1   If alcoholism is hereditary, if it's in the genes, then I think mine came from my mother's side of the family. Her brothers were all alcoholics. My mother, Lovell, and my father, Mutt, weren't big drinkers. Dad would buy a pint of whiskey on Saturday night and put it in the icebox. Then every night when he came home from working eight hours in the lead mines of Oklahoma, he'd head for the icebox and take a swig[1] of whiskey.

2   My Dad loved baseball, played semi-professional ball on the weekends and was a tremendous St. Louis Cardinals fan. In fact, he named me after Mickey Cochrane, the Hall of Fame catcher for Philadelphia and Detroit who was a great hitter. Dad had high hopes for me. He thought I could be the greatest ballplayer who ever lived, and he did everything to help me realize his dream.

3   Even though he was dog tired after long days at the mine, Dad would still pitch batting practice to me in the backyard when he got home from work, beginning from the time I was four years old. My mother would call us to dinner, but the meal would wait until Dad was finished instructing me from the right and left sides of the plate. Dad was a tough man. If I'd done something wrong, he could just look at me—he didn't have to say anything—and I'd say, "I won't do it no more, Dad." I loved my father, although I couldn't tell him that, just like he couldn't tell me.

---

[1] *swig:* a gulp of a liquid, usually alcohol

4   I joined the Yankees at 19. The following spring, when Dad died of Hodgkin's disease[2] at age 39, I was devastated, and that's when I started drinking. I guess alcohol helped me escape the pain of losing him.

5   God gave me a great body to play with, and I didn't take care of it. And I blame a lot of it on alcohol. Everyone likes to make the excuse that injuries shortened my career. Truth is, after I'd had a knee operation, the doctors would give me rehab[3] work to do, but I wouldn't do it. I'd be out drinking. . . . Everything had always come naturally to me. I didn't work hard at it.

6   After I retired at 37, my drinking got really bad. I went through a deep depression. Billy Martin, Whitey Ford, Hank Bauer, Moose Skowron [my Yankee teammates], I left all those guys and I think it left a hole in me . . . We were as close as brothers. I haven't met anyone else I've felt as close to.

7   I never thought about anything serious in my life for a continuous period of days and weeks until I checked into the Betty Ford Center.[4] I've always tried to avoid anything emotional, anything controversial, anything serious, and I did it through the use of alcohol. Alcohol always protected me from reality.

8   You are supposed to say why you ended up at the Center. I said I had a bad liver and I was depressed. Whenever I tried to talk about my family, I got all choked up. One of the things I really messed up, besides baseball, was being a father. I wasn't a good family man. I was always out, running around with my friends. My son Mickey Jr. could have been a wonderful athlete. If he had had *my* dad, he could have been a major league baseball player. My kids never blamed me for not being there. They don't have to. I blame myself.

9   During my time at the Betty Ford Center, I had to write my father a letter and tell him how I felt about him. It only took me 10 minutes to write the letter, and I cried the whole time, but after it was over, I felt better. I said that I missed him, and I wish he could have lived to see that I did a lot better than my first season with the Yankees. I told him I had four boys—he died before my first son, Mickey Jr., was born—and I told him I loved him. I would have been better off if I could have told him that a long time ago.

10   Dad would have been proud of me today, knowing that I've completed treatment at Betty Ford and have been sober for three months. But he would have been mad that I had to go there in the first place.

11   For all those years I lived the life of someone I didn't know: a cartoon character. From now on, Mickey Mantle is going to be a real person.

Epilogue

12   As one of Mickey Mantle's last wishes, he wanted to establish a donor awareness program, called "Mickey's Team," at Baylor Hospital in Texas, where he received a liver transplant. He planned to tape a series of public service announcements for the program and even invented a slogan before he died: "Be a hero, be a donor." Mickey's painful problems have inspired a twofold increase in the number of people requesting donor cards. "That program," says Mickey Jr., "will probably be the biggest thing he's going to be known for." (Richard Jerome et al., "Courage at the End of the Road," *People Magazine*)

---

[2] *Hodgkin's disease:* a cancer of the blood characterized by enlargement of the spleen, lymph nodes, and liver. It is considered hereditary. For a long time, Mickey Mantle thought he would develop the disease. One of his sons had it and died around the same age as Mantle's father.

[3] *rehab, rehabilitation:* training to restore a person to good physical condition.

[4] *Betty Ford Center:* a live-in treatment center for drug and alcohol addiction located in Rancho Mirage, California. It is named in honor of the wife of former U.S. President Gerald Ford, and many celebrities have been helped there.

B. READING FOR MAIN IDEAS

Answer the following questions based on your understanding of the reading. Write your answers on a separate piece of paper.

1. What effect did Mickey Mantle's alcoholism have on . . .

   ◆ his ability to play baseball?

   ◆ his relationship with family members?

   ◆ his friendships?

2. How did Mickey Mantle feel about his father?

To help him to be a great baseball hitter ~~great~~
missed him loved him

C. READING FOR DETAILS

Fill in the blanks on this timeline of the life of Mickey Mantle by creating sentences using the following phrases.

was cured of alcoholism at the Betty Ford Center
left baseball
father died
joined the Yankees
started a campaign for donor awareness
father began teaching him baseball

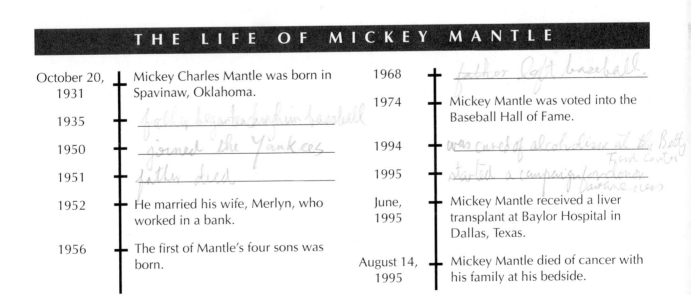

THE LIFE OF MICKEY MANTLE

October 20, 1931	Mickey Charles Mantle was born in Spavinaw, Oklahoma.
1935	*father began teaching him baseball*
1950	*joined the Yankees*
1951	*father died*
1952	He married his wife, Merlyn, who worked in a bank.
1956	The first of Mantle's four sons was born.
1968	*father left baseball.*
1974	Mickey Mantle was voted into the Baseball Hall of Fame.
1994	*was cured of alcoholism at the Betty Ford Center*
1995	*started a campaign for donor awareness*
June, 1995	Mickey Mantle received a liver transplant at Baylor Hospital in Dallas, Texas.
August 14, 1995	Mickey Mantle died of cancer with his family at his bedside.

D. READING BETWEEN THE LINES

❶ *Working with a partner, circle the choice(s) that best complete these sentences. There can be more than one correct answer. Refer to Reading One to support your choices.*

1. Mickey Mantle's father . . .

    a. had a drinking problem

    b. had nothing to do with Mickey's drinking problem

    c. had confidence in his son's abilities

    d. had an easygoing personality

2. Mickey Mantle liked to go out with his friends because . . .

    a. they had many things in common

    b. they were like family

    c. he was disappointed with his family

    d. he had trouble dealing with his father's death

3. Mickey Mantle was an American hero . . .

    a. because of his baseball career

    b. because of his organ donor campaign

    c. because he warned young people about the dangers of alcoholism

    d. because of his commitment to family

4. If Mickey Mantle's father had known about his son's alcoholism . . .

    a. he would have been very disappointed

    b. he would have been angry with him

    c. he would have forgiven him

    d. he would have made him get treatment much sooner

2 *Discuss the following questions with a partner and write your answer in the space provided.*

1. Why did Mickey Mantle become addicted to alcohol?

   _____

   _____

   _____

   _____

   _____

2. Why did Mickey Mantle say that it would have been better for him if he had told his father he loved him a long time ago?

   _____

   _____

   _____

   _____

   _____

3. Did Mickey Mantle think that his life was a success?

   _____

   _____

   _____

   _____

   _____

4. Do *you* think Mickey Mantle had a successful life? Explain your answer.

   _____

   _____

   _____

   _____

   _____

READING TWO: Mick's Toughest Inning

A. EXPANDING THE TOPIC

Mickey Mantle's illness and transplant renewed the debate about who gets priority for donated organs. Cathy Burke in this article from The New York Post *discusses Mantle's situation and gives her opinions. First answer the question and then read Burke's article.*

Do you think Mickey Mantle's celebrity status influenced the type of medical treatment he obtained?

Mick's Toughest Inning[1]

By Cathy Burke (from *The New York Post*)

1   Mickey Mantle played his way into the pantheon[2] of baseball gods, and drank his way to the brink of death.[3] So in today's cynical debate over health-care priorities, Mick's record drinking[4] would drop him to the bottom of the list for a life-saving transplant. Chilling but true. He's over 60 and was an alcoholic for most of his life, a choice that helped make him as sick as he is today. Then there's his age and medical condition, which would put his chances at about 60 percent for surviving a liver transplant for five years or more.

2   The cynics would say Mick is a poor risk indeed. They are wrong.

3   Such a heartless and politicized point of view has gained strength ever since 1984 when former Colorado governor Richard Lamm made the famous declaration that the terminally ill have a "duty to die and get out of the way. Let the others in society, our children, build a reasonable life," he said. What kind of a reasonable life is it when politicians decide whether it is a good risk to save a human life?

4   But Lamm had more to say on modern technology, exactly the kind that could save Mickey Mantle. "How many hearts should we give to a smoker . . . how many liver transplants can we afford to give to an alcoholic," he asked, implying that one was too many.

5   In Oregon, Lamm's legacy lives on in something called the Oregon Health Plan, a "medical rationing" welfare program started in February 1994. The plan prioritizes 565 diseases and their treatments based on how effective the treatments are and how much

---

[1] *inning:* a baseball team's turn at bat
[2] *pantheon:* a temple of all the gods; a group of famous people or national heroes
[3] *the brink of death:* the edge of death
[4] *record drinking:* drinking great amounts of alcohol

they cost. Transplants for liver cancer patients are not funded.

6 Can we trust the politicians to do the right thing for the sickest and poorest among us? In Oregon, the health professionals decide what diseases and treatments go on the list and then a computer determines treatment priorities based on death rates and costs.

7 But the politicians decide how much money is spent.

8 No matter what the proponents[5] say, the Oregon system rations people out of care simply by denying them medical services because some politician doesn't like the survival odds or costs.

9 Fortunately, Mick won't have to worry about getting a chance at a liver transplant. Get well, Mick, before the most cynical of the health-care reformers do us all in.[6]

---

[5] *proponents:* supporters
[6] *do us all in:* kill us all

With a partner, examine the following statements of opinion. Based on your understanding of Reading Two, decide whether Cathy Burke, a journalist, and Governor Lamm, a politician, would agree or disagree with the statements. Check off your answers.

OPINION	CATHY BURKE		GOVERNOR LAMM	
	Agree	Disagree	Agree	Disagree
1. "Deciding health-care priorities according to money or cost is lacking in compassion."				
2. "People must take responsibility for their lives. It is not the business of government to assume responsibility for them."	✓		✓	
3. "All people should be able to get health care in matters of life and death."	✓			✓
4. "It goes against medical ethics to let politicians decide who gets medical treatment just because they control the money."	✓			✓
5. "It is wiser to use money to find a cure for childhood diseases than to find a cure for diseases of old age."		✓	✓	
6. "A nonsmoker is more worthy of a lung transplant than someone who smoked for many years."	✓		✓	
7. "Taxpayers' money is being spent to make insurance companies rich."	✓			✓

B. LINKING READINGS ONE AND TWO

You have read the opinions, thoughts, and observations of the sports hero Mickey Mantle and the journalist Cathy Burke. Choose one topic below and write a paragraph in reply.

1. What do you think Cathy Burke would write about Mickey Mantle's autobiography? How does she feel about Mickey Mantle? Does she think he is a hero? Does she think he deserves special treatment as a hero? Does she think he should get an organ transplant?

2. What is your reaction to the issues that Cathy Burke raises in her article? Do you think that all people have a right to medical treatment, even if they can't pay? Should health care be rationed? What should the government's role be?

5 REVIEWING LANGUAGE

A. EXPLORING LANGUAGE: Word Forms

Working in small groups, fill in the chart with the correct forms of the words. Use your dictionary if necessary. ("X" indicates that no word belongs in that space either because no such word exists or because it is not commonly used.)

Noun	Verb	Adjective	Adverb
1. *management*	manage	*manageable*	*manageably*
2. devastation	*devastate*	*devastating*	*devastatingly*
3. priority	*prioritize*	X	X
4. *avoidance*	avoid	*avoidable*	*avoidably*
5. *toughness*	*toughen*	tough	*toughly*
6. *strength*	*strengthen*	*strong*	strongly

Noun	Verb	Adjective	Adverb
7. survival	*survive*	*survivable*	X
8. *denial*	deny	*deniable*	*deniably*
9. *determination*	*determine*	determined	X
10. *celebration*	celebrate	*celebrated*	X

B. WORKING WITH WORDS

Imagine that the letter Mickey Mantle wrote at the Betty Ford Center to his long-dead father read something like the letter that follows. Fill in the blanks with the correct form of the words from the list.

avoidance	denial	devastation	priority	survival
celebration	determination	management	strength	toughness

Dear Dad,

Your death really (1) *devastated* me. I don't think I have ever recovered from the pain and the fact that I never (2) *denied / managed* to tell you how much I loved you. The hardest thing I ever had to do was to say good-bye to you.

How do I account for my success? Your faith in me, your love, and your help. If you had lived, you would have seen my four beautiful sons. You would have shared my fame and (3) *celebrated* my success. You would have seen me realize those dreams we had so long ago.

More than anything else in the world, I wanted you to be proud of me. When I lost you, I lost my guide, my anchor in life. You were such a (4) *tough [strong]* family man, but I seem to have given my family a low (5) *priority* . I lost my way for a long time and now my very (6) _____ is in doubt. Whatever happens, I am (7) *survivable*

determination
survival

determined

to use the rest of my life to make things up to my family.

Even though I was elected to the Baseball Hall of Fame, I was not the great father to my sons during their childhood that you were to me during mine. I can't (8) _~~manage~~ deny_ that in their own ways, my kids bear the scars of my neglect. What chokes me up about all this is that they don't blame me for my failures as a parent. I only wish that I had been there for my kids in the same way that you were always there for me. You were (9) _tough_ on me, but you always wanted the best. Perhaps I could have (10) _avoided_ some of this suffering if, years ago, I had had the courage to tell you how much I loved you.

Your loving son

6 SKILLS FOR EXPRESSION

A. GRAMMAR: Past Unreal Conditionals

1 *Examine this sentence and discuss the questions that follow with a partner.*

◆ If I had done the physical rehab work after my injuries, I would have been able to play baseball after age 37.

a. Did Mickey Mantle do the physical rehab work after his injury?

b. Was he able to play baseball after age 37?

c. How are these two ideas connected in the sentence above?

Past Unreal Conditionals

FOCUS ON GRAMMAR

See unreal conditionals in *Focus on Grammar, Advanced.*

A **past unreal conditional** is used to express past untrue or past imagined situations and their result. A past unreal conditional statement can be used to explain why things happened the way they did or to express a regret about the past. A past unreal conditional statement is formed by combining an ***if*-clause** and a **result clause.** Both clauses have to be stated in terms that are opposite to what really happened.

Reality	Mickey Mantle didn't do the rehab work after his injuries; therefore, he wasn't able to play baseball after the age of 37.
Past Unreal Conditional	If Mickey Mantle had done the rehab work after his injuries, he would have been able to play baseball after the age of 37.

- -

Formation

To form a past unreal conditional statement, use ***had*** (not) + past principle in the if-clause and ***would, might, could*** (not) + ***have*** + past participle in the result clause.

If-clause	***If*** Mickey Mantle **had done** the rehab work,
Result clause	he **would have been** able to play baseball after the age of 37.
If-clause	***If*** Mantle **hadn't been** out drinking with his friends all the time,
Result clause	he **would have had** time to do the rehab work.

GRAMMAR TIP: Using *could have* or *might have* in the result clause shows more doubt about the conclusion.

2 *Combine the ideas in the following sentences by using the past unreal conditional. Remember that these conditional sentences must express the opposite of what really happened. The first sentence has been done for you.*

1. Mickey Mantle needed a transplant.

   There has been a twofold increase in the number of people requesting donor cards from Baylor Hospital.

   If Mickey Mantle hadn't needed a transplant, there might not have been a twofold increase in the number of people requesting donor cards from Baylor Hospital.

2. Mickey Mantle's father trained his son to play baseball from the age of four.

   Mickey became a champion.

   _____

   _____

3. Mickey Mantle centered his social life on alcohol.

   He neglected his wife and sons.

   _____

   _____

4. Mickey Mantle didn't think about his old age.

   He didn't take good care of himself.

   _____

   _____

5. Mickey Mantle's father died in 1951.

   He never saw Mickey Mantle become a champion.

   _____

   _____

6. Mantle went to the Betty Ford Center the year before he died.

   He reconciled with his family at the end of his life.

   _____

   _____

3 *Using the information from the readings, write your own past unreal conditionals about the following themes in Mickey Mantle's life. When you write your sentences, try to use the vocabulary words you have studied in this unit. The first sentence has been done for you.*

1. Mickey's transplant

   If Mickey Mantle had been sober all his life, he wouldn't have needed a
   liver transplant.

2. Mickey's relationship with his father

   _____

   _____

3. Mickey's relationship with his sons

   _____

   _____

4. Mickey's addiction to alcohol

   _____

   _____

B. STYLE: Elements of Autobiographical Writing

1 *Examine the following paragraph from "My Time in a Bottle" and discuss with a partner the questions that follow.*

"Even though he was dog tired after long days at the mine, Dad would still pitch batting practice to me in the backyard when he got home from work, beginning from the time I was four years old. My mother would call us to dinner, but the meal would wait until Dad was finished instructing me from the right and left sides of the plate. Dad was a tough man. If I'd done something wrong, he could just look at me—he didn't have to say anything—and I'd say, 'I won't do it no more, Dad.' I loved my father, although I couldn't tell him that, just like he couldn't tell me."

   a. Who is being described here?

   b. Who is the narrator (the person who is telling the story)?

c. During which period in the narrator's life does the action take place?

d. What verb tenses are used?

e. What statement makes us aware of an issue that caused the author a lot of pain?

CHARACTER, TECHNIQUE, AND THEME

The person being described here is Mickey Mantle's father. Because the passage is written in the first-person narrative (as shown by the use of the pronoun *I* and the possessive adjective *my*), it is clear to the reader that the narrator is Mickey Mantle himself. The verbs are all in a past tense form (the simple past: "he *was* dog tired"; the habitual past: "My mother *would call*") and the actions that are being described here all refer to the period in the author's childhood starting at age four. The statement at the very end, "I loved my father, although I couldn't tell him that, just like he couldn't tell me," makes us aware of an issue that bothered Mantle a lot.

What we can appreciate in this paragraph are the three major "elements" of autobiography: **character, technique,** and **theme**.

Character

The author of an autobiography provides details about himself and others in his life and his reactions to the events in his life. From the comfortable distance created by the passage of time, the narrator creates *self-portraits* and *portraits of the principal players* in his life. Through the portraits, we discover the writer's *character* or *system of values*. We learn how the writer views various character traits (such as generosity, sensitivity, meanness, happiness, and sadness) by examining how such traits were reflected in his own behavior and that of others in his life. In addition, we learn why the writer believes the individuals being described became the way they were and how his present values may now be different from his past values.

In the example paragraph, the author provides details about himself and his father. He writes, "Dad was a tough man," and explains further that his father "could just look at [him]" to get him to do what he wanted. The great influence the author's father had on his character development is thus revealed in these few words.

❷ *Write short answers to the following questions and discuss your answers with a partner.*

1. What did you learn about the character of Mickey Mantle's father in the example paragraph?

2. By reading Mantle's portrait of his father, we learn about the values Mickey Mantle respected. What are these values?

3. Look at the rest of "My Time in a Bottle." Does Mickey Mantle claim that he kept to these values in his own life? Underline the sentences where you find the answer.

Technique

The autobiographer must use the **past tense** and the **first-person narrative** (for example, language like "*I* loved my father") if he wants his portraits to be effective. At the same time, the writer must use interesting language and **imagery** (for example, language like "dog tired after long days at the mine," which gives us a mental picture of a sense experience) and various other **stylistic devices** (such as direct quotations or questions) to attract the reader to his writing.

3 *Discuss the following questions with a partner.*

1. Suppose that in the example paragraph Mickey Mantle had written, "Every day after work my father practiced pitching balls to me before sitting down to dinner." Would this have been an interesting sentence or a dull one? Why?

2. Underline the descriptive words Mantle uses to tell about his father's days. Why are these words effective? What do they communicate?

3. Underline the sentence where Mantle offers a direct quotation of his own words. Why does he do this? What is wrong with the grammar of the sentence?

Theme

The autobiographer must create an intimate bond with his reader by making him aware of the issues or problems that have shaped his life and that continue to be a major concern to him. For example, one of the themes that surface in "My Time in a Bottle" is Mantle's escape from loss through alcoholism.

4 *Write short answers to the following questions. Then compare your answers with another student.*

1. What is the main theme of the paragraph we examined? Underline the sentence that you think is the most significant.

2. Is there anything in this paragraph that shows the weakness or vulnerability of the narrator?

3. Does this make us feel closer to the narrator? Why or why not?

5 *Imagine that you are a character from Mickey Mantle's childhood: an older brother, a younger brother, a sister, his mother, his father, a friend. Write a paragraph from that person's point of view. For example, you may want to describe how a younger brother could have been jealous of the daily batting sessions Mantle had with his father. You could begin the paragraph this way: "Every day was the same. I sat alone in the yard while my father spent all his free time with my brother."*

*Consider **character**, **technique**, and **theme** as you plan your writing strategy. Remember to write in the first person and to use the past tense.*

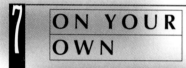

ON YOUR OWN

A. WRITING TOPICS

Write an essay on one of the following topics. Try to use the vocabulary and grammar from this unit when you write.

1. Using the three major elements of autobiography—character, technique and theme—write a portrait of yourself at a certain time in your life. Use the first-person narrative and the past tense. Express yourself in interesting and descriptive language. You can:

   a. describe your personality as it was during a particular period or at the time of a special event in your life;

   b. consider how that period or special event affected you and how it may have caused your system of values to change or remain the same;

   c. describe any individuals who had a great influence on you at the time;

   d. share with the reader the issue that was most on your mind at that time;

   e. discuss whether you now think there was anything you should have done differently.

2. Write a letter to someone who has been very important to you in your life. Mickey Mantle wrote one to his father, but the person you choose can still be alive today. If you hadn't had that person in your life, what would have happened to you? Would your life have been different? How?

3. Choose a famous sports hero, celebrity, or national leader. Make sure you know a lot about the life of this person. Put yourself in his or her shoes and write an imaginary autobiography from his or her point of view. Discuss the influence of his or her early life, the contributions he or she made, the contradictions between the person's public and private life. What are her strengths and weaknesses? What would her life have been like if her career hadn't been successful? If she hadn't made some mistakes? If certain people hadn't been there to help?

4. Some people think that alcoholics should not be eligible for organ transplants. They say that if alcoholics hadn't abused their bodies, they wouldn't have gotten so sick. Other people feel that it is unfair to deny life-saving help to another human being. Still other citizens are worried about society's limited number of donor organs and limited economic resources. What do you think? Explain your answer in a well-organized essay.

B. FIELDWORK

PREPARATION

Mickey Mantle received his liver transplant in Dallas, Texas. Organ distribution in the United States is broken down into different geographical regions (see the graph on page 22). The regions share organs on a national level when there is a surplus in a given region. All are connected on the United Network for Organ Sharing.

Using the graph and the information provided on page 22, discuss the following questions with a partner.

1. What might have happened to Mickey Mantle if he had been a patient in another geographical region of the United States?

2. According to the new rules for liver transplants since Mickey Mantle's death, which patients now get priority for liver transplants?

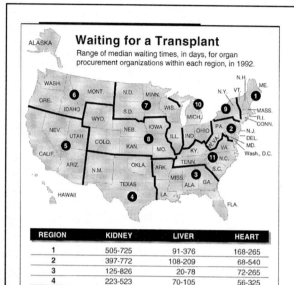

Waiting for a Transplant

Range of median waiting times, in days, for organ procurement organizations within each region, in 1992.

REGION	KIDNEY	LIVER	HEART
1	505-725	91-376	168-265
2	397-772	108-209	68-540
3	125-826	20-78	72-265
4	223-523	70-105	56-325
5	130-786	18-197	130-355
6	94-533	58	56-182
7	448-695	31-256	226-641
8	271-539	26-121	92-381
9	213-698	279-443	255-268
10	185-348	33-194	89-591
11	151-723	30-276	111-767
United States	94-826	18-443	55-707

Source: United Network for Organ Sharing.

N.Y. Times News Service

New Rules for Liver Transplants

In November 1996, the United Network for Organ Sharing changed its rules and introduced rationing. In the past, the sickest patients had top priority. But patients whose livers have been deteriorating for decades, like those with alcoholic cirrhosis or viral hepatitis, are only half as likely to survive a liver transplant as people whose livers have just suddenly failed from a viral infection or toxin (poison). The new rules state that if the two types of people are competing for one liver, it should go to the person who just became ill.

RESEARCH ACTIVITY

1. Do an Internet search or go to the library and research organ transplants in your area or country. Try to find out what the waiting period is for transplants. Also try to find out how many transplants are performed each year and whether the number has changed as a result of the new rules outlined above.

2. Take notes and organize the information.

SHARING YOUR FINDINGS

Write a report summarizing your findings and present the report to the class.

A BRIDGE ACROSS THE GENERATIONS

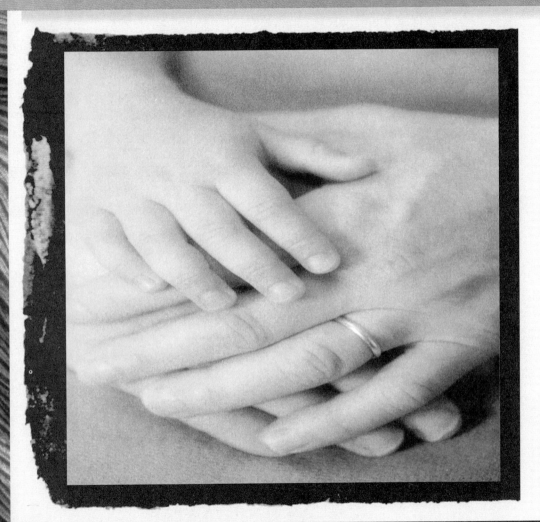

1 APPROACHING THE TOPIC

A. PREDICTING

What does the title "A Bridge Across the Generations" mean to you? What do you expect to read about in this unit? Take five minutes to write down your thoughts about these questions.

B. SHARING INFORMATION

Work in small groups. Look at the chart below. Which descriptions apply more to people over age sixty-five and which apply more to teenagers? Some of the characteristics below may apply to both or to neither. Fill in the chart and discuss your choices.

DESCRIPTION	PEOPLE OVER 65 YEARS OF AGE	TEENAGERS
1. have a lot of money	✓	✗
2. help take care of young children	✓	✗
3. work outside the home	✗	✓
4. live with one or two other generations	✓	✓
5. are often very critical and seem irritated	✗	✗
6. are well educated	✓	✗
7. have a lot of power in the family	✓	✗
8. have a lot of leisure time	✓	✗
9. sometimes feel isolated and lonely	✓	✓

2 PREPARING TO READ

A. BACKGROUND

Read the information and complete the sentences that follow based on what you have read.

Since the 1960s, Americans over sixty-five years of age have been living better lives because of the government programs they helped to build. Although citizens over sixty-five years of age represent only about 13 percent of the population, nearly half of the federal budget goes to them in two forms: Social Security pensions paid after retirement from active work, and Medicare health benefits. These programs have been very successful and have relieved families of some of the burden of caring for their older members. Older people in America are richer and more self-sufficient today.

But self-sufficiency should not mean isolation from the rest of society. Because of the pressures of modern life, many older people no longer live with, or even near, their extended families. Some may be isolated from the wider community because they live in "retirement communities" or in nursing homes. But many small towns and suburbs need the financial and moral support of their senior citizens, especially to improve the educational system, and many communities are actively seeking more solid links across the generations to strengthen the fabric of American life.

1. Today, most American families do not have the full burden of supporting older people because *Social Security pensions paid after retirement from active work and Medicare health benefits*

2. Seniors may become isolated from the wider community because *they live in "retirement communities" or in nursing homes*

3. Many small towns and suburbs need senior citizens to *be financial and moral support, especially to improve the educational system*

4. Older people in my family _____

B. VOCABULARY FOR COMPREHENSION

1 *Work in pairs. Read the following sentences and help each other to guess the meaning of the underlined words from the context of the sentences. Then write a synonym or your own definition of the word. Use your dictionaries if necessary. The first one has been done for you.*

1. The latest scientific research by the *MacArthur Foundation Consortium* * *on Successful Aging* concludes that the way we grow old is mainly a matter of how we live and that most <u>seniors</u> today are aging very successfully.

   <u>People over sixty-five years of age; elderly people</u>

2. In America today, people often have to change cities to find a job or keep a job. In this <u>mobile</u> society, older and younger generations of the same family often live in different places, making it hard to maintain close ties with grandmothers and grandfathers.

   able to move

3. Because they are often alone and like peaceful surroundings, many elderly people move to special communities where only senior citizens can live. This isolation can <u>segregate</u> them from the rest of the population.

   to separate one group of people from others because of sex race religion etc.

4. One reason some senior citizens choose to live in their own communities is that they are afraid of losing their dignity and fear <u>exposure</u> to bad treatment by people who don't understand their needs.

   an opportunity to experience new ideas events methods etc

5. Many elderly people are afraid of losing their mental abilities, but these fears are usually <u>groundless</u>. Seniors may not be able to think as fast as they used to, but they can still be lifelong learners.

   without any reason

---

* *Consortium:* a group formed to accomplish a task that no single organization could undertake alone. In this case, the consortium on aging unites researchers at many different medical schools and universities in the United States.

6. Learning new skills and taking educational courses can add a new <u>dimension</u> to the lives of senior citizens. Study after study shows that lifelong learning is good for your health.

a part of situation that affects the way you think

7. Some older citizens become <u>apprehensive</u> and depressed about the possibility of memory loss and confusion in old age.

worried & anxious especially for the future

8. According to recent studies, people who continue to be productive (with hobbies, family, and community) after they <u>retire</u> are more likely to enjoy a successful old age.

stop working usually for because of old age

9. Scientists are investigating the fact that memory loss is much less serious in <u>vigorous</u> people than in people who are physically inactive.

using a lot of energy and strength or determination

2 *Match the words from the reading that are listed on the left with a synonym from the column on the right.*

d __ 1. senior   a. separate

g __ 2. mobile   b. stop working

a __ 3. segregate   c. energetic

i __ 4. exposed   d. elderly

h __ 5. groundless   e. perspective

e __ 6. dimension   f. fearful

f __ 7. apprehensive   g. unsettled

b __ 8. retire   h. unjustified

c __ 9. vigorous   i. susceptible

READING ONE: Senior Citizens at Wilton High

A. INTRODUCING THE TOPIC

◆The Wilton Public Schools ◆

invite
Wilton Senior Citizens to a Reception
at Wilton High School

on January 23 at 2:30 P.M.

"Taking Courses at Wilton High School"

Come and learn more about the program and how to
participate in existing courses with high school students in:
ART, SOCIAL STUDIES, and ENGLISH.

"One of the most enjoyable experiences I have ever had,"
a senior citizen participant said last year.

*Look at the announcement above and discuss the following questions
with a partner. Then read the newspaper articles.*

Why do you think Wilton High School is offering space in its courses to
senior citizens? Who would benefit from participating in high school
classes? What might the drawbacks be?

A Good Idea in Wilton

The News-Times, Danbury, Connecticut

1   The town of Wilton has come up with a good idea that other communities in the Danbury area should take a look at. A select number of regular high school classes has been opened up to senior citizens. They fill unfilled seats in the classes, not costing the school system any money.

2   Donald Holt, administrator for curriculum at Wilton High, readily admits a number of motivations for opening the schools to senior citizens. He said school officials were concerned when they heard the town's older residents say that they didn't know much about what went on in the institutions that serve the town's younger residents. The educators thought bringing seniors into the classes would help them understand what the schools are doing and, perhaps, make them more willing to pay the price in education budgets and taxes.

3   Put aside that more practical reason, however, and there are many more reasons why this is a good idea. In this mobile society, we tend to be segregated by age. Many grandparents do not live near their grandchildren. The result is that the children don't have much exposure to senior citizens and vice versa.[1]

4   The Wilton senior citizens, who have enrolled in such classes as Shakespeare, drawing, parenting, and orchestra, are enriching the classes with their own special brand of experience and enthusiasm for learning. This is something any community should welcome.

---

[1]*vice versa:* the other way around

A Plan for Senior Education Takes Place

The News-Times, Danbury, Connecticut

5   "Before we began, the teachers had some real questions," Holt said. "Would the seniors dominate the classes? The answer turned out to be no. Or would they be so reticent they'd never talk? No, again. And another teacher worry: Are we going to look bad? Not a problem. All the older students are enormously enthusiastic about their teachers. I think both the teachers and the senior citizens were, in the beginning, a little frightened, a little scared. Their fears were groundless."

6   Holt met with the teachers to evaluate the program. They told him the younger students were positive about their older classmates.

7   David O'Malley, a high school student, said he thought old people spent their time in rocking chairs, adding that the seniors in class opened his eyes to attitudes about older people. "They have as much desire to learn and succeed as we do," he said.

Senior Citizens Share Classes with Teens at High School

The Hour, Norwalk, Connecticut

Shakespeare Class

8   Three new students in Sheila Henry's Shakespeare class at Wilton High School have added a new dimension to class discussions. Ms. Henry and her extra students, who have a combined age of 218 years, are part of a new project that opens a certain number of regular high school classes to older citizens. Senior citizens who turned up this year are enrolled in Shakespeare, drawing, painting, and orchestra classes.

9   "I volunteered to have seniors in my Shakespeare class," the teacher said, nodding toward Helen Murray, Metz Kahn, and Edna Jones, who stayed after class to talk about going to high school for the second time in their lives. "Wasn't it Yeats[2] who said, 'Life is a spiral staircase'? You see the same patterns and scenes but from different places on the steps," Ms. Henry said. "The kids are at the bottom of the staircase, I'm in the middle, and the senior citizens are up a little higher. The kids have talked about the contributions they [the seniors] have made to our class with their experiences and understanding of life. Their spontaneous enjoyment of Shakespeare is wonderful for the students to see."

10   None of the older people were apprehensive about being with teenagers, and all three have enjoyed the give-and-take of the class. "I was interested in things I hadn't had time for," said Helen Murray, 69, who has two grandchildren she rarely sees. "I used to say 'someday I'm going to do that.' Well, my someday has arrived."

11   "Ms. Henry's teaching is so different from my high school years," said Metz Kahn, 66, a chemical engineer. "We were told to read a play and answer questions. Here we discuss things, see films, talk about motives. And we're not segregated, as I was, by race and sex."

12   Edna Jones attends Shakespeare class every day. "The approach to the plays is quite different from when I went to school in the 1920s. Now we analyze the play, discuss the psychological background, the political and social events of the time," Mrs. Jones said. She finds the reading quite difficult. She used to read Shakespeare for the plot but now has to read it in depth.

13   Mrs. Murray agrees. "At first I decided I would do all the assignments like the young people and keep the journal Ms. Henry wants, too. By the end of the first week, it had taken over my life and I stopped. I don't see how the young people do all this work! I do find that I understand Shakespeare more now than ever before. There's a saying about the brain, 'Use it or lose it,'" she said. "I'm not going to lose mine voluntarily."

Art Class

14   John Pool, a former cancer surgeon, taught surgery to the staff at Yale and Norwalk hospitals after he retired. He still gives classes on medical ethics at Norwalk Hospital. This vigorous 83-year-old is taking drawing with Wilton High School's ninth graders in art class.

15   "Beautiful things have come of this experiment," said Bob Lassen, the art teacher. "John's friendship with the young students, the blending. Most don't have their grandparents here, don't have any relationship to older people. Working together in class helps cement something between the ages, and that is needed in today's world."

16   Pool has spent most of the semester working at a table with Kim Fernandez, Sarah Whitney, Jocelyn Baer, and Erin Smith. "We always talk. He sees things from a different point of view," Kim said. One of the girls said she couldn't imagine her grandfather joining a high school class, but, she added, "Dr. Pool looks like he's having fun."

17   He is. "I thought it would stretch my mind," Dr. Pool said, "and it has!"

---

[2] *William Butler Yeats:* Irish poet (1865–1939)

B. READING FOR MAIN IDEAS

*Compare people's expectations or preconceived notions with what really happened. Write one sentence about what the teachers, teenagers, and seniors thought **before** the program began. Then write one sentence about their views **after** they had participated in the program. Compare answers with a partner. The first one has been done for you.*

BEFORE	AFTER
1a. Wilton administrators <u>were worried that older people were uninterested in the schools and that they wouldn't sign up for high school classes.</u>	**1b.** <u>The program is a big success and has inspired similar programs in other towns and states.</u>
2a. The teachers _____	**2b.** _____
3a. The seniors _____	**3b.** _____
4a. Some teenagers _____	**4b.** _____

C. READING FOR DETAILS

*Decide if the following statements are true or false according to the reading, and write **T** or **F** on the line next to the number. If they are false, rewrite the statements on a separate piece of paper to make them true.*

__F__ 1. The Wilton program earned money for the town because the seniors paid a tuition fee for the classes.

__F__ 2. All the senior citizens were able to keep up with the assignments in the Shakespeare class.

__F__ 3. The seniors who participated in the art and Shakespeare classes did not attend high school when they were young.

__T__ 4. Students and teachers all said the older people enjoyed the classes a great deal.

__T__ 5. The teacher quoted the poet Yeats, saying that "life is a spiral staircase" because she believes that you see life from a different perspective at each age.

__F__ 6. The students over sixty-five years of age were critical of their teachers.

D. READING BETWEEN THE LINES

1 *In the reading, American senior citizens compared their educational experience seventy years ago with their experience in the Shakespeare class at Wilton High School. With a partner, decide whether the teaching methods listed in the following chart apply to English classes in the 1920s or the 1990s and check the appropriate column.*

TEACHING METHOD	SCHOOLS IN THE 1920s	SCHOOLS IN THE 1990s
1. a lot of memorizing	✓	
2. focusing mainly on the story of the play	✓	
3. lively classroom discussions		✓
4. mostly listening to the teacher talk	✓	✓
5. give-and-take between the students		
6. studying the social background of the plays		✓
7. more written work than oral work	✓	✓
8. analyzing psychology		
9. same-sex schools	✓	
10. speaking only when called on by the teacher	✓	
11. writing a journal at home to record your reactions to the readings		✓

2 *Talk about the questions that follow with your partner, and then write your answers in the space provided.*

1. Did the senior citizens like Ms. Henry's class better than the classes they remembered from their own youth? Why?

① analyze the play
② discuss the psychological background, the political and social events of the time

Yes. Mrs Jones said "The approach to the play is quite different from when I went to school in the 1920's." She said she used to read Shakespeare for the plot — but now has to read it in depth.

2. What are some of the differences between schooling in the 1920s and the 1990s?

_____

_____

_____

3. Wilton is a wealthy middle-class suburb. Do you think this program would work as well in a poor neighborhood?

_____

_____

_____

4. What does the expression "use it or lose it" mean? How does it relate to the experience at Wilton High School?

_____

_____

_____

5. What are the advantages for all participants in having programs like the one at Wilton High?

_____

_____

_____

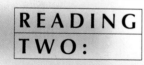

READING TWO: I Don't Feel or Look My Age

A. EXPANDING THE TOPIC

Take the following quiz on aging. Then read what Susan Scalone-Bonnici has to say about these issues in her essay entitled "I Don't Feel or Look My Age. So What?"

HOW DO YOU FEEL ABOUT AGING?   YES NO

1. Do you think people should be content to look their age?

2. Can you think of any circumstances when people would try to look older than they are? If so, when?

3. Should people try to look younger?

4. Would you spend the money for cosmetic surgery to eliminate wrinkles?

5. In your life experience, are older people treated with respect?

I Don't Feel or Look My Age. So What?

By Susan Scalone-Bonnici (from *The New York Times*)

1　Everyone wants to be and stay beautiful/handsome, clear-eyed and optimistic. Maybe this is an almost impossible task. For how can a person sustain things like raising children, with all those wrenching, heart-breaking times; carrying the responsibilities of adulthood, losing jobs, losing parents, losing spouses, without incurring a weathered look? In nature there is change: seasons, cycles, evolution. So, too, there has to be change for the human person. To remain forever young (or forever anything frozen in time) would have a stagnant[1] effect on the whole person.

2　Some things go with the territory. The stretch marks a woman gets after childbirth would not be there if she didn't bring a new life into being. Whatever we are is part of the rich history of our lives, our own unique story. It's a shame that in our youth-oriented society too much emphasis is placed on externals. Stretch marks, gray hair, a receding hairline, age freckles are signs that we are getting older, but who cares? It's not all we are about.

3　Anything that lives on this earth must age. Otherwise we wouldn't have any history! Look at a family and observe its life cycle: infant, child, adolescent, young adult, mid-life, elderly; watch how each moves on to the next position, like game pieces advancing on a board. The game of life continues and before long, baby becomes grandpa.

4　What blurs[2] perception may be a lack of compassion. Compassion allows each person at each stage of life to be, with no labels or preconceived notions[3] of what he should be, and allows that person to stand on his or her own. Thus, the young should not look upon the old with contempt; the old may

---

[1] *stagnant:* not advancing or developing
[2] *to blur:* to confuse, to make unclear
[3] *preconceived notions:* opinions that are formed before having actual knowledge or experience

not demean[4] the young. No one can afford to make a blanket judgment of anyone else or risk being judged by the same narrow-sightedness.

5 Making people aware of the need for compassion is the first step in changing their attitude. This would require a lot of effort, education and hard work. It is easier to fall back on labels (he's too old; she's just a kid; it's that middle-age thing; what does he know, he's so young; she's too old). But dispelling[5] labels has got to be done if we would dare to call ourselves a democracy of free people.

6 It is healthy to be concerned with one's appear- ance, to want to look attractive, fit, pleasant to the eye. It is an expression of how a person feels about himself to care about his looks, but only as an expression and not a total outpouring of self. Self is what is arrived at through a life of caring, loving. It is an unshakable stand of self-love and spirit where we can change and all things are possible, not by appearances only, but by how good it is to be alive and special, a vital and important part of this world in which we live—at any age.

---

[4] *demean:* to belittle, humiliate
[5] *dispelling:* eliminating, getting rid of

1 *Examine the following questions. Then discuss with a partner how Susan Scalone-Bonnici might respond to these issues about aging. There can be more than one correct answer. Circle your choice(s) and discuss them with your partner.*

1. "I have a lot of wrinkles and a sagging face. Should I have cosmetic surgery for a facelift?"

   a. No, wrinkles and other signs of age show that you have wisdom.

   b. No, don't waste your money because these operations are never very successful.

   c. OK, but don't be so concerned about the purely external aspects of the self.

   d. Yes, why should nature dictate to us if we have the technology to please ourselves?

2. "My grandmother goes ice-skating every Sunday in a short red dress."

   a. How terrible that she shames you with her inappropriate behavior!

   b. How lucky you are that she has such a strong spirit!

   c. You should try to understand her and see her point of view.

   d. Don't watch her, and it won't bother you so much.

3. "I only trust a man with gray hair."
   a. You're right, experience is very important.
   b. Younger men are not very serious.
   c. Beware of blanket judgments.
   d. Choose a more modern and up-to-date person.

4. "America is more sympathetic to youth than to old people."
   a. We ought to change this and recognize the gifts of all ages.
   b. We ought to change this and make old people the decision-makers.
   c. We're right to prefer the dynamism of youth.
   d. Dispelling labels is crucial.

5. "Young people are all reckless and thoughtless."
   a. We can't generalize about such a thing.
   b. You're right. Young people lack experience.
   c. No, young people are understanding and caring.
   d. Trying to fit people into categories only makes us more prejudiced.

2 *Based on your understanding of Susan Scalone-Bonnici's essay, answer these questions in your own words.*

1. According to the essay, why wouldn't it be a good thing if we were to be "forever young"?

   because in nature there is a change. Seasons, cycles, evolution. So, too, there has to be change for the human person. To remain forever young would have a stagnant effect on the human person.

2. What kinds of things will give a face a "weathered look," according to the author?

   _____

   _____

3. Why are "labels" bad for a democratic society?

   _____

   _____

4. The author says that appearance is important, but it is not "all we are about," not the most important thing about us. What does she say <u>is</u> more important than appearances?

   _____

   _____

B. LINKING READINGS ONE AND TWO

From your understanding of the two readings, write about one of the topics below.

1. Susan Scalone-Bonnici wrote, "the young should not look upon the old with contempt; the old may not demean the young." What would Susan Scalone-Bonnici think of the program at Wilton High School and the experiences of young and old who participated in it? Would she want to participate? Would she think this kind of program is useful to society? Why or why not? Write down some thoughts and share them with a partner.

2. Write a paragraph giving your opinion of the Wilton program and Susan Scalone-Bonnici's essay about the need to break out of stereotypes. Do you agree with her assertion that a life without change is stagnant?

5 REVIEWING LANGUAGE

A. EXPLORING VOCABULARY: IDIOMS

*You know you are reading an **idiom** when you understand the separate words in the expression but not the expression as a whole. Working in small groups, find the following idiomatic expressions in the two readings and circle the answers below that most closely approximate the meaning of the expressions in context. There can be more than one correct answer.*

1. **it would stretch my mind**   (Reading One, paragraph 17)
    a. it would expand my brain cells
    b. I would learn new things
    c. I would do mental exercises

2. **my someday has arrived** (Reading One, paragraph 10)

 a. the day I looked forward to has come
 b. the day I dreaded has come
 c. the future has become the present

3. **to stand on his or her own** (Reading Two, paragraph 4)

 a. to stand by oneself
 b. to be judged as an individual
 c. to be stereotyped or labeled

4. **opened his eyes to** (Reading One, paragraph 7)

 a. tormented him about
 b. made him discover
 c. introduced him to

5. **a blanket judgment** (Reading Two, paragraph 4)

 a. a refusal to recognize differences
 b. something to be applied in all instances
 c. something covering all members of a group

B. WORKING WITH WORDS

Both readings in this chapter discuss the need for greater intergenerational contact and understanding. The Wilton school authorities have tried to encourage the goals of lifelong learning by mixing seniors and teenagers in the high school classes. Other programs have also tried to bring together the generations; one of them is called "Adopt a Grandparent." These programs are described in the essay on page 40.

Read the essay on page 40. As you read, use the words in the left column to fill in the blanks. You may have to change the forms from noun to adjective and so on when appropriate.

apprehension
compassion
contempt
demean
dispel
enroll
incur
mobile
reticence
vice versa

The aim of this program, started in 1986 by seven Lakota Sioux grandmothers, is to help older Native Americans on the Pine Ridge Reservation in South Dakota who are all alone but may be too (1) _reticent_ to ask strangers for help. Today, many "grandchildren" in the program are Native American children who no longer live on the reservation and whose eyes are opened to their Native American heritage by this program. The generations help each other: The "grandchildren" help the elders and (2) _vice versa_. All Americans can now (3) _enroll_ in this program. Native Americans who are (4) _apprehensive_ about the coming of winter are given blankets, clothes, and household items contributed by their "grandchildren." Many people want to stand on their own and feel that accepting money is (5) _demeaning_, so the program converts money donations into gift certificates for food, electricity, and firewood.

A greatly modified urban version of "Adopt a Grandparent" began nine years later in Chicago. During the very hot summer of 1995, there was not enough electrical power to meet the city's demands. The city government (6) _incurred_ the anger of many citizens when more than 100 elderly people in poor neighborhoods died of heat all alone in their apartments, without fans or air conditioners. The government cannot always replace the ties of family in big cities, but volunteer helpers in Chicago have joined together in teams to patrol poor neighborhoods and check on seniors. They are trying to (7) _dispel_ the notion that modern cities are indifferent to the needs of older people.

Like the Native American program, the Chicago program stretches people's minds and asks them to show (8) _compassion_ for others who have made their contribution to society. Programs like "Meals on Wheels," which takes food to the elderly who have lost their (9) _mobility_, and programs where seniors help out at day-care centers for poor children, can bind the generations together and help our society show respect and not (10) _contempt_ for aging.

6 SKILLS FOR EXPRESSION

A. GRAMMAR: Noun Clauses

1 *Examine the underlined clauses in the sentences and discuss the questions that follow with a partner.*

It is important to consider <u>what the Wilton community has decided to offer its elderly population</u>. Based on the recommendation of school officials, some high school classes have been opened up free of charge to <u>whoever wishes to take courses in literature, art, and social studies with the normal high school population</u>.

a. Does each of these clauses have a subject and a verb?

b. What words do these clauses start with?

c. What is the subject-verb word order in each of these clauses?

Noun Clauses

FOCUS ON GRAMMAR

See noun clauses in *Focus on Grammar, Advanced.*

Noun clauses are like nouns in a sentence. Noun clauses can be subjects, objects of verbs or prepositions, or complements. The following words often introduce noun clauses: ***what, that, who, whom, whether, why, where, how, whatever, whoever, whomever, wherever, however.***

Noun clause as SUBJECT	**What the Wilton community has decided to offer its elderly population** is important to consider.
Noun clause as OBJECT	It is important to consider **what the Wilton community has decided to offer its elderly population.**
Noun clause as COMPLEMENT	This is **what the Wilton community has decided to offer its elderly population.**

GRAMMAR TIP: Like all clauses, noun clauses must have a subject and a verb. Although some noun clauses start with question words, the word order is not the inverted subject-verb word order that is used in questions. In all noun clauses, the subject comes before the verb.

2 *In the following paragraphs about Wilton's high school experiment, fill in the blanks with **what, that, who, why, where, how, whoever,** and correct forms of the indicated verbs. You will use some of the words more than once. The first one has been done for you.*

WILTON REVISITED

<u>Why the Wilton school officials invited</u> senior citizens to study with
     1. (the Wilton school officials/invite)

the regular high school population several years ago is now easy to

understand. _____ the program at Wilton High School today
    2. (review)

sees it for _____ : a great success. _____
    3. (it/be)   4. (educators/hope)

to gain from the blending of the generations in their high school classes—

more support from the elderly for their educational programs and less of

a communication gap between the two generations—has been realized.

Before the Wilton program was set into motion, many Wilton

teenagers made blanket judgments about _____ capable of
         5. (senior citizens/be)

seeing, doing, understanding, and feeling. The reverse was also

true.Many senior citizens didn't necessarily know _____ in
        6. (their tax dollars/spend)

public education and spoke with contempt about the teenage population.

Nevertheless, since Wilton's senior citizens and teenagers have had

the wonderful opportunity to learn together, senior citizens have come to

understand _____ to be young these days and _____
    7. (it/mean)   8. (teenagers/feel)

about different issues. Similarly, Wilton teenagers have come to appreci-

ate _____ life and _____ to be a senior
    9. (their older friends/look at)   10. (it/mean)

citizen. _____ is no longer simply _____ .
    11. (one/be)   12. (one/look)

Consequently, no one questions _____ now better communica-
        13. (there/be)

tion between the two age groups.

_____ programs like Wilton's throughout the
14. (many other communities/create)
United States makes us realize what a positive step Wilton's town leaders

took when they invited their senior citizens to enroll in regular high

school classes.

3 *Express your opinions on the following topics. Using the noun clauses given, write at least one sentence for each topic. Vary the position of the noun clauses in each sentence: Use the noun clauses as subjects, objects, and complements. After you write your sentences, identify the position you used. The first one has been done for you.*

1. how teenagers dress

   Example:

   How teenagers dress is always a sore point with me because they
   often regard their way of dress as an act of reckless rebellion. But I
   believe they wear a uniform that is as rigid as a businessman's suit.

   [Position: Subject]

   Your sentence:

   _____

   _____

   _____

   [Position: _____]

2. what makes memorizing an effective learning tool

   _____

   _____

   _____

   [Position: _____]

3. that the mobile society continues to have a negative effect on family life

   _____

   _____

   _____

   [Position: _____]

4. why parents are sometimes apprehensive when their children start to stand on their own

_____

_____

_____

[Position: _____]

5. how having preconceived notions about people can be dangerous

_____

_____

_____

[Position: _____]

B. STYLE: Introductory Paragraphs and Thesis Statements

❶ *Working with a partner, examine the introductory paragraph and discuss the questions that follow.*

Have you ever imagined a world in which time stood still? There would be no seasons, fruits would not ripen, and children would not grow up. In fact, history as a subject would not exist at all! As ridiculous as such thoughts may seem, the fact that many people go to great lengths to resist the destructive effects of time is unfortunately true. What they seem to have forgotten is that change is a natural condition in life. By refusing to accept the physical changes that their bodies are naturally undergoing, they lose sight of the beautifully invigorating psychological evolution that can accompany the aging process and condemn themselves to a stagnant and unproductive life.

a. How does the writer attract the reader's attention in the first line?

b. How do you think the ideas develop throughout the paragraph? From the general to the specific? From the specific to the general?

c. Which sentence tells the reader what the main idea of the essay is?

INTRODUCTORY PARAGRAPHS

An essay is composed of an introduction, a body, and a conclusion. In the **introductory paragraph** the writer tries to attract the reader's attention with a provocative sentence. This statement is the first of the paragraph's **general statements,** which introduce the general topic of the essay. There are many ways the writer can spark the reader's interest: a question, a humorous remark, a shocking statement.

The flow of ideas in the paragraph goes from the *general* (large, broad ideas) to the *specific* (details, examples, particular cases). The most specific statement is the thesis statement, which is usually the last sentence of the paragraph.

THESIS STATEMENTS

The **thesis statement** communicates the main idea of the essay. It reflects the writer's narrow focus and point of view, attitude, or opinion, and it also forecasts which aspects of the subject the writer will discuss to support the thesis in the body of the essay. A good thesis statement should have all of the criteria mentioned above.

The thesis statement is not a statement of fact, nor is it a statement that simply announces the general topic of the essay.

Old age is a stage of life.	THIS IS NOT A THESIS STATEMENT. It states a fact; no point of view is given here.
I am going to write about old age.	THIS IS NOT A THESIS STATEMENT. It just provides the general topic of the essay. There is no focus, no point of view, and no indication of which aspects of old age will be discussed.
Old age is a wonderful stage of life.	THIS IS NOT A THESIS STATEMENT. Although it gives us the writer's point of view, there is no specific focus here. What exactly makes old age a "wonderful" stage of life?
Old age is a wonderful stage of life because many elderly people finally come to terms with themselves in their last years as they evaluate their accomplishments and realize their true value as human beings.	THIS IS A THESIS STATEMENT. It explains why the writer believes "old age is a wonderful stage of life" and forecasts what the writer will discuss in the body of the essay: the process of coming to terms with oneself by evaluating one's accomplishments and realizing one's true value as a human being.

❷ *Read the following paragraphs and determine whether or not they would serve as good introductory paragraphs for an essay. Write down your reasons and compare your answers with a partner's.*

1. The available statistics are convincing. After using such products for only four to six months, many men can point to signs of hair regrowth in areas of their scalp where they were once completely bald. These products are now being sought by thousands of men who suffer from male pattern baldness. If you are like Oscar Wilde's character Dorian Gray, and you want to remain the picture of eternal youth for the rest of your life, you will enthusiastically read all the advertisements about the topical solutions that have been proven capable of regrowing hair. In this essay, the writer will discuss baldness.

   This [*circle one:*] is/is not a good introductory paragraph because

   _____

   _____

   _____

2. The idea of adult day care is being translated into reality more and more these days. In the 1970s, there were only a few adult day-care centers. But today there are more than 2,300 such centers across America. These centers, which are mostly run by nonprofit organizations, reflect efforts to keep elderly people out of nursing home facilities and in their homes and communities for as long as possible. Such efforts also reflect sociologists' findings that segregating the elderly creates a financial and moral burden that both families and society must shoulder.

   This [*circle one:*] is/is not a good introductory paragraph because

   _____

   _____

   _____

❸ *Work in pairs. Evaluate the following statements and put a checkmark (✔) next to the ones that are good thesis statements. In your evaluation, do not automatically think that the longer the statement, the better a thesis statement it is. For those you identify as good thesis statements, discuss how you believe the writer will develop each of these statements in the body of the essay.*

   _____ 1. Anything that lives on this earth must change.

   _____ 2. Dispelling labels has got to be done if we would dare to call ourselves a democracy of free people.

   _____ 3. Memory loss is a great problem for old people.

_____ 4. Reading literature is a lifelong process of learning.

_____ 5. Our mobile society has been responsible for the growing separation between age groups and for the growing tendency of each generation to become ignorant of and indifferent to the needs of the other.

_____ 6. Because most countries have compulsory education laws, most children in the world have to attend school until they are at least fourteen years old.

_____ 7. Bringing the young and the old together in the classroom is beneficial to both generations because the children benefit from the grandparents' wisdom and the grandparents benefit from the children's vitality.

4 *Read the following introductory paragraphs and put a checkmark (✓) next to the best thesis statements from the choices given below. Discuss your answers with your partner.*

1. In many countries, families may live in the same geographic region for generation after generation, preserving the structure of traditional family life. This is not so in the United States. From the beginning, Americans were always on the move; they were adventurers, immigrants, and settlers of the West. In the twentieth century, easy access to automobiles contributed to an even greater mobility. In the years since the end of the Second World War, record numbers of young Americans have left their hometowns and driven all over the United States to find employment and create a better future for themselves. But all this freedom of movement has come at a price, as the young and old members of families no longer live in the same communities.

   Thesis Statement?

   _____ a. Geographic mobility is an essential ingredient of the American dream of material success and independence.

   _____ b. Although this mobility has been essential to the economic growth of the country, it has led to many problems.

   _____ c. Geographic mobility has contributed to a decline in traditional family relationships and a growing sense of alienation between the young and the old.

2. People who are discriminated against on the basis of their age are victims of ageism, an attitude that demeans both young and old and prevents society from making full use of its human resources. Once we refuse to consider a person for a job because of his age, we become victims of stereotyping. That most eighty-year-old men would not qualify for physically demanding work is probably true. But isn't it

possible that a vigorous and healthy eighty-year-old man could be a better candidate for an intellectually demanding position than a man half his age? Because we would be inclined to take the application of his forty-year-old counterpart more seriously, wouldn't we be denying the eighty-year-old man not only his individuality, but also his freedom? Although such a situation may seem extreme, it is not difficult to imagine similar situations involving individuals who are much closer in age, within ten to twenty years of one another.

Thesis Statement?

_____ **a.** In light of the extended life span we enjoy today, we need to find ways to re-educate ourselves about matters of age so that we will not have preconceived notions about the abilities of people of different ages.

_____ **b.** In light of the extended life span we enjoy today, old age deserves our careful consideration.

_____ **c.** In light of the extended life span we enjoy today, stereotyping must be avoided.

5 *Choose one of the topics that you wrote about in Exercise 3 on page 43 and write an introductory paragraph for an essay on this topic. Identify your thesis statement.*

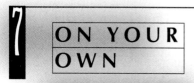

ON YOUR OWN

A. WRITING TOPICS

Write an essay on one of the following topics. In writing the essay, pay particular attention to:

a. making your introduction interesting and relevant to the topic.

b. expressing the main idea of the essay in a well-formulated thesis statement.

Try to include vocabulary and grammar you have studied in the unit.

1. In Reading One, a teacher quotes Yeats saying that "life is a spiral staircase." She continues, "You see the same patterns and scenes but from different places on the steps." In Reading Two, the author writes, "In nature there is change: seasons, cycles, evolution. So, too, there

has to be change for the human person." What do these quotes say to you about growing older?

2. Are old people entitled to special respect or special privileges because of their age? Should they be supported by their children, or should they plan for their own retirement? If old people become ill, where should they go? Do older people have a responsibility to the younger generation? Write an essay about the privileges and duties of old age.

3. Imagine a society in which people are not allowed to live beyond the age of thirty-five. Upon reaching age thirty-five, people in this imaginary society are routinely terminated because it is thought that they are no longer useful to society. Consider the strengths and weaknesses of such a society.

4. What is the meaning of the following quote from the novelist John Gardner? Do you agree or disagree? Write an essay explaining your reaction to this advice to graduating students.

   Life isn't a mountain that has a summit. Nor a game that has a final score. Life is an endless unfolding and, if we wish it to be, an endless process of self-discovery, an endless, unpredictable dialogue between our own potentialities and the life situation in which we find ourselves.

   John Gardner, Stanford University Commencement Address

5. Shakespeare wrote very amusingly and ironically about the "seven ages of man," the different stages we all go through as we move through life. Read the following extract from *As You Like It*. You may need to consult a dictionary or other reference books in the library to help you understand some of the language. Write an essay explaining what Shakespeare meant by "the seven ages," and give examples from your own experiences.

All the world's a stage
And all the men and women merely players.
They have their exits and their entrances;
And one man in his time plays many parts,
His acts being seven ages. At first the infant,
Mewling and puking in his nurse's arms.
Then the whining school-boy, with his satchel
And shining morning face, creeping like snail
Unwillingly to school. And then the lover,
Sighing like furnace, with woeful ballad
Made to his mistress' eyebrow. Then a soldier,
Full of strange oaths, and bearded like the pard,[1]
Jealous in honor, sudden and quick in quarrel,
Seeking the bubble reputation

Even in the cannon's mouth. And then the justice,
In fair round belly with good capon lined,
With eyes severe and beard of formal cut,
Full of wise saws and modern instances;
And so he plays his part. The sixth age shifts
Into the lean and slippered pantaloon,
With spectacles on nose and pouch on side,
His youthful hose, well-saved, a world too wide
For his shrunk shank; and his big manly voice,
Turning again toward childish treble, pipes
and whistles in his sound. Last scene of all,
That ends this strange eventful history,
Is second childishness and mere oblivion,
Sans[2] teeth, sans eyes, sans taste, sans everything.

William Shakespeare

---

[1] *Leopard*
[2] French word meaning "without"

B. FIELDWORK

PREPARATION

Since 1900, the life expectancy of the average American has increased about 30 years. In 1900, Americans lived an average of 45 years. Now, toward the end of the twentieth century, Americans live an average of 72 to 75 years.

Why do you believe Americans are living longer now? Write down five reasons for their longer life span, and then share your answers with a partner.

RESEARCH ACTIVITY

Go to the library and do research on the life expectancy of people in your community. Take notes and summarize the information you obtain.

1. Find out what the major causes of death are (for example, accidents, chronic diseases of the heart and the lungs, cancer, infectious diseases such as tuberculosis and AIDS) for people in your community.

2. For the elderly, those people who live the longest in your society, find out which diseases are particularly related to advancing old age and how society helps the elderly to cope with these diseases.

SHARING YOUR FINDINGS

Write a report.

1. In the introduction, give the main idea that ties your research findings together.

2. In the body, summarize your findings in detail. (How are the elderly helped to cope with the aging process in general and with the traumas of long-term illness and terminal illness? What kinds of social programs cater to the elderly? etc.).

3. In the conclusion, give your own recommendations for health care for the elderly in your community.

THE ROAD TO SUCCESS

1 APPROACHING THE TOPIC

A. PREDICTING

Do you think this photo is a good representation of the struggle for success? Why or why not? Share your thoughts with another student.

B. SHARING INFORMATION

Work in a small group. Take a survey of the people in your group to find out where they believe they belong on this "hope scale." Tally the results and indicate how many people are generally "pessimistic" or generally "optimistic" and how many fall "in-between." Next to each result, write down the general reasons that the person gave for being either optimistic or pessimistic or in-between.

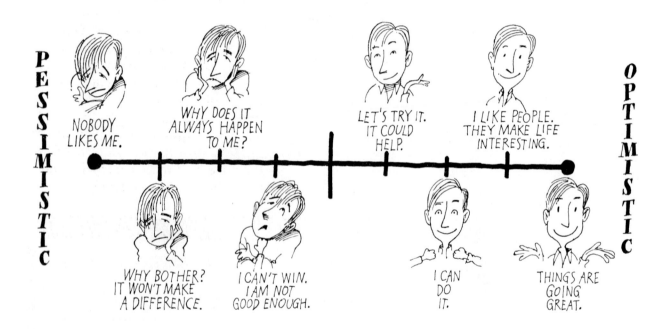

2 PREPARING TO READ

A. BACKGROUND

Read this information and take the Self-Discovery Quiz that follows. Feel free to write about your own personal experiences. Discuss your responses and your goal with a partner.

People's outlook on life has a lot to do with their potential for success. Some researchers have found a direct link between hope and success. They have found that optimists—people who always see the bright side of things—are more likely to succeed in life than pessimists, their direct opposites. Hope does not just involve having a belief in good results. It involves having both the will and the means to reach one's goal. People with hope have some traits in common: they turn to friends for advice, they regard setbacks as challenges and not as failures, they know how to break a big goal into smaller chunks and work on one aspect at a time.

Hope is the driving force of Katie, the main character in "Gotta Dance," the short story that you will read in this unit. It is the first published short story of Jackson Jodie Daviss, a freelance writer who lives in New Hampshire. In speaking of this story, the author stated that it allowed her to "say some things about the need to find acceptance on our own terms, and to define our own ideas of home and family."

SELF-DISCOVERY QUIZ

Achieving success has a lot to do with how you look at yourself.

1. Write down three things that you like about yourself.

   _____

   _____

   _____

2. Write down a goal that you would like to achieve.

   _____

3. What is your target date for achieving it?

   _____

4. What obstacles or opposition to your goal might you encounter?

   _____

5. What are some first steps you could take toward your goal?

   _____

B. VOCABULARY FOR COMPREHENSION

Work in pairs to match the underlined expressions in each sentence with the meanings listed in the columns below.

c 1. My uncle's remark that I would never succeed in life, no matter how hard I tried, <u>lit a fire under</u> me.

g 2. The orchestra leader's arms were tight and stiff when he directed his musicians to play a military march, but they were <u>loose and swaying</u> when he led them in playing a soft and gentle lullabye.

a 3. The passengers enjoy the smoothness of the new train, which <u>eases into and out of</u> stations with <u>no jolts to their systems</u>.

h 4. Waiting on tables for eight hours without a break can really <u>take it out of you</u>.

i 5. Because I was not hungry, and eating dinner was the last thing on my mind, I <u>only picked at my food</u>.

e 6. The dancer <u>tapped a step</u> and listened to its echo before continuing the dance.

j 7. Once she started dancing, she danced so well that she didn't <u>miss a beat</u>.

b 8. The beat of the music was so lively that she <u>let the rhythm take her</u>, no longer thinking about what she was doing.

d 9. When the young girl finally realized what she had to do in order to succeed, everything <u>came together</u> and she knew success was around the corner.

f 10. Because she had no doubt that the decision she had made was the right one, the woman had <u>no weights, no worries</u>.

11. reluctant
12. shabby

a. arrives in and departs from . . . quietly, without creating a shock

b. automatically followed the music

c. angered and motivated

d. made sense

e. hit the floor with her heels and toes in rapid succession according to a certain rhythm

f. no burdens, no anxieties

g. free and swinging

h. exhaust; knock . . . out

i. ate very little, with no appetite

j. make one mistake

3

READING ONE: Gotta Dance

A. INTRODUCING THE TOPIC

*NS. & U.S.A are
non-fiction* ← *text.
article
essays
reports*

Discuss these questions with a partner. Then read the story.

Did you ever have a compulsion, something you felt you *had* to do, no matter what the obstacles or consequences? Did you act on your feelings? Were you glad you did?

Gotta Dance[1]

BY JACKSON JODIE DAVISS

1   Maybe I shouldn't have mentioned it to anyone. Before I knew it, it was all through the family, and they'd all made it their business to challenge me. I wouldn't tell them my plans, other than to say I was leaving, but that was enough to set them off. Uncle Mike called from Oregon to say, "Katie, don't do it," and I wouldn't have hung up on him except that he added, "Haven't you caused enough disappointment?" That did it. Nine people had already told me no, and Uncle Mike lit the fire under me when he made it ten. Nine-eight-seven-six-five-four-three-two-one. Kaboom.

2   On my way to the bus station, I stopped by the old house. I still had my key and I knew no one was home. After ducking my head into each room, including my old one, just to be sure I was alone, I went into my brother's room and set my duffel bag and myself on his bed.

3   The blinds were shut so the room was dim, but I looked around at all the things I knew by heart and welcomed the softening effect of the low light. I sat there a very long time in the silence until I began to think I might never rise from that bed or come out of that gray light, so I pushed myself to my feet. I eased off my sneakers and pushed the rug aside so I could have some polished floor, then I pulled the door shut.

---

[1] *gotta dance:* slang expression for "I have got to dance," "I must dance"

4   Anyone passing in the hall outside might've heard a soft sound, a gentle sweeping sound, maybe a creak of the floor, but not much more as I danced a very soft shoe[2] in my stocking feet. Arms outstretched but loose and swaying, head laid back and to one side, like falling asleep, eyes very nearly closed in that room like twilight, I danced to the beat of my heart.

foreshadows

5   After a while, I straightened the rug, opened the blinds to the bright day and walked out of what was now just another room without him in it. He was the only one I said good-bye to, and the only one I asked to come with me, if he could.

6   At the bus station, I asked the guy for a ticket to the nearest city of some size. Most of them are far apart in the Midwest and I liked the idea of those long rides with time to think. I like buses—the long-haul kind, anyway—because they're so public that they're private. I also like the pace, easing you out of one place before easing you into the next, no big jolts to your system.

long distance

7   My bus had very few people in it and the long ride was uneventful, except when the little boy threw his hat out the window. The mother got upset, but the kid was happy. He clearly hated that hat; I'd seen him come close to launching it twice before he finally let fly. The thing sailed in a beautiful arc, then settled on a fence post, a ringer, just the way you never can do it when you try. The woman asked the driver if he'd mind going back for the hat. He said he'd mind. So the woman stayed upset and the kid stayed happy. I liked her well enough, but the boy was maybe the most annoying kid I've come across, so I didn't offer him the money to buy a hat he and his mother could agree on. Money would have been no problem. Money has never been my problem.

8   There are some who say money is precisely my problem, in that I give it so little thought. I don't own much. I lose things all the time. I'm told I dress lousy. I'm told, too, that I have no appreciation of money because I've never had to do without it. That may be true. But even if it is, it's not all there is to say about a person.

9   There is one thing I do well, and money didn't buy it, couldn't have bought it for me. I am one fine dancer. I can dance like nobody you've ever seen. Heck, I can dance like everybody you've ever seen. I didn't take lessons, not the usual kind, because I'm a natural, but I've worn out a few sets of tapes and a VCR. I'd watch Gene Kelly and practice until I had his steps. Watch Fred Astaire, practice, get his steps. I practice all the time. Bill Robinson. Eleanor Powell. Donald O'Connor. Ginger Rogers. You know, movie dancers. I'm a movie dancer. I don't dance in the movies though. Never have. Who does, anymore? I dance where and when I can.

---

[2] *a soft shoe:* tap dance steps but without taps (metal caps) on the shoes; a silent dance

10   My many and vocal relatives don't think much, have never thought much, of my dancing—largely, I believe, because they are not dancers themselves. To be honest, they don't think much of anything I do, not since I left the path they'd set for me, and that's been most of my twenty-three years. These people, critical of achievement they don't understand, without praise for talents and dreams or the elegant risk, are terrified of being left behind but haven't the grace to come along in spirit.

11   Mutts and I talked a lot about that. He was a family exception, as I am, and he thought whatever I did was more than fine. He was my brother, and I backed everything he did, too. He played blues harmonica. He told bad jokes. We did have plans. His name was Ronald, but everyone's called him Mutts since he was a baby. No one remembers why. He never got his chance to fly, and I figure if I don't do this now, I maybe never will. I need to do it for both of us.

12   The bus depot was crowded and crummy, like most city depots seem to be. I stored my bag in a locker, bought a paper and headed for where the bright lights would be. I carried my tap shoes and tape player.

13   When I reached the area I wanted it was still early, so I looked for a place to wait. I found a clean diner, with a big front window where I could read the paper and watch for the lines to form. I told the waitress I wanted a large cup of coffee before ordering. After half an hour or so, she brought another refill and asked if I was ready. She was kind and patient and I wondered what she was doing in the job. It seems like nothing takes it out of you like waitress work. She was young; maybe that was it. I asked her what was good and she recommended the baked chicken special, and said it was what she had on her break. That's what I had, and she was right, but I only picked at it. I wanted something for energy, but I didn't want to court a sideache, so the only thing I really ate was the salad. She brought an extra dinner roll and stayed as pleasant the whole time I was there, which was the better part of two hours, so I put down a good tip when I left.

14   While I was in the diner, a truly gaunt[3] young man came in. He ordered only soup, but he ate it like he'd been hungry a long time. He asked politely for extra crackers and the waitress gave them to him. When he left he was full of baked chicken special with an extra dinner roll. He wouldn't take a loan. Pride, maybe, or maybe he didn't believe I could spare it, and I didn't want to be sitting in a public place pushing the idea that I had plenty of money. Maybe I don't know the value of money but I do know what discretion is worth. The guy was reluctant even to take the chicken dinner, but I convinced him that if he didn't eat it, nobody would. He reminded me of Mutts, except that Mutts had never been hungry like that.

---

[3] *gaunt:* very thin

15   When the lines were forming, I started on over. While I waited, I watched the people. There were some kids on the street, dressed a lot like me in my worn jeans, faded turtleneck, and jersey warm-up jacket. They were working the crowd like their hopes amounted to spare change. The theater patrons waiting in line were dressed to the nines,[4] as they say. There is something that makes the well-dressed not look at the shabby. Maybe it's guilt. Maybe it's embarrassment because, relatively, they're overdressed. I don't know. I do know it makes it easy to study them in detail. Probably makes them easy marks[5] for pickpockets, too. The smell of them was rich: warm wool, sweet spice and alcohol, peppermint and shoe polish. I thought I saw Mutts at the other edge of the crowd, just for a moment, but I remembered he couldn't be.

16   I was wearing my sneakers, carrying my taps. They're slickery[6] black shoes that answer me back. They're among the few things I've bought for myself and I keep them shiny. I sat on the curb and changed my shoes. I tied the sneakers together and draped them over my shoulder.

17   I turned on my tape player and the first of my favorite show tunes began as I got to my feet. I waited a few beats but no one paid attention until I started to dance. My first taps rang off the concrete clear and clean, measured, a telegraphed message: *Takka-takka-takka-tak! Takka-takka-takka-tak! Takka-takka-takka-tak-tak-tak!* I paused; everyone turned.

18   I tapped an oh-so-easy, wait-a-minute time-step while I lifted the sneakers from around my neck. I gripped the laces in my right hand and gave the shoes a couple of overhead, bola-style swings, tossing them to land beside the tape player, neat as you please. I didn't miss a beat. The audience liked it. I knew they would. Then I let the rhythm take me and I started to fly. Everything came together. I had no weight, no worries, just the sweet, solid beat. Feets, do your stuff.[7]

19   Didn't I *dance*. And wasn't I *smooth*. Quick taps and slow-rolling, jazz it, swing it, on the beat, off the beat, out of one tune right into the next and the next and I never took one break. It was a chill of a night, but didn't I sweat, didn't that jacket just have to come off. Didn't I feel the solid jar to the backbone from the heavy heel steps, and the pump of my heart on the beat on the beat.

20   Time passed. I danced. A sandy-haired man came out of the theater. He looked confused. He said, "Ladies and Gentlemen, curtain in five minutes." I'm sure that's what he said. Didn't I dance and didn't they

---

[4] *dressed to the nines:* dressed in expensive clothes
[5] *easy mark:* an easy victim
[6] *slickery:* patent leather, shiny and smooth
[7] *"Feets, do your stuff":* "Feet, start dancing"

all stay. The sandy-haired man, he was tall and slim and he looked like a dancer. Didn't he stay, too.

21   Every move I knew, I made, every step I learned, I took, until the tape had run out, until they set my rhythm with the clap of their hands, until the sweet sound of the overture drifted out, until I knew for certain they had held the curtain for want of an audience. Then I did my knock-down, drag-out, could-you-just-die, great big Broadway-baby finish.

22   Didn't they applaud, oh honey, didn't they yell, and didn't they throw money. I dug coins from my own pockets and dropped them, too, leaving it all for the street kids. Wasn't the slender man with the sandy hair saying, "See me after the show"? I'm almost sure that's what he said as I gripped my tape recorder, grabbed my sneakers, my jacket, and ran away, ran with a plan and a purpose, farther with each step from my beginnings and into the world, truly heading home.

23   The blood that drummed in my ears set the rhythm as I ran, ran easy, taps ringing off the pavement, on the beat, on the beat, on the beat. Everything was pounding, but I had to make the next bus, that I knew, catch that bus and get on to the next town, and the next, and the next, and the next. Funeral tomorrow, but Mutts will not be there, no, and neither will I. I'm on tour.

glove cleaner

B. READING FOR MAIN IDEAS

"Gotta Dance" can be divided into three parts. Write a sentence that summarizes the main idea of each part of the story. Use your own words. The first one has been done for you.

Part I: Saying Good-bye (paragraphs 1–5)

After saying good-bye to her childhood home and the memory of her brother, Katie decides to change her life.

Part II: On the Road (paragraphs 6–14)

_____

_____

Part III: Meeting the Challenge (paragraphs 15–23)

_____

_____

C. READING FOR DETAILS

First circle your answers to the questions below. Then compare your answers with another student's. There is only one correct answer for each item.

1. How would you describe the attitude of the majority of Katie's family?

   a. critical of Katie's desire to be a dancer

   b. encouraging risk-taking

   c. very supportive of all her plans

2. Which statement is *not* true of Mutts?

   a. he loved playing the blues

   b. he died before he could realize his dream

   c. his sister was very upset at his funeral

3. Which of the following did Katie do before setting out for the bus depot?

   a. she went straight to her brother's room after entering her old house

   b. she danced a soft shoe in her brother's room to the beat of a famous jazz album

   c. she danced with a lot of emotion in her brother's room knowing full well that no one else was in the house

4. Which one of Katie's ideas must she re-evaluate as a result of her experiences?

   a. the pace of a long bus trip allows her time for reflection

   b. waiters and waitresses are generally impatient and unkind

   c. bus depots are usually dirty and packed with a lot of people

5. What did Katie observe when she was in the bus?

   a. on his third attempt, the little boy succeeded in throwing his hat out the window

   b. the little boy showed what perfect aim he had when his hat landed on a fence post

   c. the bus driver responded to the mother with a lot of compassion

6. Why did Katie go the diner?

   a. she needed to be in a quiet place to think more about her brother

   b. she needed to wait for her audience to arrive and to mentally and physically prepare for her performance

   c. she needed to sit down for a while to take care of a pain in her side

7. What thoughts did Katie have when she was watching the lines form in front of the theater?

   a. she considered how differences in dress can cause people to be uncomfortable with each other

   b. she realized that one should dress up when going to the theater

   c. she thought the street kids would be chased away by the police

8. Which of the following is true about Katie's performance?

   a. the theatergoers liked it so much that they missed the first five minutes of the show they had been waiting in line to see

   b. Katie was offered a job

   c. Katie was satisfied with her performance

D. READING BETWEEN THE LINES

*Based on what is implied in the short story, discuss whether these statements are true or false with your partner and write **T** or **F** on the line. Then write a sentence explaining why you made that decision. What points in the story tend to support your inference?*

_____ 1. Katie was a very private person.

   Support: _____

_____ 2. Family was important to Katie.

   Support: _____

_____ 3. Dancing came easily to Katie.

   Support: _____

_____ 4. Katie was ambitious.

   Support: _____

_____ **5.** Katie sympathized with children like herself who rebel against their families.

Support: _____

_____ **6.** Katie was careless with money.

Support: _____

_____ **7.** To Katie, "going home" meant fulfilling her dreams.

Support: _____

4 READING TWO: Keeping Your Confidence Up

A. EXPANDING THE TOPIC

Before you read "Keeping Your Confidence Up," write down three qualities that you consider essential for success and explain why. Then compare your answers with the class and discuss your reasons.

Keeping Your Confidence Up

BY DENNIS O'GRADY
(from *Taking the Fear Out of Changing*)

1   Success seeks to help you become more accepting of your genuine strengths. Self-approval unleashes[1] your best traits to be expressed in your work and family life, and in the world. How can you learn to accept your successes without panicking? Here are some practical ways to learn to celebrate all of your **SUCCESSES**.

---

[1] *to unleash:* to release

2   SELF-ESTEEM. Being a genuine achiever means you acknowledge your strengths, hunt for your secret talents and give your best to the world without being a braggart.[2]

Build Self-Confidence: Learn from your failures.

3   UNDERSTANDING. Achievement means you are an intense person who expresses who you really are while staying open to growing and changing each and every day.

Build Self-Confidence: Thrive on[3] responsibility.

4   CHILD DRIVE. You pay attention to inner urges that speak to you about what work you love to do and what insights[4] you have to give the world.

Build Self-Confidence: Make work fun.

5   CURIOSITY. You talk, talk and talk some more to people to find out what makes them tick. You soak up information like a sunbather taking in sunshine.

Build Self-Confidence: Take good advice.

6   ENERGY. You maximize your energy by eating, sleeping, exercising and working in recognition of your own special rhythms. You do what makes you feel most alive.

Build Self-Confidence: Keep your energy high.

7   SET GOALS. You dignify life with long-term goals and mark your progression toward them.

Build Self-Confidence: Choose commitment.

8   STAY FOCUSED. You intensely focus single-mindedly on the most important tasks to accomplish, and say "No way!" to nifty distractions.[5]

Build Self-Confidence: Accept self-discipline.

9   ERRORS. You make errors every day and know that if you aren't failing at least once a day then you aren't succeeding. You try again to hit the mark after you've missed it.

Build Self-Confidence: Never accept failure as a permanent state.

10   SATISFACTION. You endorse[6] yourself for your wins, follow a consistent set of values and take humble pride in all of your accomplishments.

Build Self-Confidence: Feel gratified.

11   Permit yourself to be a genuine achiever instead of an impostor. Real people aren't impostors—we are the genuine article. Take the risk and be the real McCoy![7]

---

[2] *braggart:* someone who boasts a lot
[3] *to thrive on:* to draw success from
[4] *insights:* clear, perceptive thoughts
[5] *nifty distractions:* pleasurable amusements
[6] *to endorse:* to show approval of
[7] *the real McCoy:* the real thing, not something artificial or phony (after Kid McCoy, professional name for American boxer Norman Selby, 1873–1940)

Dennis O'Grady's principles of success can be applied to typical problems that come up in business. Consider these situations and determine what O'Grady would recommend. Discuss your answers with a partner, and refer to specific parts of the text that support your interpretation. Write your answers on the lines provided.

1. You have been working seven days a week on a project that must be completed two weeks from now. Because it requires your full attention, you will need to make use of your every waking minute in the next two weeks in order to complete the project. Yet you are tempted to take advantage of an airline's cheap four-day "getaway" vacation in the Florida sun. What should you do?

_____

_____

_____

2. After being in business for several years, it is clear that you are on the road to becoming a real success. You are not sure what kind of image you need to project in public. Should you flaunt your success and boast about your great fortune, or should you act like a regular guy and behave as if you are just like everyone else?

_____

_____

_____

3. You have a very important decision to make about a policy that will have a great impact on the future of your company. You know that there will be great dissatisfaction no matter which direction you take. You usually make all your decisions on your own. Should you consult your staff or go it alone?

_____

_____

_____

4. The promotion you had been hoping for does not come through because of a poor performance evaluation. You have lost confidence in yourself. How should you deal with this situation?

_____

_____

_____

5. You are offered a high-paying job in a field that really doesn't interest you. Nevertheless, the increase in salary would dramatically change your current lifestyle. You are now earning a much lower salary while taking courses in the field of your choice. What should you do?

_____

_____

_____

6. You are a valued employee. Nevertheless, your supervisor has complained to your boss that you nap and take exercise at unauthorized times. He would like you to follow the normal break and lunch schedule. What should you explain to your boss?

_____

_____

_____

B. LINKING READINGS ONE AND TWO

Choose one topic.

1. You are a journalist in a small Midwestern town. Write a short article about a strange occurrence that happened last night at 8 P.M. A young girl named Katie began to dance in the street by the theater.

2. You are Dennis O'Grady. Write a short article answering this question: Does Katie's story illustrate any of your principles of success and if so, how?

REVIEWING LANGUAGE

A. EXPLORING LANGUAGE: Hyphenated Adjectives

When we use a two-word or compound adjective, or a group of words before a noun, we use hyphens[1] and make some minor structural changes. Hyphenated adjectives can give texture, exuberance, and poetic feeling to a work of prose.

With descriptions
  ◆ a man with sandy hair (light brown or blond) = a sandy-haired man
  ◆ a table with three legs = a three-legged table

Measurements in time or space involving plurals
  ◆ a child who is two years old = a two-year-old child
  ◆ a house with three stories = a three-story house

❶ *Change the following expressions to hyphenated adjectives.*

1. a boy with blue eyes   = _____

2. a hat with three corners   = _____

3. a woman with thin lips   = _____

4. a girl with a broken heart   = _____

5. a law that is ten years old   = _____

6. a weight of ten pounds   = _____

7. a plan for five years   = _____

---

[1] Many rules of hyphenation are complicated and may be unclear. If you are unsure, look up the word in a good dictionary.

2 *Look back at the story "Gotta Dance" and find two sentences that use a number of hyphenated adjectives in the climax of the story (the last six paragraphs). Then rewrite these expressions as hyphenated adjectives.*

1. a step that tells the audience to wait a minute =

   _____

2. an ending similar to what an actress in a Broadway musical would do =

   _____

3. a finish that makes you want to die from happiness =

   _____

4. a finish that knocks the audience out because it is so good =

   _____

B. WORKING WITH WORDS

Fill in the blanks with the following expressions as you read the possible thoughts of the sandy-haired man in "Gotta Dance."

backed	picked up the pace	the better part
for want of	reluctantly	the long haul
hold the curtain	shabby	to the nines
miss a beat	take it out of you	

It may seem glamorous, but let me tell you, working in the theater can really *take it out of you*
                                                                                              1. (wear you out)

I've been a dancer, singer, ticket taker, scenery painter, and everything else you can think of for

the better part of the last twenty years. Of course, sometimes show business can really
2. (most)

surprise you and then, all of a sudden, it all comes together.

I remember one time we were on tour in a *shabby* little theater in a small city in the
                                                    3. (run-down)

Midwest. The locals were all dressed *to the nines*, waiting for the show to begin. But
                                            4. (in their fancy clothes)

when we finally opened the doors, no one came in! No one! We couldn't understand it. All we

could hear was music from the street. ___Reluctantly___ , I went outside to announce the curtain
<u>5. (With unwilling steps)</u>

and saw a young woman in jeans and tap shoes dancing for the crowd. She didn't ___miss a beat___
<u>6. (hesitate for a minute)</u>

as she danced her heart out. I couldn't take my eyes off her and neither could anyone else. As she

___pick up the pace___, we all began clapping with her, marking the rhythm, showing our pleasure.
<u>7. (went faster and faster)</u>

___For want of___ an audience, the company even agreed to ___hold the curtain___.
<u>8. (Lacking)</u>   <u>9. (start the show late)</u>

I would've ___backed___ her to get a job dancing. I knew that right away as soon as
<u>10. (helped)</u>

I saw her, with no time needed to think it over. She was a natural! Sure, she needed training and

polish, but she had the fire and joy in her eyes that would keep her out there for ___the long haul___.
<u>11. (a long time)</u>

I guess she didn't hear what I said to her that night. We were all pretty shocked and surprised. She

asked for nothing, didn't even tell us her name. I can still see her running off into the night and

wonder what happened to her.

6 SKILLS FOR EXPRESSION

A. GRAMMAR: Identifying and Nonidentifying Adjective Clauses

❶ *Working in pairs, examine the sentences and discuss the questions that follow.*

◆ People <u>who are unwilling to risk failure</u> are not capable of achieving big successes.

◆ The waitress stayed as pleasant the whole time I was there, <u>which was the better part of two hours</u>, so I put down a good tip when I left.

a. In the first sentence, what kind of people are being discussed?

b. In the second sentence, how much time did Katie spend in the restaurant?

c. Which words come at the beginning of the phrases printed in bold letters?

d. Do you notice any difference in punctuation in the two sentences?

Adjective Clauses

FOCUS ON GRAMMAR

See adjective clauses in *Focus On Grammar, Advanced.*

Adjective clauses define, describe, or add information about nouns just as adjectives do. These clauses must have a subject and a verb, but they are fragments, not full sentences. The adjective clause can begin with the relative pronouns **who, whom, which, that,** and **whose**, or the relative adverbs **when** and **where. Who** is used for people, **which** is used for things, and **that** can be used for both people and things.

Identifying Adjective Clauses

Identifying adjective clauses give information that is *essential* to the meaning of the sentence.

- People **who are unwilling to risk failure** are not capable of achieving big successes.

If you take the adjective clause out of this sentence, the sentence itself no longer has any precise meaning. "People are not capable of achieving big successes" is vague and unclear because it implies that no one can ever succeed. The adjective clause is needed because it tells us specifically which people the statement is referring to. Identifying adjective clauses do not have any commas.

Nonidentifying Adjective Clauses

Nonidentifying adjective clauses have a different function in the sentence: they only provide extra or additional information. If nonidentifying adjective clauses are left out, the sentence still retains its basic meaning.

- The waitress stayed as pleasant the whole time I was there, **which was the better part of two hours,** so I put down a good tip when I left.

The significant clauses of this sentence are "The waitress stayed as pleasant the whole time I was there, so I put down a good tip when I left." The adjective clause is not essential to the meaning of the sentence. It provides only an additional piece of information about the time.

GRAMMAR TIP: In nonidentifying adjective clauses
—we do not use *that*
—we place commas at the beginning and end of the clause unless it comes at the end of a sentence.

2 *Underline the adjective clauses in the sentences that follow. Decide whether they are identifying or nonidentifying, and write* **I** *or* **N** *on the line. Then add the appropriate punctuation.*

_____ 1. People who lack the courage to fail also lack what it takes to achieve big successes.

_____ 2. Attitudes that help you feel positive about yourself are the key to success.

_____ 3. Dennis O'Grady who is quoted in this unit is a popular writer on motivational thinking.

_____ 4. A company whose executives are highly motivated will usually succeed.

_____ 5. A college speaker whose exact name I've now forgotten helped us to understand the power of positive thinking.

_____ 6. A modern idea which I do not share at all is that success can only be measured in financial terms.

_____ 7. The research director patiently pursued theories which others had discovered and developed.

_____ 8. The executive who wants to climb the corporate ladder will have to "go the extra mile" and work long hours.

3 *Combine the following phrases into a complete sentence, using relative pronouns and adjective clauses. The first one has been done for you.*

1. Katie was a self-taught dancer. She considered herself a "natural."

   Katie, who considered herself a "natural," was a self-taught dancer.

2. A young man entered the restaurant hungry. He left it with a full belly.

   _____

3. Katie was off to find a new place in the world. Katie's brother had just died.

   _____

4. Katie was thinking about a mother. The mother's son had just thrown his hat out the window of the bus.

   _____

5. Katie waited two hours at a diner. At the diner she had an excellent view of the people lining up for the theater.

   _____

6. Tap dancing is an American dance form. It was popularized by Hollywood movies.

   _____

B. STYLE: Paragraph Development— Supporting a Topic Sentence with Illustration and Conclusion

1 *Working in pairs, examine the paragraph and discuss the questions that follow.*

People who are unwilling to risk failure are not capable of achieving big successes. The careers of the inventor Thomas Edison and the comedian Charlie Chaplin serve as good examples. Without Thomas Edison, we might still be reading in the dark today. But did you know that Edison discovered the lightbulb after a thousand different attempts? When asked what he had learned from those one thousand mistakes, Edison responded that he had found one thousand ways in which a lightbulb could not be made. During his early days in London, people threw things at Charlie Chaplin to make him get off the stage. Would we be enjoying the starring film roles of this famous comedian today if he had taken those audiences' reactions to heart and stopped pursuing his dream to become an actor? Learning to cope with failure makes you strong enough to view every defeat as another step toward success.

a. What kind of information does the first sentence provide?

b. What do the next six sentences have to do with the first sentence?

c. Which sentence does the last sentence refer back to?

Illustration

Illustration, an essential ingredient of effective writing, is used to clarify or support the main idea that has been expressed in the **topic sentence** of a paragraph. To illustrate an idea, a writer provides clear and concise examples, persuasive explanations, appropriate statistics, and relevant anecdotes (brief stories) that support the topic sentence.

In the example paragraph, the writer provides statistics and anecdotes about the lives of Thomas Edison and Charlie Chaplin to show how both these famous people would not have become great successes if they had not risked failure. Thomas Edison's one thousand failed attempts before discovering the lightbulb and Charlie Chaplin's experiences of having things thrown at him when he first started to act are two examples that not only convince the reader of the logic of the topic sentence, but also prepare the reader for the **concluding sentence,** which reinforces the main idea of the paragraph.

② *Work with a partner on developing an appropriate topic sentence for the fully developed paragraph below.*

Topic Sentence: _____

_____

Both Judy Garland and Marilyn Monroe were wonderful entertainers. Although they died in the 1960s, they are still remembered today for their genius as performers. Judy Garland was a fine actress and singer. There isn't a child who doesn't know her as Dorothy in the classic film, *The Wizard of Oz*. Moreover, adults are still buying compact discs of her many record albums. Marilyn Monroe played comic and tragic roles in films and on the live stage. People today still watch videos of *Some Like It Hot*, *The Misfits*, and *Bus Stop*, her most famous films. Yet both these actresses tried to commit suicide many times. It is not clear if their actual deaths were the result of suicide attempts. What is clear, however, is that despite their great successes, they were not happy people.

③ *Work in a small group. Analyze Katie's character. Find the supporting statements in "Gotta Dance" which illustrate the descriptions below. Write them on a separate piece of paper.*

1. Katie is a loving and caring person.

2. Katie is a generous person.

3. Katie is an ambitious person.

④ *Develop the idea of this topic sentence. Write a complete paragraph with the necessary supporting and concluding statements. Then, in a small group, compare your paragraphs.*

Topic Sentence: "People who decide to follow their dreams sometimes have to go against the wishes of those who love them the most."

_____

_____

_____

_____

_____

_____

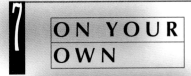

ON YOUR OWN

A. WRITING TOPICS

Write an essay on one of the following topics. Be sure to write a topic sentence for each of your paragraphs and to support your views with examples and explanations.

1. Discuss the three main qualities that you feel are needed to achieve success in your society.

2. The CEO (chief executive officer) of a major company once said that the most successful person he knew was his gardener—a man loved by his family, respected by his friends, a man who worked hard and had a full life. Would you agree or disagree with this statement? Comment on the definition of success expressed here. Do you think the CEO would agree to change places with the gardener? Would you?

3. What do you think Katie's life will be like after the end of her story? Continue Katie's story and explain how certain aspects of her life and personality will influence her future. (You may want to refer to the work you did on page 72 as you work on this topic.)

4. Read the following poem. Explain what you believe Mary Oliver is saying in her poem and compare her "journey" with Katie's in "Gotta Dance."

The Journey

One day you finally knew
what you had to do, and began,
though the voices around you
kept shouting
their bad advice—
though the whole house
began to tremble
and you felt the old tug
at your ankles.
"Mend my life!"
each voice cried.
But you didn't stop.
You knew what you had to do,
though the wind pried
with its stiff fingers
at the very foundations—
though their melancholy
was terrible.

It was already late
enough, and a wild night,
and the road full of fallen
branches and stones.
But little by little,
as you left their voices behind,
the stars began to burn
through the sheets of clouds,
and there was a new voice,
which you slowly
recognized as your own,
that kept you company
as you strode deeper and deeper
into the world,
determined to do
the only thing you could do—
determined to save
the only life you could save.

Mary Oliver

B. FIELDWORK

PREPARATION

Identifying Career Goals

Before interviewing a successful person, think about your own career goals. Use the career ladder at left to analyze your career goals.

1. At the top of the ladder, identify your **long-term goal**.

2. Consider the plan you will follow to get there. Include on each step of the ladder the **short-term goals** that you will need to meet in order to achieve your long-term goal.

3. Set a **timetable** for each step. That is, determine how long you are mentally prepared to work on each phase of your climb on this ladder.

4. Next to each short-term goal, write down the **difficulties** that you believe you will encounter and how you hope to deal with them.

RESEARCH ACTIVITY

Interviewing a Successful Person

Now that you've analyzed your own career goals, interview a successful person.

Write down the name of a successful person:

_____

1. Explain why you think this person is successful:

_____

_____

2. Prepare to interview this person. Use the four factors you have already considered—long-term goal, short-term goals, timetable, difficulties encountered—to prepare questions for the interview. Next, brainstorm with a partner to come up with a list of questions for each factor that you believe will be worth considering.

SHARING YOUR FINDINGS

1. Examine your notes taken during the interview.

2. Write a summary of the interview. What have you learned? What can be applied to your own career?

WATER, WATER EVERYWHERE...

"I Never Thought It Could Happen To Me."

1 APPROACHING THE TOPIC

A. PREDICTING

Look at this photo. Discuss with a partner what you think this man and his family are facing. What is he going to do? Who will help him?

B. SHARING INFORMATION

These pictures show people fighting a flood in the Mississippi River valley. Work in a small group and write captions for a magazine article explaining what has happened. The first caption has been written for you.

1.

Mocking an American symbol, the Mississippi River moves inland one mile to swallow a five-foot McDonald's sign.

2.

_____
_____
_____
_____
_____

3.

_____
_____
_____
_____

4.

_____
_____
_____

2 PREPARING TO READ

A. BACKGROUND

Read this information and do the map work that follows.

Water is a powerful natural force: Too little and we have deserts and drought; too much and we have storms and floods. In the United States, during the flood of 1993, rain and floodwater spread over nine states and hundreds of miles of the Mississippi River valley. Fifty people died, and damages were estimated at more than $10 billion. Officials say that it was a record once-in-a-hundred-year flood brought on by an extremely unusual eight months of very heavy rain.

1 *Look at the map below and fill in the blanks.*

The Mississippi River flows 2,350 miles from (1) _____ , Minnesota, to the (2) _____ . The area affected by the flood extended from Minneapolis, Minnesota, to (3) _____ , _____ (where the Ohio River runs into the Mississippi). This northern area is normally protected by 2,000 miles of levees or dams on the upper Mississippi.

2 *Work with a partner. Find the following towns on the map below, and fill in the blanks with their numbers to mark their location.*

1. **Ste. Genevieve, Missouri:** This town of 4,500 people was settled by French pioneers in the mid-eighteenth century. <u>100 miles north of Cairo, Illinois.</u>

2. **Hardin, Illinois:** The people of Hardin fought the flood block by block. <u>20 miles north of where the Illinois River joins the Mississippi.</u>

3. **St. Louis, Missouri:** A 52-foot flood wall protected this city of 400,000 people. <u>Where the Missouri River flows into the Mississippi.</u>

4. **Hannibal, Missouri:** This small town, birthplace of the great American writer Mark Twain, survived through sandbagging. <u>50 miles upstream from Hardin on the Mississippi River.</u>

5. **Des Moines, Iowa:** A 27-foot crest of water rolled through this city of 200,000 inhabitants. There was no drinking water for more than two weeks. <u>At the junction of the Des Moines and Raccoon rivers.</u>

6. **Valmeyer, Illinois:** This town was completely under water and has now chosen a new town site on higher ground. <u>30 miles south of St. Louis.</u>

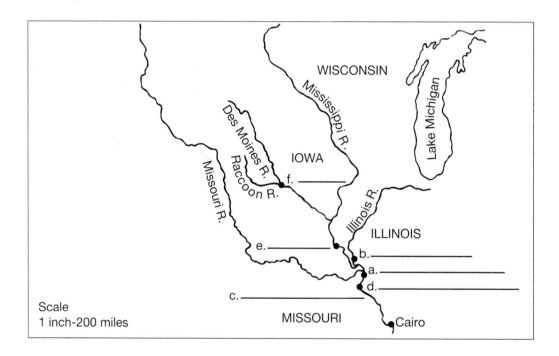

B. VOCABULARY FOR COMPREHENSION

Work in pairs. Help each other to choose a synonym for the underlined words and circle your choices. Use your dictionaries if necessary.

1. Floods can sweep into a river valley like a <u>marauding</u> army, destroying everything in sight.

   a. distressing   **b.** demolishing   **c.** decaying

2. Building levees and dams to prevent floods has been the <u>pillar</u> of modern government flood-control policies in many countries.

   a. main idea   **b.** main failure   **c.** main column

3. From earliest recorded history, humans have tried to farm fertile land <u>reclaimed</u> from floodplains.

   a. recovered   **b.** restructured   **c.** reinhabited

4. People were <u>compelled</u> to suffer through repeated flooding in order to work the fertile floodplains.

   a. permitted   **b.** obliged   **c.** persuaded

5. At the beginning of a disaster, we usually try to be brave and strong but then, after a while, we can get discouraged and our good cheer <u>wears a bit thin</u>.

   a. runs away   **b.** runs in   **c.** runs out

6. Scientists get angry and <u>bristle</u> when industries and politicians don't understand the need to protect our water and wetlands.

   a. become isolated   **b.** become depressed   **c.** become irritated

7. Scientists and engineers often say that our efforts to protect the earth's environment don't yet <u>meet the mark</u>.

   a. try hard enough   **b.** solve the problem   **c.** understand the need

8. When flood waters recede, they leave a lot of garbage, mud, and a <u>scum</u> of dirt.

   a. coating   **b.** bag   **c.** damage

9. Many flooded houses are bent over and <u>sagging</u> from the weight of the water.

   a. stinking   **b.** soaking   **c.** drooping

10. Flood waters destroy many structures and leave behind a lot of <u>debris</u>.

   a. wreckage   **b.** contamination   **c.** soil

READING ONE: The Great Flood of '93

A. INTRODUCING THE TOPIC

Before you read, write down your answers to the following questions and share them with a partner.

"You cannot tame that lawless stream, cannot save a shore which it has sentenced." Mark Twain wrote this in 1883 to describe the power of the Mississippi River, but it can apply to any major river. What did Mark Twain mean by this statement? Today we try very hard to tame and control nature. Is this a good thing?

The Great Flood of '93[1]

By Alan Mairson (from National Geographic)

1   The millions of people who live along the upper Mississippi and its tributaries[2] have long known that the generous river—source of transportation, recreation and fertile bottomland—had a mean streak. But few had imagined it could rage as it did in the summer of '93. Like a marauding army, the water invaded by day and by night to overwhelm all in its path, lay waste, and retreat, leaving in its wake death, destruction, and a colossal mess. Some 50 people were killed, and damages were estimated at more than ten billion dollars.

2   Fifteen percent of the country's freight

---

[1] As you read this article, be aware of the way the story moves back and forth from general comments on the situation to personal, eyewitness accounts.

[2] *tributary:* a stream or river that flows into a larger stream or river

moves by river barge, with a dozen or more of the 195-foot long barges tied together and guided by towboat. Principal highway for this traffic, the Mississippi was closed to shipping above St. Louis for two months, idling millions of tons of grain, fertilizer, and coal. The flood also scrambled train schedules by washing out tracks and bridges.

3 Rain and floodwaters spread over 23 million acres north of Cairo, Illinois. Downstream the Mississippi's channel was wide and deep enough to keep the flow within its banks. Soggy Midwesterners took small comfort from official pronouncements that the disaster was "in excess of a 100-year flood," placing at less than one in a hundred the chance of a similar flood happening in any given year.

* * *

4 Ste. Genevieve, Missouri, is located right beside the Mississippi River, 55 miles south of St. Louis. Because it was situated in the lower end of the flood zone, the city had extra time to heighten and extend the levee[3] that protects the downtown district.

5 Flying over the town with National Guardsmen, I saw the levee—a wall of crushed stone topped with sandbags that snaked through the streets, following the contour of the land. The people hadn't fled. I found many of them at the parking lot behind the Catholic church, filling sandbags, while others were gathered at City Hall for the daily noontime meeting. Mick Schwent, the city's emergency-preparedness director, updated everyone on the key numbers: the height of the river and the height of the levee. The National Guard commander announced new deployment of troops. Other people reported on food deliveries, electricity and telephone service, tetanus shots, and the supply of sandbags and plastic sheeting.

6 The rain came again that night, prompting the local radio station to go live with a bulletin: "We have an urgent request. It's raining and that can always cause a problem with the levee if we don't keep up. We need sandbaggers and people with pickup trucks to haul bags."

7 The people turned out. Some helped build the levee higher; others walked along the top of it with flashlights, looking for soft spots, bubbles, or leaks. "Don't worry about a slow trickle of clear water," said Bob Holst, a Ste. Genevieve cop, before I set out with three volunteers on a midnight levee walk. "But if the water's cloudy, that means material's getting washed out of the levee underneath you. Get off the levee and call us."

8 For a force of nature so threatening to many, the river seemed oddly quiet beside me. It was flat, motionless, yet I knew it was leaning hard against the levee, pushing at the stones with the weight of the summer storms.

9 Ste. Genevieve emerged from the flood of '93 in relatively good shape.

* * *

10 Levees and dams have long been the pillars of federal flood-control policy in the United States, and in the main they've done their job well, maybe too well. People moved onto the land reclaimed by levees because the soil was fertile and the property was cheap. But in the process the reconstituted river lost its bordering floodplain—the wetlands that would have held water when the river overflowed.

11 On a floodplain unaltered by levees and asphalt, floodwaters can spread slowly, depositing rich silt, causing less erosion, and potentially cresting at lower levels. Undeveloped land absorbs some water and holds the excess until it can drain off. But squeezed by levee walls designed to protect riverside cities, floodwaters swell upstream, where they may overtop earthen levees built to shield crops. Channeled tightly, water runs faster and deeper, stressing levees downstream.

12 Levees raised along the Mississippi are

---

[3] *levee*: a man-made embankment or dike to prevent flooding

usually a good bet. But the flood of '93 beat the odds. Fully 80 percent of private earthen levees in the basin failed. Most federal levees held, saving lives and land, but sending water toward less protected fields and towns. An old debate flares again: whether to rebuild the levees or let a more natural floodplain face the next big flood. "Water that was formerly allowed to spread over many thousand square miles of low lands," observed civil engineer Charles Ellet, Jr., "is becoming more and more confined to the immediate channel of the river, and is, therefore, compelled to rise higher and flow faster." Ellet wrote those words in 1853, but flood experts echoed them throughout the summer of 1993.

13   The other side of the story was crisply explained to me by K. C. Ringhausen as he sat staring at his flooded fruit-packing plant. "The problem isn't the levee," he said. "The problem is the weather. We usually get just a few inches of rain in July. This year was different." In other words, the levees did what they were designed to do, but they were never meant to control a flood like the one in the summer of '93. So the criticism of the levee system wears a bit thin on Maj. Gen. Stanley Genega, director of civil works for the Army Corps of Engineers. Genega bristled when I repeated an environmentalist's criticism, which characterized the corps' flood-control efforts as a "military campaign against nature." "It's a catchy phrase," he said. "But any look at the river that does not also consider the structures that provide for recreation, water supply, navigation, and the farm economy doesn't meet the mark. We've got all those

interests to consider, along with flood control."

* * *

14   The water finally began to retreat from the town of Hardin [Illinois] in mid-August. On the east side, the river was draining out the same way it had come in: through a hole in the Nutwood levee. In downtown Hardin the river slowly slipped back into its bed. Yet it left its muddy mark behind. A skirt of dried scum stained the sides of every building touched by the river. Trees, stripped of their leaves, were naked from their waists down. Houses sagged and stank, as if they'd aged a hundred years in just a few weeks.

15   On Kennedy Street I found Dennis and Beth Kronstable cleaning up her mother's house. Although four feet of water had filled the first floor, the walls were ruined up to the ceiling. They removed mud-caked kitchen appliances and bathroom fixtures, hosed down the floors, and shoveled debris.

16   Luckily, they had some help from the Southern Baptist disaster-relief program, which had sent volunteers from North Carolina to Hardin a few weeks earlier. They had arrived with a tractor trailer equipped to prepare hundreds of meals every day, giving local women at the canteen a much needed rest. "Those guys," said Beth, "'angels from heaven' we call them. I don't know what we'd do without them." They would probably rely on the Red Cross, the Salvation Army, or the gaggle of federal government agencies that had come to Hardin offering disaster relief. Soon Washington would authorize 5.7 billion dollars to help flood victims in the Midwest.

B. READING FOR MAIN IDEAS

*Fill in only the missing **causes** of the flood emergency. Refer to the article as necessary. Write in complete sentences.*

CAUSES	EFFECTS
1. People settled on the Mississippi floodplain.	**1a.** Levees and dams were built by the federal government.
	1b. The reconstituted river _____ _____ _____
2. Levees _____ _____ _____ _____	**2a.** There was less rich silt, _____ _____ _____
	2b. Water ran faster and over-topped the levees.
3. In the summer of 1993, it rained _____ _____ _____	**3a.** _____ percent of the private earthen levees failed.
	3b. There was a debate _____ _____ _____
4. The flood of 1993 hit the Mississippi River valley.	**4a.** Dead: _____
	4b. Damages: _____ _____
5. After the floodwaters receded, _____ _____ _____ _____	**5a.** The federal government _____ _____ _____
	5b. Private citizens _____ _____

C. READING FOR DETAILS

Go back to the chart on page 83 and fill in the missing **effects** of the situation.

D. READING BETWEEN THE LINES

1 *Based on what you have read about the flood of '93, discuss with a partner exactly who might have made the statements below. Match the statements with the following people and write their names on the lines below.*

a. Major General Stanley Genega
    Army Corps of Engineers

b. An environmentalist

c. Beth Kronstable
    Hardin, Illinois

d. The National Guard commander

e. Charles Ellet, Jr.
    Civil engineer, 1853

f. A real estate developer

1. "The flood of '93 can be viewed as one of those 'acts of God' that occur no matter how many precautions are taken. Don't let the fear of another flood get in the way of the many business opportunities that building levees can create for areas along the Mississippi."

    This kind of disaster is just part of nature and there nothing we can to do to prevent it. So let's quit worrying and start rebuilding

2. "Reinforcements of troops will be sent in tomorrow to help us keep the situation under control."

    d

    The army will come tomorrow to help us to solve the problem

3. "We shouldn't rebuild the levees. We need to let nature take its course."

    Charles Ellet Jr

    We should do nothing but let the nature do its own way.

4. "It is a law of physics that when you confine a physical element like water, it will rage fast and furious once any of the constraints that have been placed on it are removed."

e

5. "So many of us have lost our faith in our fellow man these days. I am happy to say that thanks to the strangers who traveled great distances to come here to lend a helping hand, my confidence in the spirit of human generosity has been more than restored."

Thanks for the help of the stranger, I'm confident in believing the kindness our countrymen

6. "Our ecological critics are much too absolute. They do not consider the many uses our waterways have for us."

a If we don't care of our environment, It will give us some punishment.

2 *After you answer the following questions, exchange books with a partner. Then write down whether you agree or disagree with your partner's remarks. This exchange of ideas will help you prepare for the essays at the end of the unit.*

1. Alan Mairson compares the floodwaters of the Mississippi to a "marauding army." Is this a good comparison or not? (Refer to paragraph 1 of the reading selection.)

_____

_____

_____

A partner's comments:

_____

_____

2. Are natural disasters good for the human spirit? Why or why not?

_____

_____

_____

A partner's comments:

_____

_____

4   READING TWO: The Bounty of the Sea

A. EXPANDING THE TOPIC

Answer the question and read the following essay, "The Bounty of the Sea," by Jacques Cousteau, the French oceanographer and conservationist.

If all the earth's water were put in a gallon jar, how much of it would be available fresh water and how much of it would be sea water? Consult with a partner and estimate the answer. Then check your response in the Answer Key.

The Bounty of the Sea[1]

BY JACQUES COUSTEAU

1   During the past thirty years, I have observed and studied the oceans closely, and with my own two eyes I have seen them sicken. Certain reefs that teemed with fish[2] only ten years ago are now almost lifeless. The ocean bottom has been raped by trawlers.[3] Priceless wetlands have been destroyed by landfill. And everywhere are sticky gobs of oil, plastic refuse, and unseen clouds of poisonous effluents.[4] Often when I describe the symptoms of the ocean's sickness, I hear remarks like "they're only fish" or "they're only whales" or "they're only birds." But I assure you that our destinies are linked with theirs in the most profound and fundamental manner. For if all the oceans should die—by which I mean that all life in the sea would finally cease—this would signal the end not only for marine life, but for all other animals and plants of this earth, including man.

2   With life departed, the ocean would become, in effect, one enormous cesspool. Billions of decaying bodies, large and small, would create such an insupportable stench that man would be forced to leave all the coastal regions. But far worse would follow.

---

[1] *bounty:* gift
[2] *teemed with fish:* were full of fish; overflowing
[3] *trawlers:* fishing boats
[4] *effluent:* liquid waste that flows out from a factory

3   The ocean acts as the earth's buffer. It maintains a fine balance between many salts and gases which make life possible. But dead seas would have no buffering[5] effect. The carbon dioxide content of the atmosphere would start on a steady and remorseless climb, and when it reached a certain level a "greenhouse effect" would be created. The heat that normally radiates outward from earth to space would be blocked by the CO_2 [carbon dioxide] and sea level temperatures would dramatically increase.

4   One catastrophic effect of this heat would be the melting of the icecaps at both the North and South Poles. As a result, the ocean would rise by 100 feet or more, enough to flood almost all the world's major cities. These rising waters would drive one-third of the earth's billions inland, creating famine, fighting, chaos, and disease on a scale almost impossible to imagine.

5   Meanwhile, the surface of the ocean would have scummed over with a thick film of decayed matter, and would no longer be able to give water freely to the skies through evaporation. Rain would become a rarity, creating global drought and even more famine.

6   But the final act is yet to come. The wretched remnant of the human race would now be packed cheek by jowl[6] on the remaining high-lands, bewildered, starving, struggling to survive from hour to hour. Then would be visited upon them the final plague, anoxia (lack of oxygen). This would be caused by the extinction of plankton algae and the reduction of land vegetation, the two sources that supply the oxygen you are now breathing.

7   And so man would finally die, slowly gasping out his life on some barren hill. He would have survived the oceans by perhaps thirty years. And his heirs would be bacteria and a few scavenger insects.

---

[5] *buffer:* protection
[6] *cheek by jowl:* one right next to the other, with no space in between

❶ *Write down your answers to the questions that follow, and share your ideas with a partner.*

What is your reaction to Cousteau's essay? Do you believe Cousteau sounds reasonable, or does he seem too extreme in his predictions?

_____

_____

_____

_____

_____

❷ *The following are entries from an imaginary diary written by one of the few humans left on earth, a person who has seen all of Cousteau's forecasts come true! Based on your understanding of Cousteau's essay, put these statements in the order Cousteau predicted.*

_____ 1. "Can you believe how high the waters have been rising in our coastal cities? It's a good thing we're living in the Midwest because otherwise we would have to learn to swim underwater in order to survive. My heart sank when, on a TV broadcast today, I saw the Statue of Liberty and the World Trade Center almost fully engulfed in water. You now need to be a deep sea diver if you want to visit the famous skyscrapers of New York City!"

_____ 2. "I can't believe that after all this time I am still living. There is almost no more oxygen to breathe. Despite all the work I did in the garden this year, there has been no harvest to speak of. The two heads of lettuce that I did manage to grow smelled so bad that I threw them out in disgust. I think my end is near. I have just finished eating the food I've had in storage for the past five years—and there is nothing left to eat."

_____ 3. "Because I wanted to know what was causing such a terrible odor to come from the sea, I walked toward the beach today to satisfy my curiosity. I was horrified when I approached the shore and saw all kinds of debris, dead fish, and sea life piled miles high on top of one another."

_____ 4. "We have been suffering from intolerable heat this past year. Wherever you go, there is sunlight, and people can no longer protect themselves from the burning rays of the sun. We feel as if our bodies are on fire. In addition, the air we breathe is choking us."

_____ 5. "What are we going to do? Sad to say, there are too many people living here. In addition to a severe housing shortage, there is not enough food to eat or water to drink, and the effects of disease and overcrowding are terrible."

B. LINKING READINGS ONE AND TWO

Working in pairs, choose one topic and write up an imaginary dialogue.

1. A dialogue between Jacques Cousteau and General Genega of the U.S. Army Corps of Engineers. They will argue about whether there should be conservation of our natural resources or the most economically profitable use of nature.

2. A dialogue between Beth Kronstable of Hardin, Illinois, and a volunteer ("an angel") who came to help out in her town after the flood.

3. A dialogue between you and one of the people in these readings about the importance of water in our lives.

4. A dialogue between Jacques Cousteau and someone who says, "Oh, what do I care about these creatures. They're only fish!"

5 REVIEWING LANGUAGE

A. EXPLORING LANGUAGE

Work in a small group. Divide the following words related to water into four separate categories, and place the words in the appropriate box on page 90.

barge	cresting	river	swelling	trickle
bed	debris	scum	trawler	tugboat
bubble	floodwater	silt	tributary	washout
channel	overflow	sogginess		

1. Water Vehicles

2. Bodies of Water

3. Water Movement

4. Flood Residue

B. WORKING WITH WORDS

Complete the essay using the following words.

channel	floodwaters	silt	tributaries
debris	overflowed	swelling	

The most devastating floods in this century have all taken place in China. In 1931, the Yangtze River and its smaller (1) _____ flooded their banks and killed 250,000 people. Two years later, the (2) _____ Yellow River killed 18,300. In 1938 a leader of China, General Chiang Kai-Shek, blew up the Yellow River dike at Huayuankou in an attempt to stop the Japanese army and killed an estimated 890,000 Chinese people living on the plain below that was teeming with people. In 1954, the Yangtze waters (3) _____ again and the (4) _____ killed 30,000. Since 1949, the government has invested $27 billion in water control projects aimed at altering the flow of water.

But in the summer of 1996, another of China's frequent and remorseless floods came again to the Yangtze valley. These floods left behind

(5) _____ from rotting crops and ruined farms and a terrible stench. After the deluge, a difficult period of rebuilding began. Three hundred and fifty million people now live in the Yangtze River basin.

In addition, although there was no flooding in northern China in 1996, the rain was intense and the Yellow River crested at its highest level in history. The riverbed is so choked with mud and (6) _____ that it has risen to a dangerous height above the plain. As a result, any major flood in northern China now has the potential ability to break through the main dikes that contain the river in its (7) _____ .

6 SKILLS FOR EXPRESSION

A. GRAMMAR: Adverb Clauses and Discourse Connectors Expressing Cause and Effect

1 *Working in pairs, examine the sentences and discuss the questions that follow.*

- <u>Because it was situated in the lower end of the flood zone</u>, the city had extra time to heighten and extend the levee that protects the downstream district.

- People moved onto the land reclaimed by the levees; <u>consequently, the river lost its bordering floodplain</u>.

- Billions of decaying bodies, large and small, would create <u>such</u> an insupportable stench <u>that man would be forced to leave all the coastal regions</u>.

a. In the first sentence, what word suggests that *a reason* is going to be given?

b. In the second sentence, what word suggests that *a result* is going to be given?

c. In the third sentence, what words suggest that *a reason* and *a result* are going to be given?

Adverb Clauses and Discourse Connectors Expressing Cause and Effect

FOCUS ON GRAMMAR

See adverb clauses and discourse connectors in *Focus on Grammar, Advanced.*

Adverb clauses and discourse connectors can be used to link ideas and to express cause and effect. In compound sentences these **cause-and-effect structures** reveal the connection between the reason for an event or a situation (the *cause*) and the influence this event or situation has on people, places, or things (the *result*, or the *effect*).

CAUSE: Stating a reason with adverb clauses that begin with *because* **and** *since*

- ◆ *Because/Since* **it was situated in the lower end of the flood zone,** the city had extra time to heighten and extend the levee that protects the downstream district.

- ◆ The city had extra time to heighten and extend the levee that protects the downstream district *because/since* **it was situated in the lower end of the flood zone.**

PUNCTUATION TIP: When the adverb clause beginning with *because* or *since* comes at the beginning of a sentence, a comma separates the clause from the result.

Effect: Stating a result with the discourse connectors *consequently, thus, therefore,* **and** *so*

- ◆ People moved onto the land reclaimed by the levees; *consequently/thus/therefore* **the river lost its bordering floodplain.**

- ◆ People moved onto the land reclaimed by the levees, *so* **the river lost its bordering floodplain.**

PUNCTUATION TIP: When using discourse connectors, you may write one sentence and join the two clauses as above with a semicolon (*consequently* / *thus* / *therefore*) or a comma (*so*).

DEGREE OF EFFECT: *such* **and** *so . . . that*

Compound sentences using the pattern "*such* (+ noun) or *so* (+ adjective or adverb) . . . *that* . . . "dramatically describe the great degree to which the *cause* has had an effect (*that* + the explanation) on the situation.

- ◆ Billions of decaying bodies, large and small, would create **such** an insupportable **stench that** man would be forced to leave all the coastal regions.

- ◆ The billions of decaying bodies, large and small, would be **so smelly that** man would be forced to leave all the coastal regions.

2 *Combine the following pairs of sentences to show cause and effect. Write two sentences for each item: Use patterns with **because/since** and **consequently/therefore/thus/so**.*

1. Millions of tons of grain, fertilizer, and coal were delivered late.
   The Mississippi was closed to shipping above St. Louis for two months.

   _____

   _____

   _____

   _____

2. People at first thought that the Flood of '93 was a bad dream.
   There was a one in a hundred chance of a similar flood happening in any given year.

   _____

   _____

   _____

   _____

3. The floodwaters were being squeezed tightly by levee walls.
   The water ran faster and faster, stressing the levees downstream.

   _____

   _____

   _____

   _____

4. The foundation of the house needed to be repainted.
   Four feet of water had filled the first floor.

   _____

   _____

   _____

   _____

3 *Combine the following sentences with **such/so . . . that** patterns. Write one sentence for each item.*

1. The Mississippi River raged with fury in 1993.
   The river destroyed everything that came in its path.

   _____

   _____

2. People were now certain that the levee was losing its foundation.
   The water had become very cloudy.

   _____

   _____

3. The soil of the levees was very fertile and the property was very cheap.
   People moved onto the land reclaimed by the levees.

   _____

   _____

4. The water ran faster and deeper, stressing levees downstream.
   The floodwaters had been channeled very tightly.

   _____

   _____

4 *Complete the following paragraphs by adding the appropriate cause-and-effect structure (**because/since; consequently/therefore/thus/so; such/so . . . that**).*

Living through the Flood of '93 was (1) _____ a trau-
matic experience for me and my family (2)_____ life will
never be the same for us again. (3)_____ the floodwaters
had rushed into our house until two of its three stories were fully
swallowed up by water, our house became waterlogged. Within a week,
the house had collapsed and you could see all its parts and our personal
belongings floating down the Mississippi River. While trying to
rescue some of our valuables from the house, my father was hit
(4) _____ hard in the head by a heavy pole

(5) _____ he had to spend the greater part of a month in the hospital recuperating from this injury. My mother, who was very devoted to my father, spent all her days tending to him in the hospital; (6) _____ , she, too, was removed from the scene of the catastrophe. My brother, sister, and I were determined to prove to our parents how responsible we were, (7)_____ we worked conscientiously together trying to contribute as much as possible to the neighborhood's flood emergency effort. However, all our work seemed to have been done in vain (8) _____ Mother Nature had really done her job efficiently, destroying everything that she found in her path.

After the rains stopped and the river water returned to its bed, the resettlement efforts were begun. The land in the lowland area had lost its appeal; (9) _____ , we settled in another village high up in the hills. But we have continued to be in (10) _____ a state of shock since the Flood of '93 (11) _____ we have not been able to adjust to our new home.

B. STYLE: Cause-and-Effect Essays

① *Reread and examine "The Bounty of the Sea" by Jacques Cousteau on pages 86-87.*

1. Underline the *thesis statement*, the sentence that communicates the main idea of the essay (see page 45).

2. Identify the *causes* of sea pollution, according to Cousteau.

    a. _____

    b. _____

    c. _____

    d. _____

3. List the *effects* of the death of the oceans, according to Cousteau.

a. _____

b. _____

c. _____

d. _____

e. _____

f. _____

4. Does this essay focus more on the *causes* or the *effects* of sea pollution?

THESIS STATEMENT

A **cause-and-effect essay** most often focuses on either the causes or the effects of an event or a situation. This focus is reflected in the *thesis statement*.

In a *causal* analysis, the thesis statement can briefly state the causes of an event or situation or it can mention only the most important cause. In an *effect* analysis, the thesis statement can simply summarize the main consequences of the event or situation. In Cousteau's essay, we can see that he introduces both causes and effects.

ORGANIZATION

The essay must follow a logical pattern of organization. Some common ways of organizing cause-and-effect essays are:

◆ <u>Immediate versus long-term</u>: If you are discussing the causes of the Mississippi River flood of 1993, you may want to begin with the immediate cause—prolonged heavy rains. You could explain that an unusual weather system caused the heavy rains: The jet stream went farther south than usual carrying cool, dry air and collided with a high-pressure area stalled over the Midwest bringing warm, moist Gulf air. Then you could discuss the long-term causes of the flood, such as the levee system constructed on the Mississippi and the placement of towns along the floodplain that began almost a century ago.

◆ <u>A coherent order of importance</u>: You may want to begin with the least important effects of an event and work up to the most important. Or you may find that you need to begin with the historical background of a situation and then go on to the present-day situation. The choice will be determined by the nature of the material, but you must give a logical order to your essay.

◆ <u>Order of familiarity or interest</u>: You may want to work from what your readers know or would be most interested in, to what is new and different from what they expect.

◆ <u>Causal chain</u>: Another type of cause-and-effect essay is the causal chain. As in the essay, "The Bounty of the Sea," one effect can become the cause of another effect, which, in turn, can become the cause of another effect. The carbon dioxide in the atmosphere would create a greenhouse effect, which, in turn, would melt the polar ice caps, which would flood all the major cities, and so on.

2 *Fill in the causal chain used in "The Bounty of the Sea." Compare your answers with a partner's.*

The Oceans Die

1. the sea is a cesspool ➝ _____

➝ _____

2. dead seas won't act as a buffer ➝ _____

➝ _____ ➝ flooding of coastal cities ➝ _____

3. no rain ➝ _____ and _____

4. the end of sea algae and land vegetation ➝ _____

3 *Work with a partner. The following sentences present some of the causes of floods in China (see page 90), but the causes are not explained in logical order. Decide how to reorganize the sentences into logical order to form a paragraph. You can begin with the historical background and then go on to the present-day situation.*

_____ **1.** Changing weather patterns in the Pacific Ocean, perhaps as a result of global warming, have added to China's difficulties.

_____ **2.** Increasingly strong monsoon rains now wash the Yangtze River drainage area, where 350 million people live.

_____ **3.** Over the earth's long history, nature has worked against the land area that would become China.

_____ **4.** When the Himalayan Mountains were formed over the last 40 million years, the Tibetan-Qinghai Plateau was raised to such heights that a sort of "flood machine" was created whereby powerful rivers crash down from 20,000 feet to floodplains teeming with people.

_____ **5.** Although the Chinese government has devoted more than 4 percent of all public spending since 1949 to water control projects (about $27 billion), this hasn't been enough to build disaster-proof dikes.

_____ **6.** Forest cutting in the upper reaches of the Yangtze River is also a factor in the increasing frequency of floods.

_____ **7.** There is more run-off and the land is, therefore, unable to absorb the water.

4 *Write a paragraph summarizing all you know about the consequences of the Mississippi River flood of 1993. You can refer to information contained in all parts of this unit and the notes you took on page 83. Use the cause-and-effect structures outlined on page 92. Remember that your paragraph must have an appropriate topic sentence and a logical pattern of organization.*

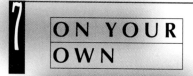

ON YOUR OWN

A. WRITING TOPICS

Choose one topic and write a well-organized essay, using the vocabulary and the grammar structures from this unit whenever possible.

1. Have you ever been involved in a natural disaster: a hurricane, an earthquake, a tidal wave, a drought, or a flood? Describe a natural disaster that you know about, and tell the causes of the disaster or the effects of the disaster on the people who lived through it.

2. What is your first reaction when you look at nature? When you see a waterfall, do you see the beauty of the light sparkling on the waters, or do you see the threat of roaring waters pounding on the rocks below? In general, do you see the beauty or the danger of nature? What causes this reaction in you? What effect does it have on your choice of a place to live?

3. Do you feel you make a contribution to the conservation of nature in your daily life? How? What changes have occurred in your daily life because of this effort?

4. During the Mississippi River flood of 1993, many people came to help the flood victims as volunteers, without getting paid. People can

volunteer to help children learn to read, to assist hospital personnel, to feed the hungry or homeless, to coach athletic games in their neighborhood, or to help out in times of disaster. Have you ever been a volunteer? Why did you volunteer? What were the results of your work, and what did you learn? Write about your experiences.

B. FIELDWORK

PREPARATION

In the first paragraph of his essay, Cousteau lists the reasons why the oceans are becoming sick:

> "The ocean bottom has been raped by <u>trawlers</u>. Priceless wetlands have been destroyed by <u>landfill</u>. And everywhere are sticky gobs of <u>oil</u>, <u>plastic</u> <u>refuse</u>, and unseen clouds of <u>poisonous effluents</u>."

Cousteau's essay was written in 1966, at a time when fishermen's trawlers were destroying the ocean floor. Since then, many national and international agencies—such as the International Maritime Organization (IMO), a United Nations agency located in London—have worked hard to protect our waterways.

Discuss with the members of your group the major water-related problems that exist in the United States or another country that you are familiar with:

1. Identify the problems.

2. Identify the major industries responsible for the problems.

3. Explain what you believe has been done in the past ten years to correct these problems.

4. Indicate what you believe still needs to be done.

5. Explain why there may have been some resistance to solving these problems.

RESEARCH ACTIVITY

Every country, state, and community has a government agency whose major concern is the protection of the environment. For the United States overall, the name of this agency is the Environmental Protection Agency, which has a division called the Bureau of Water Protection. Identify the agency in your city, state, or community that deals with water-related issues. Send a letter or e-mail to this agency. In your letter, ask for information about what has been done in the past ten years to solve *one* water-related problem. Ask questions that will help you relate to one of the issues you discussed with the members of your group.

SHARING YOUR FINDINGS

When you receive the agency information you requested, do the following:

1. Write a brief summary telling about the information you received. Is the information sufficient? Was it helpful? Where would you look further?

2. If the information was sufficient, draw a map or make a graph showing the progress (or lack of progress) in solving the problem you chose to do research on.

WHAT IS LOST IN TRANSLATION?

1 APPROACHING THE TOPIC

A. PREDICTING

Look at the title of this unit and the photo. What are the advantages of living in a multicultural society? What could be "lost in translation" for these girls? Take five minutes to write down your thoughts about these questions.

B. SHARING INFORMATION

Work in a small group and fill in your answers to the questions in the boxes that follow. Discuss your responses. Are there regional, class, gender, or age variations to these situations in your culture? Have you had any experiences in other cultures that you can share with your group?

Kissing in public
Acceptable? _____
In what circumstances?
_____
What reaction do you get if you go against this social rule?
_____
_____

Commenting on people's choice of clothing
Acceptable? _____
In what circumstances?
_____
What reaction do you get if you go against this social rule?
_____
_____

Touching people you are talking to
Acceptable? _____
In what circumstances?
_____
What reaction do you get if you go against this social rule?
_____
_____

Criticizing people directly and strongly
Acceptable? _____
In what circumstances?
_____
What reaction do you get if you go against this social rule?
_____
_____

Two women walking arm-in-arm down the street
Acceptable? _____
In what circumstances?
_____
What reaction do you get if you go against this social rule?
_____
_____

Eating as you walk down the street
Acceptable? _____
In what circumstances?
_____
What reaction do you get if you go against this social rule?
_____
_____

PREPARING TO READ

A. BACKGROUND

Read this information and fill in the values chart on page 104.

Being a teenager is difficult under any conditions. It is easy to understand how much more complicated it can be when a family immigrates to a new country. Such was the case for Eva Hoffman. Born in Poland in 1945 to Jewish parents who were Holocaust survivors, she left her homeland at age thirteen with her parents and sister to start a new life in Canada. In her autobiography, *Lost in Translation*, she tells about the impact this move had on her and her family.

Ms. Hoffman takes us on the journey from Old World Cracow to New World Vancouver; this journey prepared her for her later years at Harvard University and her literary career in New York, where she now works as an editor for the *New York Times Book Review*. Eva Hoffman writes the story of all immigrants. She describes how her Polish identity was transformed into a new Canadian identity as she underwent the physically and emotionally exhausting process of learning to communicate in English. In their attempts to "translate" the essence of their personalities from one language and culture to another, don't all immigrants find themselves both linguistically and culturally "lost in translation"?

Although Elizabeth Wong, who was born in Los Angeles, California, in 1958, was not an immigrant herself, she too may have understood Eva Hoffman's feeling of being "lost in translation" as a young girl. In "The Struggle to Be an All-American Girl," she writes how she was torn between two cultures and how she continually resisted her Chinese mother's attempts to get her to learn Chinese and be aware of her cultural background. Ms. Wong is a playwright, a teacher of playwrighting, and a writer for television.

Read the statements on page 104 about the cultural values expressed in the stories that follow. Do you agree or disagree with these statements? Circle yes or no. After you study the readings, you will be asked to return to this section to compare the authors' points of view with your own.

STATEMENTS	YOUR OPINION	POINTS OF VIEW	
		READING ONE	READING TWO
1. Children have more difficulty adapting to a new culture than their parents do.	Yes / No		
2. When people move to another culture, their native language becomes more important to them.	Yes / No		
3. Parents lose authority over their children when the family moves to another culture.	Yes / No		
4. Families become closer when they must adapt to a new culture.	Yes / No		
5. People who move to a new culture worry about betraying or forgetting their old cultural traditions.	Yes / No		

B. VOCABULARY FOR COMPREHENSION

Work in a small group and help each other to guess the meaning of the words listed below. In each set of words, underline the two words that have similar meanings to the boldfaced word on the left. Use your dictionaries if necessary. The first one has been done for you.

1. fabric	foundation	structure	factory
2. beleaguered	attacked	joined	pressured
3. abjure	abandon	forget	leave behind

4. demonstrative   affectionate   emotional   reserved
5. restraint   restriction   moderation   freedom
6. give vent to   express   suppress   release
7. stoical   unemotional   uncomplaining   impersonal
8. dissuade   pursue   hinder   advise against

3 READING ONE:
"Lost in Translation" and "The Struggle to Be an All-American Girl"

A. INTRODUCING THE TOPIC

Before you read, discuss the following information and question with a partner.

The first reading in this section portrays the difficulties of a Polish-Canadian family. This memoir is told from the point of view of Eva, a thirteen-year-old girl from Poland. Along with her mother, father, and sister Alinka, she becomes an immigrant to Canada after World War II. The second reading is about a Chinese-American family. This story is told from the point of view of ten-year-old Elizabeth. She and her brother were born in the United States. Do you think these families will have many things in common, or do you think they will be very different?

Lost in Translation

BY EVA HOFFMAN

1   "In Poland, I would have known how to bring you up, I would have known what to do," my mother says wistfully, but here, she has lost her sureness, her authority. She doesn't know how hard to scold Alinka when she comes home at late hours; she can only worry over her daughter's vague evening activities. She has always been gentle with us, and she doesn't want, doesn't know how, to tighten the reins. But familial bonds seem so dangerously loose here!

2   Truth to tell, I don't want the fabric of loyalty and affection, and even obligation, to unravel either. I don't want my parents to lose us, I don't want to betray our common life. I want to defend our dignity because it is so fragile, so beleaguered. There is only the tiny cluster, the four of us, to know, to preserve whatever fund of human experience we may represent. And so I feel a kind of ferociousness about protecting it. I don't want us to turn into perpetually cheerful suburbanites, with hygienic smiles and equally hygienic feelings. I want to keep even our sadness, the great sadness from which our parents have come.

3   I abjure my sister to treat my parents well; I don't want her to challenge our mother's authority, because it is so easily challenged. It is they who seem more defenseless to me than Alinka, and I want her to protect them. Alinka fights me like a forest animal in danger of being trapped; she too wants to roam throughout the thickets and meadows. She too wants to be free.

4   My mother says I'm becoming "English." This hurts me, because I know she means I'm becoming cold. I'm no colder than I've ever been, but I'm learning to be less demonstrative. I learn this from a teacher who, after contemplating the gesticulations with which I help myself describe the digestive system of a frog, tells me to "sit on my hands and then try talking." I learn my new reserve from people who take a step back when we talk, because I am standing too close, crowding them. Cultural distances are different, I later learn in a sociology class, but I know it already. I learn restraint from Penny, who looks offended when I shake her by the arm in excitement, as if my gesture had been one of aggression instead of friendliness. I learn it from a girl who pulls away when I hook my arm through hers as we walk down the street— this movement of friendly intimacy is an embarrassment to her.

5   I learn also that certain kinds of truth are impolite. One shouldn't criticize the person one is with, at least not directly. You shouldn't say, "You are wrong about that"—although you may say, "On the other hand, there is that to consider." You shouldn't say, "This doesn't look good on you," though you may say, "I like you better in that other outfit." I learn to tone down my sharpness, to do a more careful conversational minuet.

6   Perhaps my mother is right after all; perhaps I'm becoming colder. After a while, emotion follows action, response grows warmer or cooler according to gesture. I'm more careful about what I say, how loud I laugh, whether I give vent to grief. The storminess of emotion prevailing in our family is in excess of the normal here, and the unwritten rules for the normal have their osmotic effect.[1]

---

[1] *osmotic effect:* an effect of being gradually absorbed

The Struggle to Be an All-American Girl

BY ELIZABETH WONG

1   It's still there, the Chinese school on Yale Street where my brother and I used to go. Despite the new coat of paint and the high wire fence, the school I knew ten years ago remains remarkably, stoically, the same.

2   Every day at 5 P.M., instead of playing with our fourth- and fifth-grade friends or sneaking out to the empty lot to hunt ghosts and animal bones, my brother and I had to go to Chinese school. No amount of kicking, screaming, or pleading could dissuade my mother, who was solidly determined to have us learn the language of our heritage. Forcibly, she walked us the seven long, hilly blocks from our home to school, depositing our defiant tearful faces before the stern principal. My only memory of him is that he swayed on his heels like a palm tree and he always clasped his impatient, twitching hands behind his back. I recognized him as a repressed maniacal child killer, and that if we ever saw his hands, we'd be in big trouble.

3   We all sat in little chairs in an empty auditorium. The room smelled like Chinese medicine, an imported faraway mustiness[1], like ancient mothballs[2] or dirty closets. I hated that smell. I favored crisp new scents like the soft French perfume that my American teacher wore in public school. There was a stage far to the right, flanked by an American flag and the flag of the Nationalist Republic of China, which was also red, white and blue but not as pretty.

4   Although the emphasis at school was mainly language—speaking, reading and writing—the lessons always began with exercises in politeness. With the entrance of the teacher, the best student would tap a bell and everyone would get up, kowtow,[3] and chant, "Sing san ho," the phonetic for "How are you, teacher?"

  Being ten years old, I had better things to learn than ideographs copied painstakingly in lines that ran right to left from the tip of a *moc but*, a real ink pen that had to be held in an awkward way if blotches were to be avoided. After all, I could do the multiplication tables, name the satellites of Mars, and write reports on *Little Women* and *Black Beauty*. Nancy Drew, my favorite heroine, never spoke Chinese.

---

[1] *mustiness:* moldy dampness; a smell of decay
[2] *mothballs:* made of a strong-smelling substance; used to keep moths away from clothes
[3] *kowtow:* to bow with respect

6   The language was a source of embarrassment. More times than not, I had tried to dissociate myself from the nagging loud voice that followed me wherever I wandered in the nearby American supermarket outside Chinatown. The voice belonged to my grandmother, a fragile woman in her seventies who could outshout the best of the street vendors. Her humor was raunchy,[4] her Chinese rhythmless, patternless. It was quick, it was loud, it was unbeautiful. It was not like the quiet, lilting romance of French or the gentle refinement of the American South. Chinese sounded pedestrian. Public.

7   In Chinatown, the comings and goings of hundreds of Chinese on their daily tasks sounded chaotic and frenzied. I did not want to be thought of as mad, as talking gibberish. When I spoke English, people nodded at me, smiled sweetly, said encouraging words. Even the people in my culture would cluck[5] and say that I would do well in life. "My, doesn't she move her lips fast," they would say, meaning that I'd be able to keep up with the world outside Chinatown.

8   My brother was even more fanatical than I about speaking English. He was especially hard on my mother, criticizing her, often cruelly, for her pidgin speech[6]—smatterings of Chinese scattered like chop suey in her conversation. "It's not 'What it is,' Mom," he'd say in exasperation. "It's 'What *is* it, what *is* it, what *is* it.'" Sometimes Mom might leave out an occasional "the" or "a," or perhaps a verb of being. He would stop her in mid-sentence: "Say it again, Mom. Say it right." When he tripped over his own tongue, he'd blame it on her: "See, Mom, it's all your fault. You set a bad example."

9   What infuriated my mother most was when my brother cornered her on her consonants, especially "r." My father had played a cruel joke on Mom by assigning her an American name that her tongue wouldn't allow her to say. No matter how hard she tried, "Ruth" always ended up "Luth" or "Roof."

10   After two years of writing with a *moc but* and reciting words with multiples of meanings, I was finally granted a cultural divorce. I was permitted to stop Chinese school.

11   I thought of myself as multicultural. I preferred tacos to egg rolls; I enjoyed Cinco de Mayo more than Chinese New Year.

12   At last, I was one of you; I wasn't one of them.

13   Sadly, I still am.

---

[4] *raunchy:* obscene
[5] *cluck:* a clicking sound with the tongue showing conern or interest
[6] *pidgin speech:* simplified, uneducated speech

B. READING FOR MAIN IDEAS

Work in pairs. Go back to the chart on page 104. In the "Points of View: Reading One and Reading Two" columns of the chart, put a checkmark (✓) next to the statements supported by the readings and an "x" next to the statements not supported by them. Discuss your own answers with your partner. Are your answers different from the answers expressed by the authors of these readings?

C. READING FOR DETAILS

1 *Compare and contrast the cultural customs of Poland and Canada as Eva describes them in "Lost in Translation." Try to find at least five examples. The first one has been done for you.*

Polish Ways	Canadian Ways
1. In Poland, Eva was comfortable about showing her feelings openly.	1. Eva felt Canadians were more reserved about their feelings.
2.	2.
3.	3.
4.	4.
5.	5.

2 *Compare and contrast Elizabeth's attitude toward Chinese things and her attitude toward American things when she was young, as told in "The Struggle to Become an All-American Girl." Try to find at least five examples. The first one has been done for you.*

Elizabeth's Attitude Toward Chinese Things	Elizabeth's Attitude Toward American Things
1. Chinese smells were musty like old mothballs or dirty closets.	1. American smells seem new and crisp like French perfume.
2. _____	2. _____
3. _____	3. _____
4. _____	4. _____
5. _____	5. _____

D. READING BETWEEN THE LINES

1 *Based on what is implied in the readings, discuss with your partner who might have made the following statements. In the blank space, write **Ev** (Eva), **El** (Elizabeth), **B** (both girls), or **N** (neither of them).*

_____ 1. "My mother has no idea what I'm going through."

_____ 2. "I am hurt by my mother's criticism of me."

_____ 3. "I miss the old country."

_____ 4. "I just want to fit in and stop thinking about the past."

_____ 5. "I feel comfortable in two cultures."

_____ 6. "Sometimes I want to express myself in one language and sometimes in another."

_____ 7. "Now that I am older, I regret losing so much of the past."

_____ 8. "When people just look at me, they don't really know who I am."

2 _Answer the following questions based on your understanding of the readings. Then compare your answers with those of your partner._

a. "'In Poland, I would have known how to bring you up, I would have known what to do,' my mother says wistfully, but here, she has lost her sureness, her authority."

Why do you think Eva's mother has lost her authority?

_____

_____

_____

_____

b. "I don't want us to turn into perpetually cheerful suburbanites, with hygienic smiles and equally hygienic feelings."

Explain the meaning of this statement.

_____

_____

_____

_____

c. At the end of the story, "The Struggle to Be an All-American Girl," Elizabeth Wong writes, "At last, I was one of you; I wasn't one of them. Sadly, I still am."

What do you think she means?

_____

_____

_____

_____

4 READING TWO: In One School, Many Sagas

A. EXPANDING THE TOPIC

Before you read "In One School, Many Sagas," write a short answer to the following question.

A **saga** is a story. Judging from this title, what do you expect Reading Two to be about?

In One School, Many Sagas

By Alan Riding (from *The New York Times*)

1   Sabine Contrepois well remembers the day two years ago when she explained to her high school class how the Vietnam War eventually spilled into Cambodia. Suddenly, Meak, an Asian girl in the front row, burst into tears. "I asked her what was wrong," Mrs. Contrepois recalled. "She said her father was shot the day the Khmer Rouge took power in Cambodia in 1975. She and her mother spent years in concentration camps before they escaped through Thailand. There was absolute silence in the classroom."

2   The incident set the teacher thinking. A traditional role of French schools is to prepare children of immigrants to become French citizens. Yet Meak's reaction made Mrs. Contrepois realize that she knew nothing of the background of the young people of different races whom she faced every day. Clearly, some students' parents came to France simply to find work. Others came fleeing wars and dictatorships. Yet Mrs. Contrepois, who comes from an immigrant family herself, also wondered whether the teenagers themselves knew why they were in France. Did they know their own family history?

3   A year ago, seeking answers, she gave the 120 students in her six classes a research project titled: "In what way has your family been touched by history?" If they did not know, she told them, they should ask their parents and grandparents. The result is "History, My History," a document in which 41 students, mostly in their late teens, describe the tumultuous paths—wars in Armenia, Spain, Algeria, Vietnam and the former Yugoslavia, repression in Poland, Portugal and Cameroon—that brought their families here.

4   Mrs. Contrepois sees the problem through the prism of her students[1] at Frederic Mistral High School in this town south of Paris. Her job is to teach youths who are considered by the school system to be slow learners. Many are immigrant children who have trouble finding jobs after school.

5   To Mrs. Contrepois, the youths' main liability[2] is not a lack of ability, but confusion about their identity. "It's easier for them to accept being

---

[1] *through the prism of her students:* through the eyes of her students

[2] *liability:* a disadvantage

French if they can also come to terms with their roots," she said. "This project tried to do that. It made them communicate with their parents. In many cases, they discovered things that made them proud. And I think it taught them tolerance towards each other."

6 Yassine, a 19-year-old born in France of Algerian parents, said he discovered that his grandfather had been tortured and killed by French troops during Algeria's war of independence. "I didn't know anything about this," he said. "We never spoke about Algeria at home. I had never dared ask before."

7 Stephanie, also 19, said she learned that her grandfather was shot by invading German troops in Poland in 1939. "My father came here illegally in 1946, but this topic was taboo[3] at home," she said. "He died two years ago and my mother told me the story. When she saw the final project, she cried. She was very proud."

8 To insure the authenticity[4] of the stories, Mrs. Contrepois asked her "student authors," as she now calls them, to provide documentation. Sevana, 16, found newspaper photos of the Turkish atrocities[5] against Armenians in 1915, when her great-grand-parents were killed. Slawomir, whose father, a Pole, sought asylum[6] in France in 1981, offered a photograph of her grandmother with Lech Walesa.[7]

9 This month, the work was awarded the "Memories of Immigration" prize by the Foundation for Republican Integration, headed by Kofi Yamgnane, a former Minister for Integration who was born in Togo.

10 Mrs. Contrepois was well equipped to oversee the project. The 36-year-old teacher was born in a run-down Paris hotel shortly after her Spanish-born father and Algerian-born mother arrived here fleeing the Algerian War. "They were penniless immigrants, and they knew all about discrimination," she said. While her family eventually found a place in French society, she knows that it is more difficult for immigrants today. But at least with this group of young people, she has made an impact. "She has changed our lives," Yassine said, speaking for the "student authors" at a recent ceremony here attended by Mr. Yamgnane and the town mayor, Gabriel Bourdin.

11 "History, My History" will soon be published as a book here, and the students have made another plan—they want to visit New York. Their prize brought them $5,000, but they must raise $39,000 more. "We want to compare our experiences with those of young Americans like us, how they study, what their culture is," Yassine said. "The only New York I've seen is on television."

---

[3] *taboo:* forbidden
[4] *authenticity:* truthfulness
[5] *atrocity:* an act of great evil, especially cruelty
[6] *asylum:* refuge, shelter
[7] *Lech Walesa:* leader of a workers' movement in Poland who became the head of state after Poland gained its independence from the former Soviet Union

Read the following quotes from the article above and write short answers to the questions. Compare your answers in a small group.

1. Sabine Contrepois: "It's easier for them to accept being French if they can also come to terms with their roots."

What does this statement mean? Do you agree with Mrs. Contrepois?

2. Yassine: "I didn't know anything about this. We never spoke about Algeria at home. I had never dared ask before."

Why do you think Yassine never asked his family any questions?

3. Stephanie: "When [my mother] saw the final project, she cried."

Why do you think Stephanie's project made her mother cry?

B. LINKING READINGS ONE AND TWO

From your understanding of the three stories in this unit, write a paragraph about one of the topics below.

1. You are Elizabeth from the story "The Struggle to Be an All-American Girl." Imagine that your grandmother said to you one day, "Only your outside is Chinese; inside you are all American-made." Write a letter to your grandmother explaining how you feel about what she said.

2. You are the father of Yassine, or the mother of Stephanie, students in Mrs. Contrepois's classroom. Write a letter to your child explaining why you kept the family history a secret.

3. You are Eva Hoffman as a young girl. What do you think about the history project the French students are doing? Would you like to do such a project for your class to read in Canada? Do you think it would help your classmates to understand you, or would it just make you seem too different from the others?

4. You are Elizabeth from "The Struggle to Be an All-American Girl," but you are now an adult. Write a letter to the grown-up Eva explaining how your attitude toward your cultural background changed as you got older.

5 REVIEWING LANGUAGE

A. EXPLORING LANGUAGE: Noun Suffixes

The suffixes **-ness, -ty, -ity,** and **-ment** mean "the state, quality, or condition of being." When you add *-ness, -ty,* and *-ity* to certain adjectives and *-ment* to certain verbs, you create nouns that relate to *the state, quality, or condition of being a particular way.* For adjectives of two syllables or more that end with a *y,* the *y* changes to *i* after *-ness* is added.

Examples

quiet (adjective)

quietness (noun = "the state, quality, or condition of being quiet")

happy (adjective)

happiness (noun = "the state, quality, or condition of being happy")

authentic (adjective)

authenticity (noun = "the state, quality, or condition of being authentic")

move (verb)

movement (noun = "the state, quality, or condition of moving / being moved")

*Work with a partner. Read the following sentences and identify the **noun** that can be created from the underlined words. Then write a sentence using the noun form. The sentence you create should not change the meaning of the original sentence, even though some words will have to be changed. The first sentence has been done for you.*

1. Elizabeth likes the <u>refined</u> manner in which Southerners speak English.

   Noun form: <u>refinement</u>

   Sentence: <u>Elizabeth likes the refinement of Southerners' speech.</u>

2. Penny does not understand that Eva is being <u>friendly</u> when she shakes her arm in excitement.

   Noun form: _____

   Sentence: _____

3. Eva learns that hooking her arm through Penny's as they walk down the street together <u>embarrasses</u> Penny.

   Noun form: _____

   Sentence: _____

4. Eva does not want her father, mother, and sister to stop being <u>loyal</u> to one another.

   Noun form: _____

   Sentence: _____

5. Many French immigrant children are surprised to learn that their ancestors were the unfortunate victims of <u>atrocious</u> crimes.

   Noun form: _____

   Sentence: _____

6. The Hoffman family's <u>stormy</u> emotional state is far beyond the norm in Canada.

   Noun form: _____

   Sentence: _____

7. Eva is <u>ferocious</u> about protecting her family's common bond.

   Noun form: _____

   Sentence: _____

B. WORKING WITH WORDS

Read these thoughts that may have gone through the mind of Alinka, Eva's younger sister. Complete the following paragraphs with words and expressions from the list below; they are synonyms for the words indicated.

asylum	cluster	giving vent to	storminess
atrocities	come to terms with their roots	hygienic	trapped
beleaguered	fabric	loose	
blend in	fragile	perpetually	

These have been difficult years for my parents. The _____ of
                                                        1. (structure)

their emotional lives has been made ever so _____ because of
                                              2. (delicate)

their own suffering and their firsthand knowledge of the terrible

_____ suffered by so many of their loved ones during World
3. (torment)

War II. My parents sought to make a new life for us in Canada.

Although they had hoped that their new home in Canada would provide

an _____ for them from their tragic past, my parents' sense
     4. (haven)

of sorrow still dominates them. Their every gesture is still _____
                                                              5. (troubled)

by their memories of the past.

You may think that as the youngest family member of our _____
6. (group)

of four, I have been untouched by all this. Yet it was not until we moved

to Canada that I realized how very _____ I had been by my
7. (imprisoned)

parents' sadness. I had never realized how simple life could be. None of

my Canadian friends seem to have a history or to be troubled by the

need to _____. Their
8. (understand who they are in light of their family history)

_____ happy faces, which my sister sarcastically describes
9. (constantly)

as reflecting not only _____ smiles," but also
10. (clean, healthy)

_____ feelings," are a welcome sigh of relief to me.
10. (clean, healthy)

While my sister may laugh at my friends and their parents because

of their superficiality, I disagree. I want more than anything else to

_____ with this Disneyland mentality, with this fairy tale of
11. (feel comfortable)

a life where "everyone lives happily ever after."

So, if I am putting a lot of makeup on my face and behaving in ways

that make my mother think of the _____ girls in our Polish
12. (immoral)

town, be happy for me! I am doing two things at once. I am rebelling as

only teenagers know how to rebel and, in so doing, I am "painting" a

new life for myself. Through my actions, not only am I _____
13. (expressing)

my frustrations and liberating myself from the _____ of my
14. (turmoil)

family's inner life, but I am also creating a new identity for myself. I am

becoming free!

6 SKILLS FOR EXPRESSION

A. GRAMMAR: Adverb Clauses of Comparison and Contrast

1 *Working in pairs, examine the following sentence from "Lost in Translation" and discuss the questions that follow.*

◆ "You shouldn't say, 'You are wrong about that,' although you may say, 'On the other hand, there is that to consider.'"

a. Is this one sentence or two?

b. Which part of the sentence contains words that are polite to say in Canadian culture?

c. What is the difference between the two parts of the sentence?

d. What is a synonym for *although* in this sentence?

Adverb Clauses

FOCUS ON GRAMMAR

See adverb clauses in *Focus on Grammar, Advanced.*

Adverb clauses can be used to combine two ideas into one sentence. They can be used in the first or second part of the sentence. They provide variety for the sentence and smooth transitions from one idea to another in your paragraphs. The following adverbials will be particularly helpful in comparison and contrast essays. Look at the examples carefully to see where commas are needed.

Comparison or Similarity	Examples
just as	*Just as* Eva is struggling to be accepted in Canada, Elizabeth is struggling to be accepted in the United States.
in the same way that	*In the same way that* many immigrants have chosen to come to North America, many are choosing France as their new home.

Contrast or Difference	
whereas	**Whereas France has an official ministry to help with assimilation of immigrants,** the United States does not have such an institution.
while	Mrs. Contrepois felt that children need to know their roots, **while** their parents felt the past was too painful.
despite the fact that	**Despite the fact that Americans have tolerated the use of many immigrant languages,** they remain profoundly attached to the English language.
although	**Although Americans have tolerated the use of many immigrant languages,** they remain profoundly attached to the English language.

GRAMMAR TIP: Sentences with *despite the fact that* often include an unexpected idea or a contradiction. *Although* may also be used in this way. In these sentences, the subject of both clauses is the same.

2 *For each of the following topics, write one or two sentences with words of comparison and contrast. By using the cues given, write sentences using **although, despite the fact that, in the same way that, just as, whereas, while.** The first topic has been done for you.*

1. *Telling the truth*

   Poles/Canadians

   <u>While Poles may prefer to be honest and direct when giving criticism,</u>
   <u>Canadians may choose to be more diplomatic and keep their opinions</u>
   <u>to themselves.</u>

2. *Cultural identity*

   Elizabeth / Eva

   _____
   _____
   _____

3. *Respecting one's parents*

   Elizabeth's brother / Alinka (Eva's sister)

   _____
   _____
   _____

4. *Showing intimacy*

   Eva / Penny (Eva's friend)

   _____
   _____
   _____

5. *Obedience*

   American children / Chinese children

   _____
   _____
   _____

6. *American ways / Canadian ways*

Elizabeth / Eva's mother

_____

_____

_____

7. *Independence*

Elizabeth / Eva

_____

_____

_____

8. *Personal stories*

"Lost in Translation" / "History, My History"

_____

_____

_____

B. STYLE: Comparison and Contrast Essays

1 *Examine this essay and discuss the questions that follow. Work with a partner.*

Elements of Structure

Introductory Paragraph

Thesis Statement

A Comparison of Eva and Elizabeth

Whoever once said that the children of immigrants have an easy time adapting to life in their new country was surely mistaken. Because they usually learn to speak the new language sooner than adults, immigrant children often become the family spokesperson. As the oldest children in their families, both Eva Hoffman and Elizabeth Wong play an active role in helping their family members communicate with the outside world. As a result, they often suffer from the pain and frustration that people who live in two cultures can experience. By examining the relationships that these two girls have with their mothers and other important people in their lives, we can see that although Eva and Elizabeth may have certain hopes and feelings in common, they are at the same time very different from one another.

Body

Like Eva, Elizabeth wants to be accepted by her peers, and she is embarrassed when she is made to feel different from them. In the same way that Eva becomes self-conscious about expressing her feelings, Elizabeth is ashamed as she wanders through the American supermarket and hears her grandmother calling after her in Chinese. Elizabeth also hates it when her mother speaks English. But on the surface at least, she does not seem to be as bothered by this as her younger brother. This brings us to another common area of concern. Eva and Elizabeth are both unhappy about the ways in which their brother and sister treat their mother. Just as Eva is angered when her sister Alinka challenges her mother's authority, Elizabeth views her brother's constant criticisms of her mother's English as fanatical and cruel. Both Eva and Elizabeth are more outwardly protective of their mothers' feelings than their brother and sister are.

Although Eva and Elizabeth share similar attitudes, they also differ from each other in many respects. Unlike Eva, Elizabeth does not feel that her identity is bound to her family's cultural heritage and history. Whereas Eva embraces her Polish heritage, Elizabeth flees her Chinese background. While Eva wants to hold on to the memory of the family's sad past, Elizabeth is happy when her mother grants her a "cultural divorce" and says she no longer has to attend the Chinese school. In contrast to Elizabeth, Eva is flexible: She is willing to compromise and accept the best of both cultures. Whereas Eva sees herself becoming bicultural, Elizabeth adores the sights and sounds of everything American and wants only to be an "all-American girl." How could she want anything else if Nancy Drew, her favorite heroine, never spoke Chinese? Of course, all this can be explained by the different ages and the different circumstances of the two girls. Eva is thirteen years old, while Elizabeth is only ten years old. In addition, whereas Eva herself is an immigrant, Elizabeth was born and raised in the United States. Such basic differences in their lives leave a wide gap between them.

Conclusion

Eva and Elizabeth have made different adjustments to their crosscultural experiences. When children like Eva immigrate, they understand the sacrifices their parents have made in order to provide them with a better life because they themselves have participated in the immigration process. However, children like Elizabeth often don't understand the sacrifices their parents have made for them until they become adults. And when they finally do, can it sometimes be too late?

1. Which words and phrases does the writer use to point out similarities and differences?

2. In the body of the essay, can you readily identify the paragraph that deals with the similarities and the paragraph that deals with the differences? Explain how the writer makes this easy for the reader.

3. What does the writer do to connect the two paragraphs of the body?

4. Are the similarities between the two characters more important than the differences, or are the differences more important than the similarities? Explain.

PURPOSE OF COMPARISON AND CONTRAST ESSAYS

When you write a comparison and contrast essay, the purpose is not just to point out similarities and differences or advantages and disadvantages. The purpose is—as with all essays—to persuade, explain, or inform. The emphasis should be on either the similarities or the differences, and details should be included according to which emphasis is chosen.

The *thesis statement* of the essay you have just read, the last sentence of the *introductory paragraph*, tells the reader something about the emphasis that will be developed in the *body of the essay.* "By examining the relationships that these two girls have with their mothers and other important people in their lives, we can see that although Eva and Elizabeth may have certain hopes and feelings in common, they are at the same time very different from each other." We know by the last sentence of the body of the essay that the differences outweigh the similarities: "Such basic differences in their lives leave a wide gap between them." This point of view is reinforced in the *conclusion* of the essay.

PATTERNS OF ORGANIZATION

There are two ways to organize a comparison and contrast essay: through block organization or point-by-point organization.

Block Organization	Point-by-Point Organization
◆ Similarities: *all subjects are discussed*	◆ Subject One: *similarities and differences are discussed*
◆ Differences: *all subjects are discussed*	◆ Subject Two: *similarities and differences are discussed*
	◆ Subject Three: *similarities and differences are discussed*

Block Organization

In a **block organization** essay, the writer discusses each part of the comparison in clearly distinct parts (or blocks) of the essay. For example, the writer could first refer only to Eva and then only to Elizabeth, or, as in the essay "A Comparison of Eva and Elizabeth," he could first discuss the *similarities* between the two girls and then the *differences* between them.

The paragraph dealing with similarities contains many words and expressions that point out likenesses: *like, in the same way that, just as, both,* and so on. Similarly, the paragraph revealing the differences contains words and expressions that show differences: *unlike, whereas, while, in contrast to,* and so on.

In order to connect one block of the essay with the other, the writer uses a *transitional sentence* that prepares us for the change in emphasis of the next block: "Although Eva and Elizabeth share similar attitudes, they also differ from each other in many respects."

Point-By-Point Organization

In *point-by-point organization,* the writer organizes the development of ideas according to "points," or categories, that are common to both subjects. In each paragraph of the body, a different point is discussed. For example, a comparison of Eva and Elizabeth might (after the introductory paragraph) begin with a paragraph exploring the differences in their *age and background.* A second paragraph might discuss the similarities and differences in their *family life,* and so on. It is usually better to limit the categories to three or four.

A point-by-point organization is usually chosen when there are many complex aspects to a comparison; a block organization is more suitable for a simpler subject.

Organizing Information through Outlines

Whether you choose block or point-by-point organization for your comparison and contrast essay, preparing an outline can help you to organize your main ideas, topic sentences, and supporting details. After you prepare an outline, you know exactly what you want to write and how you want to write it.

2 *Re-read the body of the essay "A Comparison of Eva and Elizabeth." Then work with a partner and complete the block organization outline that follows by filling in the blanks. Do not copy the sentences that appear in the essay. Instead, write notes that reflect the information that is conveyed in each sentence.*

Outline: A Comparison of Eva and Elizabeth
(Block Organization)

I. How Eva and Elizabeth are like each other

    A. Embarrassment

       1. Eva:

       _____

       2. Elizabeth:

       _____

    B. Siblings

       1. Eva:

       _____

       2. Elizabeth:

       _____

II. _____

    A. Cultural Heritage and History

       1. Eva:

       _____

       2. Elizabeth:

       does not want to go to Chinese school

    B. Cultural Identity

       1. Eva:

       _____

       2. Elizabeth:

       _____

    C. _____

       1. Eva:

       immigrant

       2. Elizabeth:

       _____

3 *With your partner, plan an outline according to point-by-point organization for the same essay, "A Comparison of Eva and Elizabeth." Use the following framework as a guide.*

Outline: A Comparison of Eva and Elizabeth
(Point-by-Point Organization)

I. Age and Background

    A. Eva:

    _____

    B. Elizabeth:

    _____

II. Family Life

    A. Eva:

    _____

    B. Elizabeth:

    _____

III. Cultural Identity

    A. Eva:

    _____

    B. Elizabeth:

    _____

ON YOUR OWN

A. WRITING TOPICS

Write an essay about one of the following topics. In order to organize your ideas effectively, write a clear thesis statement and create an outline in response to it. Follow the outline as you write the essay. Try to use the vocabulary and grammar structures you have studied in this unit.

1. Have you ever had a friend whose culture, background, talents, or qualities were different from yours? Consider how your similarities and differences contributed to your friendship. Did your friendship grow because you were similar or because you were different?

2. When immigrants arrive in a new country, should they assimilate into the new culture or try to preserve their old culture? In what ways do you think people need to assimilate? What kinds of things do people usually want to preserve from their old culture? What is the risk to the nation if assimilation is too extreme? What is the risk if immigrants do not assimilate?

3. What is the meaning of the following extract? In what ways might Luc Sante have felt "other"? How has your own identity been formed? Have you ever had the experience of being "other"?

Ethnically, I am about as homogeneous as it is possible to be: aside from one great-grandmother who came from Luxembourg, my gene pool derives entirely from an area smaller than the five boroughs of New York City. I was born in the same town [Verviers, Belgium] as every one of my Sante forebears at least as far back as the mid-sixteenth century, which is as far back as the records go. Having been transplanted from my native soil [to live in the U.S.], and having had to construct an identity in response to a double set of demands, one from my background and one from my environment, I have become permanently "other."

Luc Sante, "Living in Tongues"
(from *The New York Times Magazine*)

B. FIELDWORK

PREPARATION

In what way has your family been touched by history? Prepare to write an essay in response to this question. Interview family members, either in person or by mail to gather information for your essay. Before starting your research, brainstorm with a partner for other questions that you believe would be worth investigating. Here are some points you may want to consider when you make up the questions for your interviews.

1. Has your family always lived in the same place? What influenced the decision to stay or go?

2. Has your country undergone any great changes in the last fifty years? Wars? Revolutions? Divisions? Reunifications? Changes in the political system? What effect have these events had on your family?

3. Have the economic circumstances of your family changed in recent generations? What are the reasons for these changes?

4. How has your family adjusted to change?

5. Do you think it is important for children to know the history of their family?

6. Has your family ever had any secrets that were not immediately told to the younger generation? Why were certain facts not openly discussed in your family?

7. Is there any documentation that you would like to show to illustrate your family's history? This can include photos, newspaper articles, or magazines from the period. It can include personal items if you and your family agree to do so.

RESEARCH ACTIVITY

When you interview family members, be sure to take good notes. You may want to request permission to use a tape recorder if you are interviewing in person. Ask them if they have any photos, newspaper articles, official announcements, letters, or personal records that you can include in your essay.

SHARING YOUR FINDINGS

Write an essay in which you summarize your findings and explain how this information has affected you. Include relevant documentation.

THE LANDSCAPE OF FAITH

1 APPROACHING THE TOPIC

A. PREDICTING

Look at the title of this unit and the photo above. In spite of different practices, why do you think religion is such an important part of life all over the world? Write down your ideas and share them with the class.

B. SHARING INFORMATION

Interview a partner using this questionnaire about religion. You will need to summarize in a few sentences your partner's answer to question 5. After you have finished, show your summary to your partner to check the content. Then, discuss your answers in a small group.

◆ RELIGION IN YOUR LIFE ◆

QUESTION	YES	NO
1. Were you brought up in a particular religion?	_____	_____
2. Do you still feel a part of that religion today?	_____	_____
3. Do you participate fully in a religion today?	_____	_____
4. Do you follow all the customs, rules, and traditions of this religion?	_____	_____

5. How has the religion affected your life or your family's life?

_____

_____

_____

_____

_____

_____

2 PREPARING TO READ

A. BACKGROUND

Read the information below and discuss the questions that follow in a small group.

In this chapter, there is an interview with one of the most well-known Buddhists in the world, the Dalai Lama, the religious leader of the Tibetan Buddhist community.

The Buddhist religion is based on the teachings of Siddhartha Gautama, a Hindu prince who lived about 2,500 years ago in India. (This was about the same time Confucius was teaching in China.) Siddhartha became the Buddha, or "Enlightened One," after a personal journey of spiritual awakening, and he spent the rest of his life teaching people. Buddhist teachings have spread all over Asia and are followed today by more than 255 million people. Buddhism is divided into many different schools and sects, but all Buddhists share certain basic beliefs.

For Buddhists, all life is suffering. This suffering is caused by selfish efforts and desires. A life goes through many cycles of rebirth because there is always something more to learn. The end of rebirths and suffering, the release into the highest stage of happiness—nirvana—is achieved only by learning to give up self-interest. Buddhists are taught to speak kindly, to do no harm, and to avoid killing, stealing, lying, drinking alcohol, and committing sexual offenses. Buddhists believe there is no beginning and no end, no creation and no Higher Being.

Tibetan Buddhism has suffered greatly in recent years. In the 1950s the Chinese Communist government invaded Tibet and almost destroyed the spiritual and cultural basis of the religion. In 1959 the Dalai Lama, the head of the religion there, had to leave his country with 70,000 of his followers; he now lives in exile.

1. Do you know of any other religions whose philosophy is based on respect for the life and teachings of an individual? What religions are they?

2. Do you know of other religions that have suffered from government persecution during the twentieth century?

3. Why do you think some Westerners are attracted to Eastern religions? Why do you think some Easterners are attracted to Western religions?

B. VOCABULARY FOR COMPREHENSION

Work in pairs. Read the sentences and match the underlined word or expression with a synonym from the list. The first one has been done for you.

___e___ 1. The Buddhist religion believes in <u>the idea that individual people can come back in a new life form after death</u>.

_____ 2. Spiritual concerns are usually associated with religion, but <u>worldly, material</u> concerns are usually identified with government authority. In some cultures, however, the spiritual leader is also the head of government.

___h___ 3. When someone asks you to guess what the future will bring, you are being asked to <u>theorize</u> about what may happen.

___b___ 4. In some countries, an unpopular political, spiritual, or artistic leader can be forced into <u>leaving his country and living in a foreign land</u>.

___a___ 5. In many religions, the leaders are not elected. The heads of the religion <u>choose</u> their successors.

___c___ 6. Many parents give their children a religious education, hoping that when the children grow up they will be <u>observant</u> members of the religion.

___f___ 7. Some young people feel that religious concerns are no longer <u>related</u> to modern life.

___g___ 8. History shows that brutal dictators do not think much about the long-term interests of their people. They are often reckless and <u>interested only in the moment</u>.

___d___ 9. Some religions are practiced only among their own people, but other religions seek to <u>spread</u> their ideas among as many people as possible.

a. designate ✓
b. exile ✓
c. practicing
d. propagate
e. reincarnation
f. relevant ✓
g. short-sighted ✓
h. speculate ✓
i. temporal

3 READING ONE: Peace Prevails

A. INTRODUCING THE TOPIC

Before you read the interview with the Dalai Lama, answer the following question in a written paragraph. Then discuss your answer with a partner.

Do you think the world will be better or worse 100 years from now?

Peace Prevails

By Claudia Dreifus (from *The New York Times Magazine*)

1   In the Buddhist tradition, the future counts for little. Nonetheless, when Tenzin Gyatso, fourteenth Dalai Lama and the spiritual and temporal leader of Tibet in exile, was asked to speculate on the landscape of faith a century from now, he gave it his best try. He was interviewed in Bloomington, Indiana, on a brilliant summer morning, after having laid the cornerstone[1] for a new Buddhist temple.

2   **Question:** In the next hundred years, thanks to organ transplants and genetic therapies, people may be able to live much longer lives. If you had the chance to do that, would you take it?

3   **Dalai Lama:** The mere living is not so important. The important thing is useful-ness. So if I could get another hundred years more and be useful, then . . . good. Otherwise, you just create more problems for others. And then, from the Buddhist viewpoint, isn't it better to have another young body [through reincarnation]? There's a Buddhist story about an old monk who was dying and everyone was very sad. He said, "Don't be sad. Right now, I have an old, decaying body. But very soon . . . I will get a fresh young body."

4   **Question:** Three years ago, you predicted that the next hundred years would be a century of peace, hope and justice. Since then, there have been massacres in Rwanda and Burundi, the Northern Irish peace discussions have been blown apart and the Chinese have kidnapped the young boy you designated to be the Panchen Lama.[2] Are you still optimistic about the future?

5   **Dalai Lama:** Oh, yes. Of course. A hand-ful of shortsighted people have always existed. But overall, their day is over because the public's attitude towards war and violence has become much healthier than at any time in history. People used to be much more jingoistic[3] and nationalistic compared with the way they are now.

6   Recently I was talking with the English Queen Mother. She is 96, and I asked her,

---

[1] *cornerstone:* a foundation; a stone laid at a formal ceremony
[2] *Panchen Lama:* chief spiritual adviser to the Dalai Lama
[3] *jingoism:* extreme nationalism, usually marked by an aggressive, warlike attitude toward other countries

"What changes have you seen in your life-time?" She answered, "When I was young, we had not much concern about the outside world. Now people have a great concern about what is happening all over the world." This is a very positive change.

7   So I believe that due to [the revolution in] information, generally speaking, any leader, if he tried to mobilize the whole nation for war, would find it impossible. In previous times, it was quite possible. Well, small-scale wars, perhaps they can still do. But large-scale wars, I think, are not likely. I do believe that in the next century we have to seriously think about putting a complete stop to the arms trade.

8   Q: Buddhism has become quite popular in the West. Could you see a future American president who is a practicing Buddhist?

9   DL: No, I think someone in the Judeo-Christian tradition would be better. I prefer that people in Western countries follow their own traditions. I have no desire to propagate [my religious beliefs].

10   Q: A hundred years in the future, what will be the role of women in religion?

11   DL: I think improved. Because the women want it.

12   Q: Can you see a situation where there might be a woman as Pope, a woman as Archbishop of Canterbury, a woman as Dalai Lama?

13   DL: In the Buddhist world, there's not much of a problem. Some of the Lamas of high reincarnation are women.

14   Q: Is it possible that you, the 14th Dalai Lama, might be the last Dalai Lama?

15   DL: It is possible. Not as a result of external force, though. If the majority of the Tibetan people feel that the Dalai Lama institution is no longer relevant, then the institution will automatically cease. Now, if that happens while I'm alive or just after my death, then I am obviously the last Dalai Lama. But if my death comes in the next one or two years, then most probably the Tibetan people will want to have another incarnation. Of that I'm quite certain. Of course, there is the possibility that Tibetans become insignificant in our land and all decisions are made by the Chinese. It is possible and very sad.

16   Q: Are you concerned that you might have a violent death?

17   DL: It is possible, I don't know. Airplanes trouble me. Dying in the ocean. And ending up in the stomach of a shark.

18   Q: One hundred years from now, what would you like to be remembered for?

19   DL: As a Buddhist practitioner, I have no interest in that. So long as I am alive, my time and my life must be utilized properly. Then after my death, I don't care how people remember me.

20   Q: Is it true that you like to go shopping when you travel?

21   DL: I like it. I'm a human being. I think human beings have a lot of curiosity. I go to Los Angeles; sometimes I shop for myself. Shoes . . . small electronic equipment . . . cat food. I go to shopping malls just like they were museums.

22   Q: Many people get a sense of God by observing nature. What will religions be like in a hundred years if there is little nature left on earth?

23   DL: The world itself is nature. The sun, the moon, they are nature. Even if there were no more animals, nature would still be here. For those religions that believe in a creator, they would have to find reasons to explain why our beautiful blue planet became a desert.

24   If you ask me whether it's good or bad, of course it's bad. But in the Buddhist tradition, something like that would not change our attitude. We believe the whole world will come and disappear, come and disappear—so eventually the world becomes desert and even the ocean dries up. But then again, another new world is reborn. It's endless.

B. READING FOR MAIN IDEAS

Under each of the main themes of this reading, write a few sentences summarizing the Dalai Lama's point of view.

1. What does the Dalai Lama say about his philosophy of death?

_____

_____

_____

_____

2. What does the Dalai Lama say about his attitude toward war?

_____

_____

_____

_____

3. What does he say about the role of the Dalai Lama in the future?

_____

_____

_____

_____

4. What does he say about the future of the earth?

_____

_____

_____

_____

C. READING FOR DETAILS

Read the sentences on the left. Cross out the sentences that are not part of the Dalai Lama's predictions. Then, decide which major theme of the reading the remaining sentences support. Write the number of the sentence under the appropriate main idea on the right.

PREDICTIONS

1. The Chinese government may go further in opposing the Tibetan people's religion.

2. Buddhists will be converting thousands of Americans to their religion.

3. Improvements in information technology will continue to create concern for people in other countries.

4. World wars will be less likely than in the twentieth century.

5. Nature may go through a cycle where much is destroyed.

6. Tibetans will be true to their religion unless external force obliges them to change.

7. Nationalism will decrease as different peoples draw closer together.

8. The Dalai Lama will not worry about how people will remember him 100 years from now.

9. Buddhists will have to accept the idea of a creator.

10. Concern for others will diminish the power of nationalism in local wars.

11. Old bodies should be discarded.

MAIN IDEAS/THEMES

The Role of the Dalai Lama in the Future

The Dalai Lama's Attitude toward War

The Dalai Lama's Philosophy of Death

The Future of the Earth

D. READING BETWEEN THE LINES

Based on what you have read in the interview, imagine what the Dalai Lama would say if he were asked the following questions. Write short answers and explain your conclusions, referring to specific parts of the interview. The first one has been done for you. Then compare your answers with those of another student.

The Dalai Lama

1. **Question:** Should the Tibetans take arms against the Chinese?

   Answer: <u>The Dalai Lama would probably say no because he</u> <u>speaks out against war and violence in paragraph 5 of</u> <u>the interview.</u>

2. **Question:** Should religious people refuse to go to the movies?

   Answer: _____

   _____

3. **Question:** Should society invest a great deal of money in keeping very old and ill people alive as long as possible?

   Answer: _____

   _____

4. **Question:** Should society be concerned about endangered species?

   Answer: _____

   _____

Now invent two questions of your own for the Dalai Lama, and ask a classmate to answer them.

5. **Question:** _____

   Answer: _____

   _____

6. **Question:** _____

   Answer: _____

   _____

   _____

4 READING TWO: Religion

A. EXPANDING THE TOPIC

*Before you read this excerpt from an essay that offers a general definition of the word **religion**, answer the question below. Write a short definition and discuss it with a partner. Although there can be diverse views on this question, the passage tries to make broad generalizations applicable to many religions and different periods of history.*

How would you define the word *religion*?

Religion

FROM COMPTON'S INTERACTIVE ENCYCLOPEDIA

1   It has been said that thoughts of death lead necessarily to the development of religion. It is difficult to imagine what need there would be for religion in a world in which no one ever died or became ill. The literatures of all religions attempt to give answers to basic questions: From where did the world come? What is the meaning of human life? Why do people die and what happens afterward? Why is there evil? How should people behave? In the distant past, these questions were answered in terms of mythology. In literature, they are dealt with in poetry. Modern sciences try to investigate them.

2   As a word religion is difficult to define, but as a human experience it seems to be universal. The twentieth century German-born American theologian Paul Tillich[1] gave a simple and basic definition of the word. "Religion is ultimate concern." This means that religion encompasses that to which people are most devoted or that from which they expect to get the most fundamental satisfaction in life. Consequently, religion provides adequate answers to the most basic questions posed above.

3   Four centuries earlier the German social reformer Martin Luther[2] spoke in similar terms about God. He stated that to have a god was to "have something in which the heart trusts completely." Putting Tillich's

---

[1] *Paul Tillich:* Protestant theologian (religious thinker), 1886–1965
[2] *Martin Luther:* German leader of the Protestant Reformation, 1483–1546

and Luther's definitions together, it is possible to see that religion does not necessarily have to be involved with shrines, temples, churches or synagogues. It does not need complex doctrines or clergy.[3] It can be anything to which people devote themselves that fills their lives with meaning.

4   In Western civilization, religion has traditionally been defined as belief in and worship of one God. This is true for Judaism, Christianity, and Islam. The statements by Tillich and Luther make it clear, however, that such a definition may be too narrow. In original Buddhism in India and Confucianism in China, there was no recognition of a supreme being. Both of these philosophies were basically concerned with patterns of human behavior.

5   Regardless of definition, all religions (as the word is normally used) have certain elements in common: rituals to perform, prayers to recite, places to frequent or avoid, holy days to keep, means by which to predict the future, a body of literature to read and study, truths to affirm, charismatic[4] leaders to follow, and ordinances[5] to obey. Many have buildings set aside for worship, and there are activities such as prayer, sacrifice, contemplation, and perhaps magic.

6   Closely associated with these elements is personal conduct. Although it is possible to separate ritual observances from moral conduct, worship has normally implied a type of relationship with a god from which certain behavior patterns are expected to follow. A notable exception in history is the official state religion of ancient Rome, which was kept separate from personal commitment and morality.

On a separate piece of paper, write an explanation of the following quotes from the text. Compare your answers with those of a partner.

1. "In the distant past, these questions were answered in terms of mythology. In literature, they are dealt with in poetry. Modern sciences try to investigate them." (Paragraph 1)

2. "Putting Tillich's and Luther's definitions together, it is possible to see that religion does not necessarily have to be involved with shrines, temples, churches or synagogues. It does not need complex doctrines or clergy. It can be anything to which people devote themselves that fills their lives with meaning." (Paragraph 3)

3. "Although it is possible to separate ritual observances from moral conduct, worship has normally implied a type of relationship with a god from which certain behavior patterns are expected to follow." (Paragraph 6)

---

[3] *clergy:* a group of men and women who are religious leaders and servants of God
[4] *charismatic:* embodying a personal magic of leadership, creating great loyalty and enthusiasm among followers
[5] *ordinances:* orders or regulations to follow

B. LINKING READINGS ONE AND TWO

Work in pairs. Choose Exercise 1 or 2, and fill in the appropriate answers.

1 *In Reading Two, the writer lists five basic questions which the literatures of all religions attempt to answer. Based on the interview with the Dalai Lama, how do you think he would respond to these questions? Discuss with a partner what answers you would expect to find in Buddhist literature. Then write your answers in the spaces provided.*

**How Would the Dalai Lama Answer
the Five Basic Questions of All Religions?**

1. From where did the world come?

The world itself is nature. Even if there were no animals, nature would still be there. For those religions that believe in a creator, they would have to find reason to explain

2. What is the meaning of human life?

The mere living is not so important. The important thing is usefulness suffering) characteristic

(The life is

3. Why do people die, and what happens afterward?

Don't be sad. Right now I have an old decaying body. But very soon I will get a fresh young body

4. Why is there evil?

because a shortsighted people have always existed

(all life is suffering
The suffering is caused selfish.)

5. How should people behave?

We should have a great concern about what is happening all over the world

2 *Discuss the following questions with a partner, and then write your opinions in the space provided.*

A Student Interview

1. Do you agree that world wars are not likely today or in the future? Why or why not?

_____

_____

_____

2. Do you think we should be worried about endangered animal species and the protection of the earth?

_____

_____

_____

3. Do you care how people will remember you after you die?

_____

_____

_____

5 REVIEWING LANGUAGE

A. EXPLORING VOCABULARY

The words at the top of page 142 are all related to religion. Working in a small group, put them in the correct categories on the chart that follows. Add any other words you can think of to these categories.

bishop	Confucianism	mosque	rituals	worship
Buddhism	Hinduism	ordinances	shrine	
Christianity	Islam	prayer	synagogue	
church	Judaism	priest	temple	
clergy	monk	rabbi	theologian	

NAMES OF RELIGIONS	PLACES OF WORSHIP	RELIGIOUS LEADERS	RELIGIOUS PRACTICES
_____	_____	_____	_____
_____	_____	_____	_____
_____	_____	_____	_____
_____	_____	_____	_____
_____	_____	_____	_____
_____	_____	_____	_____
_____	_____	_____	_____
_____	_____	_____	_____

B. WORKING WITH WORDS: Analogies

Analogies compare relationships between things that are alike in some ways. The analogy **Buddhism : temple = Judaism : synagogue** is expressed in English as follows: "Buddhism is to a temple as Judaism is to a synagogue." In other words, "Buddhism is practiced in a temple just as Judaism is practiced in a synagogue."

Use the words that you worked with in the previous exercise to complete the following analogies. Circle the correct answer from the choices given.

1. church : Christianity = ? : Islam

A church is to Christianity as a _____ is to Islam.

   a. church   **b.** mosque   **c.** synagogue

2. ? : temple = priest : church

A _Monk_ is to a temple as a priest is to a church.

a. pope   b. mullah   c. monk

3. Islam : Turkey = ? : China

Islam is to Turkey as _Confucianism_ is to China.

a. Confucianism   b. Christianity   c. Judaism

4. politician : political scientists = clergy : ?

Politicians are to political scientists as clergy are to _theologians_.

a. theologians   b. practitioners   c. worshipers

5. Roman Catholicism : France = ? : the United States

Roman Catholicism is to France as _Protestantism_ is to the United States.

a. Protestantism   b. Catholicism   c. Christianity

6. mullah : Islam = ? : Protestantism

A mullah is to Islam as a _minister_ is to Protestantism.

a. rabbi   b. priest   c. minister

7. perform : rituals = recite : ?

Perform is to rituals as recite is to _prayers_.

a. ordinances   b. prayers   c. practitioners

8. laws : customs = ? : rituals

Laws are to customs as _ordinances_ are to rituals.

a. prayers   b. ordinances   c. theologians

9. Mecca : ? = Vatican City : Roman Catholicism

Mecca is to _Islam_ as Vatican City is to Roman Catholicism.

a. Judaism   b. Buddhism   c. Islam

10. ? : Christianity = Christianity : Islam

Judaism is to Christianity as Christianity is to Islam.

a. Hinduism   b. Buddhism   c. Judaism

SKILLS FOR EXPRESSION

A. GRAMMAR: Definite and Indefinite Articles with Count and Non-Count Nouns

1 *Examine the sentences below and discuss the questions that follow with a partner.*

◆ Islam is <u>a religion</u>.

◆ Islam is <u>the religion</u> practiced by all believers in the Koran.

◆ Islam and Hinduism are <u>religions</u>.

◆ Islam and Hinduism are <u>the religions</u> practiced by the majority of people on the Indian subcontinent.

◆ <u>Honesty</u> is a virtue.

◆ <u>The honesty</u> of the man is his greatest virtue.

a. Which sentence means that Islam is one of many religions?

b. How do the meanings of the nouns change when *a* and *the* are used and when they are not used in the above sentences?

Definite and Indefinite Articles

FOCUS ON GRAMMAR

See definite and indefinite articles in *Focus on Grammar, Advanced.*

For Singular Count Nouns

Whether or not an article is needed before a singular noun depends on whether the noun is a count noun or not. All singular count nouns must be preceded by either an **indefinite article** [*a(n)*] or a **definite article** [*the*]. You choose *a(n)* or *the* depending on the situation.

If you are describing "one of many," use the indefinite article *a(n)*.	Islam is *a religion.*
If you are describing "the specific one," use the definite article *the.* Imagine that definite article, unlike the indefinite article, creates a "finite limit" and refers precisely to "a specific one."	Islam is *the religion* practiced by all believers in the Koran.

For Plural Count Nouns

The same concepts apply to count nouns in the plural. When it is obvious that the plural count noun does not represent all the nouns in a group, no article comes before it.

In the example sentence, we know that Islam and Hinduism are only two of many religions.	Islam and Hinduism are **religions.**
When information given in the sentence limits the plural count noun to a specific category, the definite article **the** is used.	Islam and Hinduism are **the religions** practiced by the majority of the people on the Indian subcontinent.

For Non-Count Nouns

Non-count nouns are always singular because they cannot be counted. **Honesty, knowledge, wisdom, ignorance, information, evidence, research** and **advice** are examples of non-count nouns. No articles comes before them when a specific reference is not being made. But when it is obvious that a specific reference is being made, the definite article is used.

In the example sentence "the man's honesty," and not just "honesty" in general, is the subject.	**The** honesty of the man is his greatest virtue.

---

2 *With a partner, decide whether the singular nouns on page 146 are count or non-count nouns. Circle your choice. Then write two sentences for each one. Show in the case of count nouns how both the definite and indefinite articles can be used. Show in the case of non-count nouns how the indefinite article is omitted and the definite article can be used. The first two have been done for you.*

1. purity   Count /(Non-Count)

Purity is a state sought by many religious people.

The purity of his intentions was admired by all his friends.

2. church   (Count)/ Non-Count

The people saw a church in the distance.

The church that they saw was the one that had just been built.

3. belief   Count/Non-Count

_____

_____

4. spirituality   Count/Non-Count

_____

_____

5. ceremony   Count/Non-Count

_____

_____

❸ *Work with a partner. In the following paragraphs about the Society of Friends, a Protestant religion, add a definite article or an indefinite article in the spaces provided if you believe that an article is necessary. If you believe no article is necessary, put an "X" in the space.*

(1) _____ Religious Society of Friends, commonly referred to as

(2) _____ Quakers, was founded in 1652 after George Fox received

(3) _____ vision from God on Pendle Hill in Northwest England.

(4) _____* vision helped Fox to realize that (5) _____

spiritual presence of God was (6) _____ source of all religious truth.

Such (7) _____ realization became the basis for (8) _____

Quaker doctrine of the inner light. The Quakers believe that (9) _____

spirit of God enters (10) _____ consciousness of both men and

women equally and that it is evidenced in human beings' most honorable

behavior.

_____

*Wherever a definite article is possible, you may also consider using demonstrative adjectives (*this, that, these, those*) if the noun to which they refer has been mentioned—as this one is—in a preceding sentence.

The Quakers believe in (11) _____ equality and in (12) _____ pacifism, which involves an opposition to war and service in an army. Their insistence on (13) _____ equality of all human beings has been demonstrated in their refusal to show any signs of respect such as removing one's hat to (14) _____ person regarded as (15) _____ social superior. It has also been evident in (16) _____ leadership roles that Quaker women Susan B. Anthony and Lucretia Mott assumed in (17) _____ struggle for women's rights in (18) _____ United States.

Because of their beliefs, the Quakers faced many conflicts with the political and religious authorities in England, and they were often persecuted as a result. (19) _____ founding in 1681 of (20) _____ colony of Pennsylvania by William Penn, (21) _____ Quaker, provided (22) _____ haven for many Quakers and exiles of other persecuted religious groups. Some Quakers also settled in Rhode Island, Massachusetts, and the South. They were not welcome in the South because of their opposition to (23) _____ slavery. Nevertheless, despite their pacifist views, they played (24) _____ major role during the American Civil War (1861–1865) by helping (25) _____ African-American slaves make their way to (26) _____ safety of the North.

B. STYLE: Writing a Definition Essay

1 *Examine Reading Two and discuss the questions below with a partner.*

a. In the first paragraph, how does the writer "unify" all the religions in the world?

b. In the second and third paragraphs, what does the writer do to come closer to a definition of the word *religion?*

c. What kind of comparison do you find in the fourth paragraph?

d. How is the fifth paragraph similar to the first paragraph?

WHAT IS A DEFINITION?

When writing a **definition essay,** the writer enters the world of classification. Through **classification,** we analyze a subject by dividing it into categories. First we find what all of the categories have in common—the "common characteristics"—and then we seek to determine how each of the categories can be distinguished from one another.

This is precisely what a definition is: the process of putting nouns in categories or "classes." In a definition, we show how the item or concept to be defined is part of a broader category and how it is different from the other members of this category. The box that follows gives examples.

Classification

Member/Smaller Class	Larger Class	Specific Details
1. a rabbi	a religious leader	Judaism
2. a mullah	a religious leader	Islam
3. rabbis and mullahs	religious leaders	

1. "A rabbi is a religious leader in the Jewish community."

2. "A mullah is a religious leader in the Islamic community."

3. "Rabbis and mullahs are religious leaders."

RESEARCH AND PREPARATION

The writer of the definition essay "Religion" went through a similar process of analysis throughout the research stage. After studying "all religions" and analyzing their "common characteristics" and differences, as in the classification box above, the writer was then ready to write an essay defining "religion."

ESSAY STRUCTURE

As is evident in Reading Two, the definition essay goes from the realm of the "indefinite" (*a* religion is . . . /religions are . . .) to the realm of the "definite" (*the* Moslem religion, unlike *the* Buddhist religion, is . . .). The writer first tells us what "all religions" have in common ("*all religions* attempt to give answers to basic questions"). Then, after interpreting the quotes by Paul Tillich and Martin Luther, the writer shows that the Western belief in one God is not shared by followers of the Eastern religions. The writer then refers to other "*elements in common:* rituals to perform, prayers to recite, holy days to keep." It is apparent from the way this brief excerpt unfolds that in the rest of the essay the writer will continue to show a pattern of common characteristics and specific differences.

In a definition essay, as in all other kinds of essays, the writer introduces examples, shows similarities and differences, uses quotations, and so on, in order to make sure the information is communicated as effectively as possible. The writer provides a **thesis statement** ("As a word religion is difficult to define, but as a human experience it seems to be universal."). The writer also permits his **point of view** to surface. For example, at the beginning of the essay "Religion," the statement—"It is difficult to imagine what need there would be for religion in a world in which no one ever died or became ill"—immediately familiarizes the reader with the writer's point of view. Thus, despite the difficult task of objective analysis that the writer must go through when preparing a definition essay, one thing is certain: The writer's point of view remains very important.

2 *Work with a partner and write a definition for each of the following words. Break down each word according to the "Member/Smaller Class—Larger Class—Specific Details" categories before you actually write its definition. Use a dictionary if necessary. The first one has been done for you.*

1. **a synagogue**

Member/Smaller Class	Larger Class	Specific Details
a synagogue	a house of worship	Judaism

Definition: A synagogue is a house of worship where Judaism is practiced.

2. **a prayer**

Member/Smaller Class	Larger Class	Specific Details

Definition: _____

_____

3. **a sin**

Member/Smaller Class	Larger Class	Specific Details

Definition: _____

_____

4. a prophet

Member/Smaller Class	Larger Class	Specific Details
_____	_____	_____

Definition: _____

_____

5. a ritual

Member/Smaller Class	Larger Class	Specific Details
_____	_____	_____

Definition: _____

_____

3 *Work in a small group. Brainstorm a definition for the word* **love.** *Many religions preach "love your fellow man." But what exactly is love? Analyze at least five types of love. Two types of love have been suggested to you below. Find the common characteristics and differences of each type of love. Then write down the definition of* **love** *that the group agrees upon.*

Member/Smaller Class	Larger Class	Specific Details
1. self-love	_____	_____
2. the love of a parent for a child	_____	_____
3. _____	_____	_____
4. _____	_____	_____
5. _____	_____	_____

Definition of *Love:* _____

_____

4 *Write an essay defining and explaining the meaning of love to you.*

ON YOUR OWN

A. WRITING TOPICS

Choose one question and write a well-organized essay. Remember to provide a thesis statement and sufficient explanations, examples, and support to develop your definition. Use the vocabulary you have studied in this unit.

1. Write a brief definition of the religion you follow or the dominant religion in your country. Explain its most important beliefs and practices.

2. George Bernard Shaw[1] wrote, "There is only one religion, though there are a hundred versions of it." Do you agree or disagree? Explain your answer.

3. How has religion influenced and affected your life? Write an essay defining the positive and/or negative effects of religion on various aspects of your life.

4. Would you marry someone of a different faith? Why or why not? What difficulties would you have to overcome, and what would be the positive or negative results?

5. Can a person be "religious" without following a formal religion? Answer the question with reference to the following poem by Emily Dickinson.[2]

Some keep the Sabbath going to church;
I keep it staying at home,
With a bobolink[3] for a chorister,[4]
And an orchard for a dome.

Some keep the Sabbath in surplice;[5]
I just wear my wings,
And instead of tolling the bell for church,
Our little sexton[6] sings.

God preaches,—a noted clergyman,—
And the sermon is never long;
So instead of getting to heaven at last,
I'm going all along.

Emily Dickinson

---

[1] *George Bernard Shaw* (1856–1950), Irish-born British playwright and author
[2] *Emily Dickinson* (1830–1886), American poet
[3] *bobolink:* an American songbird
[4] *chorister:* a singer in a church choir
[5] *surplice:* a loose, white robe worn by clergymen
[6] *sexton:* a church officer or employee who takes care of church property and, in some churches, rings the bell for services

B. FIELDWORK

PREPARATION

In Reading Two you read a general definition of religion. There are many religions in the modern world. Choose one religion with which you are not familiar, and find out as much as you can about it. Begin with the following questions and add to them as you do your research.

- ◆ Does this religion have a belief in a creator? Is there one god or many?

- ◆ What kind of behavior is expected of believers? What is the definition of "a good life" according to this religion?

- ◆ Where is this religion practiced in the world?

RESEARCH ACTIVITY

If possible, interview a member of the religious community you are interested in, or you can conduct your research in the library or on the Internet. Be sure to consult several sources of information so that you can reduce the likelihood of prejudice or distortion in your treatment of the religion.

SHARING YOUR FINDINGS

1. After you have taken notes about the religion you chose, write up your findings as a definition essay. The title can be, for example, "What Is the Hindu Religion?" or "What Is Zen Buddhism as Practiced in Japan?" or "What Is the Baptist (Protestant) Religion?"

2. Form a small group and read your essay to the other members of the group. Comment on each other's essays, and discuss what you have learned.

MANAGING A CAREER

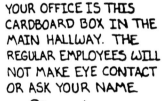

APPROACHING THE TOPIC

A. PREDICTING

Discuss the humor of this cartoon with another student. According to the cartoon, how are temporary employees treated in the business world? Why do you think this happens?

B. SHARING INFORMATION

❶ *In your experience, how do people usually get a job? Number the ways listed below from 1 to 8, with 1 being what you consider to be the most frequent way to get a job and 8 being the least frequent way. Do this individually. Then discuss the reasons for your answers in a small group.*

How to Get a Job

_____ school placement offices

_____ family members

_____ personal contacts

_____ advertisements in the newspaper

_____ temporary work in the office or company

_____ volunteer (unpaid) work in the office or company

_____ mailing your resumé directly to many companies

_____ an employment agency that contacts companies for you

❷ *Circle what you consider the three most important aspects of a good job in the list below. Compare your answers in a small group and tally your findings; that is, record how many times each answer was chosen.*

What Does a Good Job Mean to You?

1. a high salary
2. opportunities for advancement
3. good benefits (health insurance, retirement pension)
4. job security
5. independence
6. travel
7. interesting co-workers
8. good location

2 PREPARING TO READ

A. BACKGROUND

cost-cutting
cut cost
downsize

Read the information and write short answers to the questions that follow. Then discuss your ideas with a partner.

Because of global competition, advances in technology, and corporate cost-cutting, the fear of losing a job has become a fact of life for many employees, both blue-collar workers and professionals. Many employees who are laid off from full-time jobs can find only temporary jobs or part-time jobs as a replacement. For example, in the United States in the 1990s, more than two-thirds of new jobs were temporary positions and these temporary workers made up more than 25 percent of the work force. "Temps" generally receive no health insurance, no retirement pensions, no benefits at all aside from an hourly wage. Many economic specialists fear that temporary jobs widen the gap between "haves" and "have-nots" in society.

1. Does temping serve a useful purpose for society? Or, is temping just a way to take advantage of employees?

2. In addition to workers who have lost their full-time jobs, who might find temping helpful?

B. VOCABULARY FOR COMPREHENSION

Work in pairs. Read the sentences below and on page 156 and circle the correct synonym for the underlined word from the choices given. Use the dictionary if necessary. The first one has been done for you.

1. Large corporations cannot interview all the people who wish to work for them, so they <u>screen</u> the resumés first, often by computer, to choose the best applicants.

    a. filter   **b.** block   **c.** investigate

2. These computer screenings are not always very fair, and many applicants would rather skip them and speak directly to a human being.
    a. oppose   **b.** avoid   **c.** cheat

3. There is a glut of lawyers on the market, and many law school graduates cannot get good jobs.
    a. excess   **b.** shortage   **c.** decline

4. A blue-chip corporation is usually a good investment because it has given its stockholders reasonable and steady dividends for a long time.
    a. risky but worth the risk **b.** new and unique **c.** financially stable

5. This employee has no discernible skills in computer work now, but we may be able to teach her quickly.
    a. obvious   **b.** careful   **c.** long-term

6. Many prospective business school students must demonstrate a working knowledge of English before being accepted.
    a. unlikely   **b.** hopeful   **c.** potential

7. He can enhance his chances of finding a good job by getting a graduate degree in Business Administration.
    a. diminish   **b.** clarify   **c.** improve

8. Enrolling in this course can give you access to a network of professors and students who can help you find work.
    a. the need for   **b.** the right to use   **c.** the security of

9. But getting a good education is not a panacea. Unfortunately, it will not automatically get you a good job.
    a. solution   **b.** problem   **c.** cure-all

3 READING ONE: The Expanding Role of Temps

A. INTRODUCING THE TOPIC

Discuss these questions with a partner before you read the article from the "Managing Your Career" column in The Wall Street Journal.

What do you think job seekers can do to get noticed by an employer? How can they "get in the door?"

The Expanding Role of Temps Offers Avenues to Good Jobs

By Hal Lancaster (from *The Wall Street Journal*)

1   Is the job of your dreams beyond your reach because some company's computerized screening device doesn't find the right buzzword on your resumé? "If I could just get in the door for an interview," you groan, "I could knock their socks off." That's where temping comes in. No longer just a fill-in for vacationing secretaries and receptionists, temps are now brought in for special projects and long-term assignments. They increasingly include white-collar technical and professional workers—even the occasional executive.

2   Temping can help you learn new skills or bridge the gap between jobs. Some people are even making a career of temping—mostly those who like the independence or need more flexible work schedules, such as working mothers. All told, companies shelled out $4.9 billion to temps in 1995, more than double what they paid four years earlier, according to the National Association of Temporary and Staffing Services. More to the point, companies are increasingly using temporary assignments to fill full-time jobs. About 40 percent of those sent out on temp assignments get offered full-time positions, estimates the association. If hiring the right people is so critical, why not test drive the merchandise first?

3   Many people who might not otherwise get within smelling distance of an interview are getting permanent jobs through temp work. For one thing, they skip companies' elaborate screening processes. Once they get the temporary jobs, they can quickly build experience. For their part, the companies, knowing they've got a free trial period, are more willing to take a chance on someone who might not fit exactly their job profile.

4   When attorney Michael Mayer moved to the lawyer-glutted Washington, D.C., area last year, he couldn't find a job, despite sending out countless resumés. So he signed up with Lawcorps, a temping agency for lawyers and paralegals. Last June he got a one-week assignment at Weil, Gotshal, & Manges, a blue-chip firm where he had considered job prospects so unlikely he hadn't even sent a resumé. He reviewed an article one of the partners was preparing for publication. The firm liked his work, and asked him to stay beyond the one-week period. Eventually he was hired full-time as an attorney.

5   "Lawyers coming out of law school have found that one of the best things they can do to find a job is to sign up with an agency," says Brice Arrowood, president of Lawcorps. "You get some real experience; that's better than just a nice degree." About 25 percent to 30 percent of Lawcorps' people find full-time employment through the agency, he estimates. Temping can also help you to pursue new career routes, through the training that many temp agencies now offer and through assignments that stretch people's skills.

6   After college, Carolyn M. Harper, of King of Prussia, Pennsylvania, wasn't having much luck finding a job in human resources[1] or corporate training, logical possibilities for someone with a psychology degree. But she sent her resumé out to some temp agencies and got a nibble: The Bradley Burns agency had a "temp-to-perm" job as the database administrator for Pinpoint Communications, a start-up Internet advertising company. While she had no discernible high-tech skills, she and the company decided to give each other a two-week whirl. Six months later, Ms. Harper, now full-time, is putting together Web pages for the company's new Web site.

7   Brian Altman dropped out of a Ph.D. program in organizational psychology at Temple University

---

[1] *human resources:* personnel management, the department that makes policies for hiring, training and firing employees

in Philadelphia to seek a career on Wall Street. But prospective employers didn't take him seriously. They changed their tune after he accepted a temp assignment as an administrative assistant for Zurich American Insurance. "It showed I had a commitment to not going back to school," he says. And the assignment involved considerable computer work, which also spruced up his resumé. A week ago he landed a job as an analyst of asset[2] portfolios at Merrill Lynch. "They were interested in finding someone with good computer and quantitative skills," he says.

8   To enhance your chances of landing good temp jobs that can lead to full-time work, talk to your temp agency counselor daily, says Richard M. Rogers, a veteran temp who wrote "Temping: The Insider's Guide." Also make sure the counselor knows your skills and the kinds of permanent jobs you'd like. "You want to become more than a name," he says. One way to do that: Pick up your paychecks instead of having them mailed, giving you an excuse to chat and show the counselor how personable and presentable you are. The idea, he says, is to get inside a company, where you can impress managers with your performance and attitude and where you have access to internal job intelligence, such as water-cooler chat and job postings.

9   As with everything else involved in careers these days, temping is no panacea. You may simply spend a lot of time doing mind-numbing labor. It can also be a professionally lonely life, because you are rarely in one place long enough to form ties. And, as more jobseekers turn to temporary assignments, the competition is getting stiffer, meaning there's little assurance of regular work. But, as Mr. Rogers notes, "The question isn't how insecure temping is, but how secure is full-time employment these days? The gap between the two is narrowing."

---

[2] *assets*: possessions in the form of stocks, bonds, and savings accounts that have value and can be sold

B. READING FOR MAIN IDEAS

Complete this letter from Max, a recent college graduate, to his friends. Use your understanding of the reading selection and give three reasons to explain why temping might be a good career move.

Dear Dan and Jessie,

I know you've been having a lot of trouble finding a job now that college is over. I'm having a bad time, too. But you know what? I've been thinking about temping. Here are some reasons why I think it may help us. _____

_____

_____

What do you think of my idea? Call me as soon as your trip is over.

See you soon,

Max

C. READING FOR DETAILS

Read the questions that follow and circle the best answer. Then discuss your answers with a partner.

1. Why is it often hard to find "the job of your dreams"?

    a. The computers don't have all the job listings.

    b. You can't get an interview.

    c. You don't wear the right socks.

2. Who is typically regarded as a temp worker?

    a. technical and professional workers

    b. people on vacation

    c. receptionists and secretaries

3. Why do job-seekers like temping?

    a. They can earn money and learn new skills at the same time.

    b. They can work several jobs at the same time.

    c. They can leave work to have children.

4. Why do employers like to hire temps?

    a. The employers can offer more full-time jobs.

    b. The employers can produce better merchandise.

    c. The employers end up considering a wider range of candidates for their full-time positions.

5. What kind of job-counseling advice might Michael Mayer give to a fellow law student?

    a. Write a good resumé. Your resumé helps you get your foot in the door.

    b. Try temping. It may lead you somewhere.

    c. Don't move to Washington, D.C., if you want to get a job as an attorney.

6. Choose the correct statistic.

a. In 1991, companies paid $9.8 billion in wages to temp employees.

b. Three out of every five people sent out on temp assignments get full-time positions.

c. At least one out of every four people who sign up with Lawcorps gets a full-time job.

7. What do Carolyn Harper and Brian Altman have in common?

a. They both had high-tech skills before starting their new jobs.

b. They both lacked work experience.

c. They both work on Wall Street now.

8. According to Richard Rogers, how can you become more than a name to your temp counselor?

a. by going to the temp agency to pick up your checks in person

b. by practicing water-cooler chat

c. by letting your counselor know what you thought of your jobs

9. What is a disadvantage of temping?

a. The job may not be so interesting.

b. Temps have to break ties with other employees.

c. Temping fills the gap between unemployment and full-time work.

D. READING BETWEEN THE LINES

Fill in the advantages of temping as they have been presented in Reading One. Then list the disadvantages of temping for employees based on your general understanding of the text. Although the article does not present the disadvantages of temping for employers, there are some. What do you think they are? Add your ideas to the list. Then discuss your answers in a small group.

ADVANTAGES OF TEMPING

For Employers   **For Employees**

1. <u>The screening process is reduced.</u>   1. <u>Temps avoid the usual screening</u>
   _____   <u>process and "get in the door."</u>
   _____   _____

2. <u>Skilled temps can be paid less</u>   2. <u>Temps learn . . .</u>
   <u>money than full-time employees.</u>   _____
   _____   _____

3. <u>The company does not commit</u>   3. _____
   <u>itself to anything more than</u>   _____
   <u>short-term employment.</u>   _____

4. _____
   _____
   _____

DISADVANTAGES OF TEMPING

For Employers (your ideas)   **For Employees**

1. _____   1. _____
   _____   _____
   _____   _____

2. _____   2. _____
   _____   _____
   _____   _____

3. _____   3. _____
   _____   _____
   _____   _____

READING TWO: Coca-Cola Thinks International

A. EXPANDING THE TOPIC

Discuss this question with a partner, and then read the following article from International Business.

What qualities do you think multinational corporations like Coca Cola are looking for when they hire management trainees (people they plan to train as managers)?

from *International Business*

Coca-Cola Thinks International[1]

By Alan M. Rugman and Richard M. Hodgetts

1   Coca-Cola has been operating internationally for most of its 100-year history. Today the company has operations in 160 countries and employs over 400,000 people. The firm's human resource management (HRM) strategy helps to explain a great deal of its success. In one recent year Coca-Cola transferred more than 300 professional and managerial staff from one country to another under its leadership development program, and the number of international transferees is increasing annually. One senior-level HRM manager explained the company's strategy by noting:

We recently concluded that our talent base needs to be multilingual and multicultural. . . . To use a sports analogy, you want to be sure that you have a lot of capable and competent bench strength, ready to assume broader responsibilities as they present themselves.

2   In preparing for the future, Coca-Cola includes a human resource recruitment forecast in its annual and long-term business strategies. The firm also has selection standards on which management can focus when recruiting and hiring. For example, the company likes applicants who are fluent in more than one language because they can be transferred to other geographic areas where their fluency will help them be part of Coca-Cola's operation. This multilingual, multicultural emphasis starts at the top with the president, Roberto Goizueta, a Cuban-

[1] From *International Business: A Strategic Management Approach*, by Alan M. Rugman and Richard M. Hodgetts, McGraw Hill, 1995, p. 323. Reproduced with permission of the McGraw Hill Companies.

born American who has been chairman for over a decade, and with the 21 members of the board, of whom only four are American.

3   The firm also has a recruitment program that helps it to identify candidates at the college level. Rather than just seeking students abroad, Coca-Cola looks for foreign students who are studying in the United States at domestic universities. The students are recruited stateside and then provided with a year's training before they go back to their home country. Coca-Cola also has an internship program for foreign students who are interested in working for the company during school break, either in the United States or back home. These interns are put into groups and assigned a project that requires them to make a presentation to the operations personnel on their project. This presentation must include a discussion of what worked and what did not work. Each individual intern is then evaluated and management decides the person's future potential with the company.

4   Coca-Cola believes that these approaches are extremely useful in helping the firm to find talent on a global basis. Not only is the company able to develop internal sources, but the intern program provides a large number of additional individuals who would otherwise end up with other companies. Coca-Cola earns a greater portion of its income and profit overseas than it does in the United States. The company's human resource management strategy helps to explain how Coke is able to achieve this feat.[2]

---

[2] *feat:* a great accomplishment

Classic Coke
from Egypt

You are doing a first screening of candidates for an international internship program at the Coca-Cola Company. Based on your understanding of Reading Two, decide whether or not the people below might be good candidates for such a program. Indicate your decision with a yes or no and give your reasons. Then share your findings with a partner.

1. Mr. X is a brilliant student who excelled in his courses on marketing. He likes to work alone and speaks only when his plans are fully developed. He doesn't react well to criticism or join in discussions.

   *Decision/why?*_____

   _____

2. Mr. Y is an ambitious, extroverted candidate who tries hard to please and knows how to get along with others. He has studied engineering in the United States for two years.

   *Decision/why?*_____

   _____

3. Ms. A has lived and studied outside her country for several years. She has many friends from different backgrounds and fits in well with the American family she lives with in North Carolina. She is easygoing and flexible and got satisfactory grades in business school.

*Decision/why?*_____

_____

4. Ms. B has studied two foreign languages and has an excellent reading knowledge of each one. She is very nationalistic and only likes the way things are done in her country. She has had a first-rate education and is ambitious and smart.

*Decision/why?*_____

_____

5. Mr. Z has wonderful ideas about marketing and comes highly recommended from his graduate business school teachers. He is shy and speaks slowly. It is hard for him to make presentations in a large group, but he prepares excellent written reports.

*Decision/why?*_____

_____

B. LINKING READINGS ONE AND TWO

Read the case study about the career decision Daniel Prieto must make, and do the activity that follows.

A Case Study: Daniel Prieto's Options

Daniel Prieto has just completed a four-year B.S. (Bachelor of Science) degree at an American university. He is a shy student who never really fit in very well with others, but he received good grades in college and is fluent in Spanish and English. He does not have much money, and his family—who immigrated from Colombia, South America—worked hard to pay for his studies. Now his parents are getting old, and they expect Daniel to contribute money so that his younger brother can go to school and have the same opportunities he had. Daniel is unsure about what he should do next.

One possibility is to enter an M.B.A. (Master of Business Administration) program in the United States. This degree will add a great deal to his earning power, whether he stays in the United States or returns to Colombia. But he is not sure that he can get accepted to a very good business school at this time because he doesn't have enough work experience. Temping in the United States may be the way to improve his resumé, learn new skills, and earn money. He may even attract the attention of an employer and be offered a full-time job for a year or two. On the other hand, Daniel has also heard that the Coca-Cola Company is looking for candidates in its internship program. The job doesn't pay anything, but it could be a way to "get in the door." And he would be learning about real management tasks, not fooling around with entry-level work in a temp agency.

In a small group, consider Daniel's options. In the space below, make a list of the advantages and disadvantages of each career choice. Then choose the one that you consider the best choice for him now. Try to come to a consensus in your group.

DANIEL'S CHOICES	ADVANTAGES	DISADVANTAGES
Business School		
Temping		
Coca-Cola Company		

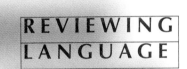

REVIEWING LANGUAGE

A. EXPLORING LANGUAGE: -er / -ee Noun Suffixes

The suffix *-er* tells us that the person is "the one who is doing something" (active) and the suffix *-ee* tells us that this is the person "to whom it is being done" (passive). Thus, an *employer* is the one who employs others and an *employee* is the one who is being employed.

◆ The employ<u>er</u> was not pleased with her employ<u>ee</u>'s attitude.

Complete the story on page 166 by filling in the blanks with the correct word.

MY TIME WITH A TYPE-A ADVERTISING EXECUTIVE

Hi! My name is Meredith. Last week I was given a great assignment by my career _____ at the temp agency . . . or so I thought. She
(1) trainer/trainee
said it would be the chance of a lifetime. Oh sure, a chance to go crazy!

She sent me to an advertising agency on Madison Avenue, where I was questioned by an _____ who had no patience at all. He
(2) interviewer/interviewee
quickly assigned me to work for Mr. Rose, the head of the agency. I never even got a chance to say hello to Mr. Rose. "Do this, get that, make sure the prints are ready, call the photo lab, cancel that appointment, and get me a coffee" was all I heard from 8:00 in the morning to 7:00 at night with no extra pay for extra hours. To Mr. Rose, I was just a nameless _____ . But he was a fugitive from a madhouse!
(3) employer/employee

He talked too fast and did three things at once. And everything had to be ready five minutes before he said it. Even though he was old enough to retire, he kept working because he had created the agency twenty-five years ago. All the new _____ feared him, and so did I. But
(4) hires/hirees
I thought I would have a chance to show my new _____
(5) employer/employee
what I knew about graphic design and maybe make him see I could be more than just a secretary. Forget it! For the next four days all I did was make phone calls and appointments, send out memos and e-mails, and get him coffee. The crisis came when someone needed help correcting a computer payroll program. Mr. Rose never took the time to explain things clearly, and I had no idea how the payroll program worked. I confused all the names of the _____ on the salary checks
(6) payers/payees
for three departments! Secretaries received managers' pay, and Mr. Rose's check went to the head of the mailroom. Needless to say, many employees were happy, but I was told to leave.

Now I'm back to being a _____ at the temp agency
(7) trainer/trainee
again. But this time I'm going to insist that the agency find me a job that has *something* to do with graphic design.

B. WORKING WITH WORDS:
Idiomatic Expressions

Match these idioms, which have been taken from the readings, with their meanings on the right. Write the correct letter in the blank space next to each idiom.

___b___ 1. "get in the door"
(Reading One, paragraph 1)

___e___ 2. "knock their socks off"
(paragraph 1)

___l___ 3. "shelled out"
(paragraph 2)

___c___ 4. "test drive the merchandise"
(paragraph 2)

___k___ 5. "stretch people's skills"
(paragraph 5)

___d___ 6. "get a nibble"
(paragraph 6)

___a___ 7. "give [it] a whirl"
(paragraph 6)

___i___ 8. "changed their tune"
(paragraph 7)

___f___ 9. "spruced up"
(paragraph 7)

___g___ 10. "landed a job"
(paragraph 7)

___f___ 11. "water-cooler chat"
(paragraph 8)

___h___ 12. "what worked"
(Reading Two, paragraph 3)

a. have a trial period
b. have an opportunity
c. try it out
d. get a positive response
e. improved
f. the successful part
g. obtained employment
h. information that employees exchange
i. altered a decision or attitude
j. make a good impression
k. teach something new
l. paid money

6 SKILLS FOR EXPRESSION

A. GRAMMAR: Specific Uses of Infinitives and Gerunds

❶ *Examine the underlined words in the sentences below, and discuss the questions that follow with a partner.*

 ◆ He had the opportunity <u>to spruce up</u> his resumé.

 ◆ He had no commitment to <u>going</u> back to school.

a. What form is underlined in the first sentence?

b. What form is underlined in the second sentence?

c. Why are these forms used?

The Infinitive

FOCUS ON GRAMMAR

See infinitives in *Focus on Grammar, Advanced.*

The **infinitive (to + verb;** *to play, to watch)* is commonly used:

1. When it answers the questions "Why?" or "For what purpose?"	He dropped out of school **to seek** a career on Wall Street.
2. In certain verb + infinitive + object patterns	The firm's recruitment program **helps to identify** candidates at the college level.
3. After many adjectives	Companies are more **willing to take** a risk on someone.
4. After certain expressions	

Many expressions are followed by the infinitive when "*to do* what?" is the answer that the infinitive gives the reader or the listener. In the sentence, "He had the opportunity to spruce up his resumé," the

infinitive *to spruce up* tells us "what" he had "the opportunity *to do.*"
Here is a list of expressions that follow this pattern:

be ready	*have a tendency*
have the ability/have an inability	*have the time*
have the courage	*have the will*
have the need	*it is difficult*
have the opportunity	*it is easy*
have the option	*it is economical*
have the right	*it is practical*

The Gerund

FOCUS ON GRAMMAR

See gerunds in *Focus on Grammar, Advanced.*

The **gerund** (a verb form ending in **-ing** used as a noun; *playing, watching*) is commonly used:

1. After such verbs as ***avoid, consider, enjoy, include, involve, spend***

   You should *consider* **changing** your career if your talents are not used at your present job.

   You may simply *spend* a lot of time **doing** mind-numbing work.

2. After all prepositions (for example, ***about, from, in, to, with***)

   The job applicant was concerned *about* **making** a good impression.

3. After certain expressions

Many expressions are followed by the gerund because they end with prepositions (for example, "have a commitment *to going,*" "be concerned *about going,*" "be interested *in going*"). The rule regarding the use of gerunds after all prepositions is simple to apply if you remember that the preposition is "a part of" the expression. Thus, in the sentence at the beginning of this section, "He had no commitment to *going* back to school," the gerund (*going*) is used because the *to* is part of the expression.

Because it is difficult to remember which expressions end in prepositions, familiarize yourself with the most common expressions that are followed by the gerund. Here is a list:

be accustomed to	***have (no) difficulty (in)****
be committed to/have a	***have (no) experience (in)****
commitment to	
be concerned about	***have (no) luck (in)****
be dedicated to	***have (no) trouble (in)****
be devoted to	***insist on***
be interested in	***look forward to***
be involved with	***object to***
be responsible for/have the	***plan on***
responsibility of	
choose between/among	***succeed in***
deal with	

❷ *Read the following job announcement from a local newspaper. Underline the gerunds and the infinitives first. Then list the verbs or expressions that take the infinitive and those that take the gerund. The first example for each category has been done for you.*

IICG

These are fascinating times for IICG (International Investment Consulting Group) as we take bold steps to serve our clientele better. If you have the ability to lead a team and want the opportunity to build a new future for yourself, we invite you to join our dynamic organization in the following capacity:

Technical Office Manager

You will be responsible for supervising the daily operation of an office team of financial advisers, accountants, and clerical workers. Your duties will include supervising and providing technical and managerial direction. Your first project will involve designing and putting into operation a new office-wide billing system.

The successful candidate must have a degree in accounting and a minimum of five years' experience working in a supervisory capacity, and must be comfortable communicating with large groups of people.

If you are committed to achieving excellence in whatever you do and are challenged by the idea of creating new services for one of the world's leading investment consulting firms, contact us by mailing/faxing your resumé and cover letter to: Stephen Elliott, Recruiting Manager, Department of Personnel, IICG, 229 Water Street, New York, New York 10038 [FAX: 1-212-338-4912].

---

*Note: The preposition *in* is implied. You need not use it; in fact, it is better usage to leave it out.

Expressions with Infinitives

1. <u>take bold steps to serve</u>

2. _____

3. _____

4. _____

Expressions with Gerunds

1. <u>be responsible for supervising</u>

2. _____

3. _____

4. _____

5. _____

6. _____

7. _____

3 *Think of a job you would like to have. Using the expressions listed on pages 169 and 170, write ten sentences about your personal strengths that you hope would convince a prospective employer to hire you.*

1. _____

2. _____

3. _____

4. _____

5. _____

6. _____

7. _____

8. _____

9. _____

10. _____

4 *The cover letter on page 172 was written in response to the job announcement shown on page 170. Fill in the blanks with either the gerund or the infinitive of the verb provided.*

11709 Andros Isle

Potomac, Maryland 20854-3175

(301) 571-1282

May 5, 1998

Stephen Elliott, Recruiting Manager

Department of Personnel

IICG

229 Water Street

New York, New York 10038

Dear Mr. Elliott:

I would like to be considered for the position of Technical Office Manager.
Your job announcement in today's issue of *Financial Weekly* made me
aware of this opening. My resumé is enclosed for review and consideration.

I have been responsible for _____ the accounting and billing
                                    1. (supervise)
departments of three successful businesses in the past ten years. That is why
I am more than ready _____ the challenges of your position.
                          2. (take on)
Although the position I now hold with Allyn, Douglass & Frank is a very
demanding and satisfying one, I have the desire _____ profession-
                                                      3. (grow)
ally. I would like _____ for a firm that deals primarily with invest-
                       4. (work)
ment consulting. Furthermore, I am most interested in _____ to
                                                            5. (respond)
the challenges of _____ and _____ into operation a new
                      6. (design)   **7. (put)**
office-wide billing system. I have been successful with such projects in the
past and enjoy _____ involved in such problem-solving tasks.
                   8. (be)
I believe my background provides the technical and managerial expertise you require for the position of Technical Office Manager. I look forward to
_____ from you in the near future to schedule an interview at your
9. (hear)
convenience. I would like to have the opportunity _____ more about
                                                        10. (learn)
your firm's plans and goals and how I might contribute to its continued success.

                                    Sincerely,

                                    Ben Arvin

                                    Ben Arvin

BA

Enclosure

B. STYLE: Cover Letters and Resumés

1 *Examine the cover letter shown on page 172 with a partner, and answer the following questions.*

> **a.** How do we know who is writing the letter (the addresser) and to whom the letter is being written (the addressee)?
>
> **b.** Where does the writer tell us the reason for his letter?
>
> **c.** How does the writer try to interest the addressee in his qualifications?
>
> **d.** What does the writer do before he concludes the letter?
>
> **e.** How do we know what the "enclosure" is?

WRITING COVER LETTERS

If you are really interested in landing a job, your typed **cover letter** that you send with your resume is the first step toward getting your foot in the door. The cover letter is what the prospective employers or human resources representatives read first. If it does not make a good impression, you are not likely to get a nibble at the job you are applying for.

1. How to Begin

First of all, write your address and the date on the upper left-hand side of the page. Then write the name and address of the person to whom you are sending the letter (the addressee) on the left-hand side of the page.

2. Get the Addressee Interested in You

Next, explain why you are writing. Tell how you know about the job opening and why you believe you have the necessary qualifications. For example, in the model cover letter, the writer refers to the job announcement and to the similar positions that he has held for the last ten years.

3. Speak to the Addressee's Needs

Then, make the reader see why he or she needs you. Tell him, as does the writer of the sample letter, that you have had a great deal of success working on projects similar to the one that is being advertised ("designing and putting into operation a new office-wide billing system," for example).

4. Ask for an Interview

Finally, tell the reader that you would like the opportunity to have an interview to show how you could best contribute to the business's needs. Sign your name after an appropriate expression of courtesy (*Sincerely, Very truly yours*, and so on). At the same time, by putting the word "enclosure" under your initials on the lower left-hand side of the page, remind the reader of what you wrote in the first paragraph of the letter: that you have enclosed your resumé for his examination.

Tips for Your Cover Letters

1. Make sure the appearance of the letter is attractive. You make a good impression if your cover letter and your resumé are on the same stationery.

2. Be brief. Don't write a letter that is more than one page in length.

3. Write relatively short sentences.

4. Show that you are an enthusiastic and willing worker. Describe other personality traits that may be relevant to the job in question.

5. If you are currently employed, explain why you are looking for a new job at the present time.

2 *Examine the resumé on page 175. Then, working in pairs, answer the following questions:*

a. What are the different sections of the resumé, and what function does each section serve?

b. In what order is work experience listed?

c. What kinds of verbs are used to indicate the person's accomplishments?

BEN ARVIN

11709 Andros Isle Potomac, Maryland 20854-3175
Tel: (301) 571-1282 Fax: (301) 571-1283 E-mail: ba25@aol.com

OBJECTIVE

Supervisory Accounting/Finance Management position with a company seeking experienced operations and systems design managers

QUALIFICATION SUMMARY

Leader—Team Builder—Communications Expert
Troubleshooter and Problem Solver
Knowledge of Lotus 1-2-3, EXCEL, and other software

EXPERIENCE

1997–Present

Allyn, Douglass & Frank, Esq. Potomac, Maryland

OFFICE MANAGER

* Operate entire billing and payroll system of this major real estate law firm
* Supervise staff of bookkeepers and clerical personnel
* Design and refine computerized billing systems
* Evaluate efficiency of the bookkeeping division and streamline[1] office work procedures

1993–1997

Font, Samuels & Albamonde New York City, New York

COLLECTIONS MANAGER

* Organized collections and job estimates for this Hispanic advertising agency
* Performed cost-benefit analysis
* Resolved problems arising from previous accountants' errors
* Recommended and realized full-scale computerization of company's accounts

1988–1993

General Tours New York City, New York

CONTROLLER

* Supervised staff of bookkeepers and clerical personnel
* Controlled 16,000 individual accounts
* Purchased foreign currency and dealt with domestic banks and hotels
* Generated substantial savings for company

EDUCATION

M.B.A. Columbia University School of Business, 1988
B.A. Brooklyn College, 1986
Economics and Accounting Major

---

[1] *streamline:* make more efficient

WRITING RESUMÉS

Think of your **resumé** as a summary of your personal profile. Therefore, to write an effective resumé, you must be brief but detailed enough to give the reader a pretty good idea of who you are. As in the sample resumé, a resumé can have the following sections: (1) Name, address, and phone number; (2) Objective; (3) Qualification Summary; (4) Experience; (5) Education. These sections usually appear in the order given here.

1. Name, Address, and Phone Number

Make sure this information is centered at the top of the page. After all, you don't want anyone to doubt that you are the center of attention here.

2. Objective

It is good to include this section if you want employers to know that you are looking for a particular job or if you want to show that you have a clear idea of where you are going.

As is evident in the "Objective" and other sections of the sample resumé, the text of a good resumé is not written in complete sentences. You can even omit articles (*a/the*), subjects (*I*) and forms of the verb *to be*.

3. Qualification Summary

Whereas in the Objective section you tell employers where you want your career to go, in this section you tell employers what you have already done. The Qualification Summary section gives a brief picture (a "snapshot") of your accomplishments or character traits.

4. Experience

Prospective employers consider this section to be the most important part of the resumé. Your current or most recent job is listed first. Although it is important to give the titles of the positions you have held, it is more important to describe your responsibilities and your accomplishments. In addition, be sure to include all unpaid and paid experience that relates to the job objective—for example, any volunteer work you have done which gave you a chance to develop useful business skills.

As in the sample resumé, the use of action verbs, such as *operate*, *design*, and *evaluate*, is essential.

5. Education

In this section, you summarize your academic history. List the most recent academic institution first.

This section should be longer for people who are just graduating from school or who have very little work experience. In such cases, the Education section should appear before the Experience section. If this is your situation, you should list all awards, fellowships and scholarships you have received and describe your responsibilities in internships and all extracurricular activities (for example, working on the school newspaper) and volunteer activities (for example, working in a soup kitchen for the homeless).

It is very important to remember that you are not limited to the sections in the sample resumé when you design your own. There are other sections that can be included. For example, if you are applying for a position with an international company, and your language skills are impressive or you have studied abroad, a Languages section and a Study Abroad section will be very important. Remember that your resumé should be tailored to meet your needs. Consequently, the sections you choose to develop must represent who you are in the way you want to be reflected.

Tips for Your Resumé

1. Make sure the resumé looks good. It should be easy to read, neat, and uncluttered in format.

2. Don't include the word resumé.

3. Don't include salary information.

4. Don't write "References available upon request." Although some people write these words at the end of their resumés, they are not necessary. You can be sure that your prospective employer will not hire you without speaking to people who can talk about your previous job performance!

5. Don't give personal statistics: date of birth, marital status, health status, height, weight, and so on.

6. Don't include a photograph. Remember that the resumé itself should be your best photograph.

SENDING A "THANK YOU" LETTER

If all this advice works for you, and you are invited to an interview, your "job" is not over yet. You must make it your business to send a personalized "thank you" letter to the interviewer immediately after the interview. This simple expression of courtesy may eventually land you the job!

3 *After reading the following job announcement in the* Boston Chronicle, *Janet Eaglethorpe decides to send her resumé to Rita Agata. Read the announcement and the facts about Janet. Then write her resumé for her.*

Takata, Shana & Jerome, Esq., a Japanese-American law firm that specializes in international trade and contract law, is conducting a search for a recent law school graduate who is comfortable speaking in both Japanese and English. The successful candidate will take on many challenging responsibilities. Please write to Rita Agata, Personnel Director, Takata, Shana & Jerome, Esq., 8 Oxford Street, Cambridge, Massachusetts 02138 for further information.

Facts about Janet Eaglethorpe

1. Janet Eaglethorpe was born in Ithaca, New York, in July 1970. She lived there until she was nine years old and then moved with her parents to Tokyo, Japan, where her father was an account executive for an international marketing company.

2. Janet learned to speak Japanese fluently within ten months and stayed in Japan until March 1988, when she graduated from high school.

3. In August 1988 she began to study for her B.A. degree at the University of California at Los Angeles (U.C.L.A.), where she majored in Japanese and East Asian studies.

4. During her first two years at U.C.L.A., she did volunteer work for an organization that helped Cambodian refugees adapt to life in the United States. She was also the captain of U.C.L.A.'s debating team. In her third and fourth years, she wrote articles for the school newspaper and worked as an intern for *The Los Angeles Times*. Janet graduated from U.C.L.A. with the highest academic honors in May 1992.

5. After U.C.L.A., she attended New York University Law School. She received her law degree in June 1995 and passed the California, New York, and Massachusetts bar exams in November 1995.

6. From September 1995 until the present, she has worked for Joshua, Dobbs, & Ira, Esq., a prominent Boston law firm that specializes in contract law.

7. Janet now resides at 302 Garfield Street, Cambridge, Massachusetts 02138. Her phone number is (617) 681-1318.

4 *Write the cover letter that will accompany the resumé Janet Eaglethorpe will send to Takata, Shana & Jerome, Esq.*

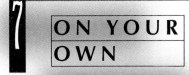

ON YOUR OWN

A. WRITING TOPICS

Choose one of the writing topics. For the essay questions (3–5), remember to provide a thesis statement and sufficient explanations, examples, and support to develop your main idea. Wherever possible, use the vocabulary and grammar from the unit.

1. Write your resumé. Be sure to include in each section of the resumé information that relates to the goals defined in the Objective section of your resumé.

2. Describe the funny things that have happened to you or a friend of yours while on the job. Send this piece of writing to *The New York Times* Website: onthejob@nytimes.com or to On the Job, Money and Business, The New York Times, 229 West 43rd Street, New York, NY 10036.

3. What are the advantages and disadvantages of temping for employers and employees?

4. Imagine the perfect career pattern for yourself. Would it involve working for several different companies, or for only one company during the course of your career?

5. Some multinational firms are not welcome in the countries where they do business. This may be because the multinational corporation doesn't understand the culture and customs of that country, or because the multinational corporation is taking over or replacing local companies. Show how a particular multinational corporation ended up being resented by the natives of a country in which it had established operations.

B. FIELDWORK

PREPARATION

You will write a letter to the personnel director of a large corporation in order to get information about the corporation's attitude toward hiring temp employees.

Form a small group. Work with the members of this group on identifying the key corporations to which each of you could write.

RESEARCH AND BRAINSTORMING ACTIVITY

1. Find out the names of the personnel directors to whom you are writing so that the letters you send are given the attention they deserve. Give each other suggestions about how to get this information.

2. Then brainstorm with each other on the kinds of questions you will need to ask in your letters. You may want to ask about temporary positions offered in the firm, the number of temp employees versus permanent full-time employees, the number of temp employees who are eventually offered permanent positions, the number of interns, the corporation's relationship with temp agencies, and changes in hiring practices in recent years. Add your own questions as well.

3. Use the business letter format, which is the same as the format of the model cover letter that appears on page 172.

4. Work together to improve your letters.

SHARING YOUR FINDINGS

Write a summary of the information you received. Explain how this information has added to your knowledge of temping and its advantages and disadvantages.

WHEN THE SOLDIER IS
A WOMAN . . .

APPROACHING
THE TOPIC

A. PREDICTING

What do you think women's lives are like in the military? Write a list of
the problems you think women might face in the armed forces. Then
make a list of the satisfactions you think they might find in military work.
Compare your lists with a partner's.

B. SHARING INFORMATION

How do you feel about women in the military? First answer the survey individually. Then work in groups of four or five people. Tally the answers from your group and discuss the reasons for each person's opinions.

Women in the Military: What Should Their Role Be?

	YOUR ANSWER (CIRCLE ONE)		GROUP TALLY
1. Women should be allowed to serve in the military.	Agree	Disagree	Agree _____ Disagree _____
Explain your answer: _____			
2. Like men, women should be allowed to fight the enemy in direct combat situations.	Agree	Disagree	Agree _____ Disagree _____
Explain your answer: _____			
3. Women with children should not be allowed to serve in the military.	Agree	Disagree	Agree _____ Disagree _____
Explain your answer: _____			
4. Women officers should never command men.	Agree	Disagree	Agree _____ Disagree _____
Explain your answer: _____			
5. Both women and men should have the right to refuse military service if it goes against their beliefs.	Agree	Disagree	Agree _____ Disagree _____
Explain your answer: _____			

PREPARING TO READ

A. BACKGROUND

Read this information and do the exercise that follows.

Women have served in the American military throughout most of this century, but mostly in support roles: as nurses, supply workers, and transportation personnel. During World War II, some women flew Air Force planes as test pilots, trainers, and transport auxiliaries, but they were not recognized for their contribution. After the war, women were forced out of their jobs in the armed forces and factories, and were replaced by men returning from the war. Later, even during the Vietnam War, in the 1960s and 1970s, women in the United States armed forces represented only 1 in 70 soldiers.

But in the 1990s a new generation of American women participated in the Gulf War: repairing tanks, piloting supplies, doing intelligence work, flying helicopters, working computers, and training to save the wounded as women firefighters. In the new American military, which is an all-volunteer force, about 1 in 9 soldiers is a woman. Part of the reason for this higher proportion is that technological advances have replaced purely physical strength in many military operations, allowing women to fill new roles. In addition, in an effort to attract the best candidates the Army, Navy, and Air Force offer educational opportunities and significant financial rewards to all soldiers, making a soldier's life more attractive to women.

In some countries, women soldiers can fight in combat missions with men, but not in the United States. Although women soldiers are now eligible for fighter pilot training (and will eventually be able to earn the flying hours required to later qualify as highly paid civilian airline pilots), they cannot volunteer for combat missions even though many may wish to do so.

Work in a small group. Compare the situation of American women in the military to the situation of women in the military in other countries. Discuss the following topics and any others your group may think of:

- the role of women soldiers, if there are any
- women's participation in war efforts of the past
- the role of women soldiers after the wars ended
- men soldiers' attitudes toward women soldiers

B. VOCABULARY FOR COMPREHENSION

*Work in a small group. Study the military vocabulary and the definitions below. Then consider the relationship between these vocabulary words and important concepts you will encounter in the readings in this unit: **danger, teamwork, suffering, and peace.** If a word relates to the category, put a "+" sign in the corresponding column on the chart on page 185. If the word does not relate to the category, put in a "−" sign. If you are unsure, or if the word relates only partially to the category, put a "?" in the column. Explain your choices. Try to reach a group consensus. The first line of the chart has been filled in for you.*

Military Vocabulary: Definitions

ammunition	bullets, bombs, explosives; anything fired from a weapon
battalion	a group of 500–1,000 soldiers
bunker	a strongly built shelter for soldiers
casualties	military people lost through death, wounds, or illness
civilian	a person who is not in the armed forces
coalition	a union of political parties or countries for a special purpose, usually for a limited time, often during wars
convoy	an armed group of ships or vehicles traveling together for protection
enlisted personnel	people who enter the army voluntarily
missing in action	soldiers lost in battle and not identified
mission-capable status	a condition of being ready to go out for special duty
red alert	the most urgent warning to be ready for an emergency
survivors	people who continue to live after coming close to death or after others have died

	DANGER	TEAMWORK	SUFFERING	PEACE
1. ammunition	+	?	+	–
2. battalion				
3. bunker				
4. casualties				
5. civilian				
6. coalition				
7. convoy				
8. enlisted personnel				
9. missing in action				
10. mission-capable status				
11. red alert				
12. survivors				

3 READING ONE: Women at War

A. INTRODUCING THE TOPIC

List three topics that you would expect to read about in these letters written to Glamour *magazine from American women soldiers who participated in the Gulf War in 1991. Compare notes with a partner. After you finish the reading, check to see if your predictions were correct.*

1. _____

2. _____

3. _____

from *Glamour*

Women at War

◆ *Women at war—what was it like? Via an ad in the military newspaper, Stars and Stripes, Glamour magazine asked American women serving in the Gulf to write and describe their day-to-day life. What did they think about, dream about, worry about? Here are some of the letters received.*

Letter 1

1   I am a First Lieutenant serving with coalition forces in the Middle East. Most of all I am afraid my husband will find out that I am within range of Iraq's Scud missiles. I don't want him to worry about me. Of course, I worry about chemical attacks. You move as fast as you can but if you get the shakes during a red alert, you can't put on your GCE [ground crew ensemble]. You can't let the fear get to you.

2   I am a weather forecaster in charge of two men, both staff sergeants. Our job is to bring accurate weather information to air crews. Sounds easy, yes? No! Sparse satellite data really hurts and the weather during the late winter/early spring is subject to rapid change.

3   I dream of not having to walk one hundred yards to the shower. I dream of taking a long, warm bath. And wearing a dress would be marvelous. Also, eating at certain favorite restaurants in Oregon, my home state.

4   I write home all that I want to remember. The collection will be my "Desert Diary" to read to my husband and children on cold winter nights.

Thyra A. Bishop

Letter 2

5   I am an E-6 [Petty Officer First Class] in the Navy and the mother of two: a three-year-old boy and an eleven-month-old girl. It breaks my heart to be here, so far away from them. I put their pictures up on the wall in my room. I can barely look at them without crying, though. But I am fortunate because they are being very well cared for in the loving hands of their father. When all the death and destruction of this war starts to get me down, all I have to do is go to any of my fellow service members and see all the mail they have received from people *they don't even know,* the caring and concerned people of the U.S.A. When I think of all the yellow ribbons worn and all the American flags so proudly displayed, I get a great feeling in my heart.

Dawn Bell

Letter 3

6   I am a Second Lieutenant in the U.S. Army. I'm the executive officer [second in command] of a military intelligence head-quarters com-pany. I'm one of 17 females in a company of 127 personnel. My battalion flies aerial intelligence missions.

7   I keep myself busy by writing my fiancé, Jeff Devine, daily and planning our December seventh wedding.

8   My father is a Methodist minister in Appleton, Wisconsin. My parents are against the war and have marched for peace. They say that if the church doesn't stand up for peace, who will? That may seem strange to some people, as their only daughter is in Saudi Arabia. But the military paid for my college education and I'm paying that debt.

Jennifer Freese

Letter 4

9   Many people are curious to know how it is here for us females. Usually they ask the officers rather than the enlisted soldiers.

Enlisted personnel are the backbone of the Army—we're the ones who get our hands dirty.

10 I am twenty-four years old and I've been in the Army for almost two years. My biggest fear is being captured. We were told that if captured, we would be raped, tortured and murdered. I could only say that they would have to murder me. I can't give up my ground to anyone.

11 I sometimes dream of shallow things like getting my hair and nails done or going shopping. When I see the natives and how poor they are, it hurts to see how I take some things for granted.

12 You do things here that you would never before dream of doing. If you're in a convoy that will not make many stops, you learn how to urinate in a Pringles or Planters can in a moving vehicle. It's really difficult but you develop great balance.

Jillian Manderville

Letter 5

13 I am a twenty-seven-year-old soldier in the U.S. Army. Being in a Patriot [missile] unit, we have to move quite frequently. I saw torched bunkers, vehicles, shells from ammunition. It was truly unreal. The Iraqi soldiers were barely living from day to day on beans and rice. You could tell that they weren't expecting such an early ground war because they left their boots behind. You could also tell that an Allied tank not only shot at the bunker but ran right over the top of it. That is the price these soldiers had to

pay. The thoughts that ran through me almost made me cry.

14 I honestly don't believe I'll continue my career in the Army, not because of the war but because the Army is tough and if you don't get tough with it and become strong, you are lost. I've learned to respect others, to survive in whatever conditions arise.

15 For those women who think that the service is for them, please think seriously about it. It's not a picnic. Getting up at 3 A.M. to move is scary and deep down you know you have to go on and get it over with. I feel truly thankful to have made it through this war safely.

Carla Yvette Henry

Letter 6

16 I've been here for a month and I really wish I were back home. I miss my daughters Kimberly and Candice. There are six of us on the midnight to 0800 shift. It's kind of lonely but we always hope and pray that nothing happens because we're all working Casualties, which deals with personnel who are hurt, injured or dead. We work eight hours a day, seven days a week. Before, it was twelve hours a day, but they worried about our getting burned out. The stress level in this place is very high.

17 They have just opened the sports complex so we can get a little recreation. The females can only go from 1300 to 1500 hours. We have to enter through the back door; the front door is for males. We're not allowed to drive civilian cars, only military vehicles,

so to get anywhere they have public transportation for our use.

Barbara Ann Malone-Verduin

Letter 7

18   I am a sergeant in the Army. My job is equipment, records and parts specialist. I make sure that equipment and parts are maintained properly and are at a fully mission-capable status.

19   My most dreadful moment was collecting two dead Iraqi soldiers and putting them in body bags. Normally, this wouldn't have been my mission. A crew who did this line of work was not available, so my unit asked for volunteers. I turned white as a ghost when I was asked to volunteer. But I felt someone should care for them properly instead of just letting them rot away as soldiers missing in action. At least their families would know their whereabouts. If I had died in this war, I would have wanted people to take care of my body. Despite the fact that they were the enemy, they *were* still human beings fighting this crazy war, who were just as frightened as all of us.

Lisa Richards

Letter 8

20   When Iraq invaded Kuwait on August 2, my unit—the 11th Air Defense Artillery Brigade at Fort Bliss, Texas—was put on alert. I was scared, not of the war, but because I didn't want to leave my family behind. Now it's two o'clock in the morning, sixty miles from the Iraqi border, and all I think about is whether I'm going to get out of here alive and be with my family again.

21   This is one of the hardest things I'll ever have to face. Sometimes when I'm lying on my cot I find myself gazing up at the ceiling, and I start crying because my son is now walking and running on his own and I'm not there to see it. He's growing up without me. But at least he's safe with his Dad. (My husband got out of the Army in June of 1990, so he started playing the role of house-husband while I worked, paid the bills and was still a mom.) The only things my son and I have together right now are the few opportunities I get to talk to him on the phone and the letters my husband writes.

22   I know every mother over here feels just as I do about being away from her children. My friend has five children; her husband is also at home taking care of the kids, and she misses them dearly.

23   We try not to think about home too much, so we keep busy. Sometimes we don't even know what day it is. I just know it's been five months since I've been able to hold my baby and my husband—five months since someone told me he loved me—and still we don't know how much longer we will be here. A few months, maybe a year.

24   But we are strong, we are survivors. We are here to fight if we have to, to keep the rest of the world, especially U.S. citizens, from harm. When I do get out of here, I'll be able to pass down war stories to my son and be proud of them. The fact that I am an American woman in a male-dominated country and am being given the chance to fight for what I believe in shows our women have come a long way.

Veronica Martin

Letter 9

25   "I think if you talk to women in the military, we see ourselves as soldiers. We don't really see it as man versus woman. What I'm doing is no greater or less than the man who is flying next to me or in back of me."

Army Major Marie T. Rossi
Aviator and soldier, daughter and wife.
Killed in the Persian Gulf.

B. READING FOR MAIN IDEAS

*Read the following statements. Based on the reading, would you say they are true or false? Write a **T** or **F** next to each statement.*

_____ 1. None of the women were worried about appearing unfeminine.

_____ 2. All the women decided to remain in the Army or Navy after the war.

_____ 3. The women were afraid of the enemy and wanted revenge.

_____ 4. The Army separated the men and women soldiers in their work teams.

_____ 5. All the women were patriotic.

C. READING FOR DETAILS

Use the letter writers' exact words (with quotation marks) to explain their thoughts on the following subjects. Also, identify the letter writer by name. One has been done for you.

1. **Thinking about Fear**
   Choose direct quotes from four letters (#1, 4, 5, 8) on this subject:

   a. *"Of course, I worry about chemical attacks . . ." "You can't let the fear get to you." Thyra Bishop*

   b. _____

   c. _____

   d. _____

2. Thinking about the Enemy
Choose direct quotes from three letters (#4, 5, 7) on this subject:

a. _____

b. _____

c. _____

3. Discussing Their Jobs as Officers
Choose direct quotes from two letters (#1, 3) on this subject:

a. _____

b. _____

4. Writing about Discrimination Against Women
Choose direct quotes from three letters (#6, 8, 9) on this subject:

a. _____

b. _____

c. _____

5. Thinking of Their Children Back Home
Choose direct quotes from three letters (#2, 6, 8) on this subject:

a. _____

b. _____

c. _____

6. Thinking about Their Husbands
Choose direct quotes from three letters (#1, 2, 8) on this subject:

a. _____

b. _____

c. _____

D. READING BETWEEN THE LINES

Work in a small group. Go back to the nine letters in Reading One and evaluate how dedicated each woman is to military service. Rate each writer on a scale of 1 to 6, with 1 as not very dedicated to 6 as very dedicated. Some ratings may be very clear, but others may be open to considerable discussion and interpretation in the group. Try to convince each other by referring back to the letters. For each letter, circle the appropriate number on the scale.

Letter 1	1	2	3	4	5	6
Letter 2	1	2	3	4	5	6
Letter 3	1	2	3	4	5	6
Letter 4	1	2	3	4	5	6
Letter 5	1	2	3	4	5	6
Letter 6	1	2	3	4	5	6
Letter 7	1	2	3	4	5	6
Letter 8	1	2	3	4	5	6
Letter 9	1	2	3	4	5	6

READING TWO: In Peace, Women Warriors Rank Low

A. EXPANDING THE TOPIC

In Reading Two, you will learn about the lives of women soldiers after they return home from a war in Eritrea, a country in East Africa. Before you read, discuss the following question with a partner.

How do you think women soldiers feel about their military experience after they return home?

Asmara Journal: In Peace, Warrior Women Rank Low

By James C. McKinley (from *The New York Times*)

1   Some days Nuria Mohammed Saleh says she actually finds herself missing the war—not the fear and horror, not even the adrenaline kick and camaraderie of soldiering. She misses being treated like a man. Like thousands of other Eritrean women, Mrs. Saleh fought side by side with the men in the rebel army that freed this rocky land from Ethiopian rule in 1991. Like most women who are veterans here, she has found it hard to return to the deeply traditional and patriarchal[1] society she left behind as a teenager.

2   A few years ago, she recalled, she was hammering the enemy with mortar fire. Now she sweeps floors for a dollar a day in an office building near the capital she helped liberate. The only hints of her past are the shrapnel[2] scars around her lips. Mrs. Saleh is one of about 20,000 women who have been discharged from the Eritrean Army in the last two years as part of a larger demobilization of nearly 52,000 troops. Though about 3,000 remain in the army, the vast majority of women were sent home. Some had spent their entire adult lives in the Eritrean People's Liberation Front. Most have little education, having quit school to join the guerrillas.

3   The front[3] changed their lives, they said. The rebel commanders were Marxists by training and treated women as equals. The front's soldiers were taught to ignore sexual, tribal and religious differences. Women were trained to drive tanks, fight and handle big guns. Though not many women had the education to become officers, a handful rose to command rebel battalions. Many married fighters from other religions and tribes.

4   Even outside the army in rebel-controlled regions, because the Liberation Front required most men to be in combat, women broke out of traditional molds, working as dentists, medical technicians, administrators, factory workers, mechanics and teachers, a United Nations report said.

5   But if women who were guerrillas had hoped that fighting and dying in the war would change their status in Eritrean society, they have discovered instead that society's traditions die hard. Several said their families had rejected their mixed marriages and employers had been reluctant to hire them for skilled jobs. Even more galling[4] for some women is that, once they put on civilian clothes, men started expecting them to play subservient roles again.

6   Aster Haile was 12 when she joined the rebels. While she fought and worked for the front as a teacher, her sister spent the war in Saudi Arabia. After liberation, Ms. Haile said, she could not find work teaching, so she borrowed from her sister and opened a dress shop on Victory Avenue. Despite her military service, she said many men she meets still resist treating her like a businesswoman.

7   Other women who were veterans have banded together in cooperatives, pooling their savings and severance pay to start textile and honey-making businesses. Along with male veterans, they have been undergoing retraining at Government expense to work as truck drivers and carpenters.

8   Here in Asmara, the capital, one group of women who were fighters have opened a fish

---

[1] *patriarchy:* a social system controlled only by men
[2] *shrapnel:* pieces of artillery, mortars, or hand grenades
[3] *the front:* the war zone
[4] *galling:* aggravating; frustrating

market, the Gejeret Fish Retail Shop, built with the help of grants from the United States and the United Nations. Nine women work there, having traded in their AK-47s for fillet knives. They share the profits with other female veterans who are partners. Each woman takes home about $72 a month. Ghenet Berhe, a 30-year-old mother, said she did not mind filleting fish, since the whole country is struggling to get back on its feet economically. But when she was asked if she missed her life in the rebel army, she smiled and said, "Of course." "We had equality," she said. "We had common goals and common ends."

1 *Examine the following incomplete statements. Then, with a partner, decide which choices could complete the sentences according to the point of view expressed in the reading. Circle your choices. There is always more than one correct answer.*

1. Women veterans of the Eritrean Army miss their army days because . . .

   a. many became officers

   b. they didn't want to get married

   c. they were treated as equals to men

   d. they did not face religious or tribal discrimination

2. A subservient position is . . .

   a. when you take orders, not give them

   b. when you do unskilled labor

   c. when you don't own your own land

   d. when you are partners in a cooperative

3. During the war, women made progress because . . .

   a. they could take jobs only men had before

   b. they could train for skilled jobs

   c. they could choose their husbands more freely

   d. they could go to school more easily

4. Many former women soldiers find life in peacetime very frustrating because . . .

   a. they can't find good jobs

   b. their marriages have become unacceptable

   c. they are no longer traditional women

   d. they thought their country would be more grateful to them

2 *Write the answers to the following questions in your own words. Compare your answers to those of a partner.*

1. Why did the United Nations encourage the women to form cooperatives?

   _____

   _____

   _____

2. What, if anything, had the women gained by being soldiers?

   _____

   _____

   _____

B. LINKING READINGS ONE AND TWO

You have read about the thoughts and feelings of several women soldiers in Readings One and Two. Choose one of the topics below and write the letter indicated.

1. You are Veronica Martin. Write a letter to Nuria Mohammed Saleh discussing your family and your military service. Tell her about the similarities and differences between your life and hers. How do you see the future?

2. You are Ghenet Berhe. Write a letter to Dawn Bell telling her about how you felt being in the military and what your life is like now in the U.N. cooperative.

3. You are Aster Haile. Write to Carla Yvette Henry, who wants to leave the U.S. military. Tell her about your experiences and about your life after you left the army.

5 REVIEWING LANGUAGE

A. EXPLORING LANGUAGE:
Adjective Suffixes

The suffixes *-al, -ial, -an, -ar, -ary* mean "pertaining to," "related to," "connected with." When you add one of these suffixes to a noun, you create an adjective that means "pertaining to," "related to," "connected with" the subject of the noun.

Example: education (noun)
              educational (adjective = "pertaining to education")

1 *Work with a partner. The noun forms of adjectives that appear in the reading selections are listed below. Add the correct suffixes to form adjectives.*

1. medic _____   5. technic _____

2. militia _____   6. sex _____

3. tradition _____   7. tribe _____

4. patriarch _____   8. air _____

2 *Work with a partner. The following nouns appear in the reading selections. Change them to adjectives by adding the correct suffixes.*

1. volunteer _____   3. vehicle _____

2. recreation _____   4. minister _____

B. WORKING WITH WORDS:
Idioms with *Get*

1 *The following idioms are only a few of the many expressions with **get** in the English language. Find the correct meaning for each idiom or expression according to the way the expression is used in the readings and circle your choice. There is only one correct answer for each question.*

1. "get the shakes" (Reading One, paragraph 1)
   a. become chilly
   b. become nervous
   c. become dizzy

2. "get to you" (Reading One, paragraph 1)
   a. approach you
   b. enter you
   c. bother you

3. "get me down" (Reading One, paragraph 5)
   a. depress me
   b. irritate me
   c. pull me under

4. "get our hands dirty" (Reading One, paragraph 9)
   a. become involved in illegal activity
   b. assume responsibility for all negotiations
   c. do all the heavy, physical work

5. "get it over with" (Reading One, paragraph 15)
   a. complete the task
   b. overcome all difficulties
   c. ignore all inconveniences

6. "getting burned out" (Reading One, paragraph 16)
   a. becoming exhausted or disinterested because of overwork
   b. becoming overly enthusiastic because of overwork
   c. becoming inspired by too much work

7. "get back on its feet economically" (Reading Two, paragraph 8)

　　a. assess its economic situation

　　b. come to terms with its economic weaknesses

　　c. recover its economic stability

2 *Working in a small group, write a list of any other expressions with* **get** *that you know.*

SKILLS FOR EXPRESSION

A. GRAMMAR: Direct and Indirect Speech

1 *Examine the two sentences below and discuss the questions that follow with a partner.*

◆ "The military paid for my college education and I'm paying that debt." (Jennifer Freese)

◆ Jennifer Freese said that the military had paid for her college education and she was repaying that debt.

a. Do these two sentences have different meanings?

b. Why are they written in a different way?

c. Why does the second sentence have no quotation marks?

d. How have the pronouns and verb tenses been changed?

Direct and Indirect Speech

FOCUS ON GRAMMAR

See direct speech and indirect speech in *Focus on Grammar, Advanced.*

Direct speech is a quotation or recording of a person's exact words. Quotation marks are used to make this clear to the reader.

Indirect speech paraphrases or reports what someone said without necessarily using the person's exact words. Quotation marks are not used. The verbs *agree, answer, believe, decide, explain, realize, say, tell,* and *think* are commonly used to introduce direct speech.

"The military paid for my college education and I'm repaying that debt."

Jennifer Freese

Jennifer Freese **said** that the military had paid for her college education and she was repaying the debt.

Changing Direct Speech to Indirect Speech

Verb forms and tenses and pronouns change when direct speech becomes indirect speech.

Direct Speech	Indirect Speech
1. Present tense changes to the past.	
"I **am** an E-6 in the Navy."	She said she **was** an E-6 in the Navy.
2. Simple past changes to the past perfect.	
"I **put** up pictures of my kids on the wall."	She said she **had put** up pictures of her kids on the wall.
3. Present perfect changes to the past perfect.	
"I **have been** here for a month."	She explained that she **had been** here for a month.
4. The future **will** changes to **would**.	
"I **will** read this diary to my children someday."	She thought that she **would** read this diary to her children someday.
5. The modal **can** changes to **could**. When **must** means **have to**, it changes to **had to**. **May, might** and **should** remain the same.	
"I **can** barely look at them without crying."	She realized that she **could** barely look at them without crying.

❷ *Rewrite the following direct quotes in indirect speech. Compare your answers with a partner's.*

August 1990

Lieutenant Veronica Martin is an Army Reserves Officer stationed at Fort Bliss, Texas. At her interview today, she said, "My unit, the 11th Air Defense Artillery Brigade, was put on alert last night."

Indirect Speech: (1) _____

_____

She said, "I am scared but not of the war."

Indirect Speech: (2) _____

_____

"I don't want to leave my family behind," she explained.

Indirect Speech: (3) _____

_____

October 1990

It is two o'clock in the morning and Veronica Martin is sixty miles from the Iraqi border.

"All I have been able to think about is my family," she said.

Indirect Speech: (4) _____

_____

"Will I ever see them again?" she wondered.

Indirect Speech: (5) _____

_____

"This is one of the hardest things I will ever have to face," she said.

Indirect Speech: (6) _____

_____

"But the soldiers are strong," she told us. "We are here to fight if we have to, to keep the rest of the world, especially U.S. citizens, safe from harm," she added.

Indirect Speech: (7) _____

_____

3 *Rewrite the following indirect speech statements in direct speech. Compare and check your answers with a partner.*

November 1991

Lieutenant Martin's husband was interviewed in his home about his wife's service in the Gulf War. Mr. Martin told us that he had been in the Army until June 1990.

Direct Speech: (8) _____

_____

He explained he had started taking care of the children at that time.

Direct Speech: (9) _____

_____

He said his son was learning to walk and run and that he missed his mother.

Direct Speech: (10) _____

_____

He said they talked to her on the phone every two weeks.

Direct Speech: (11) _____

_____

④ *Go back to Reading One and find Letter 2 by Dawn Bell. Rewrite the letter as indirect speech. Compare your letter with a partner's.*

B. STYLE: Paragraph Development— Writing a Summary

① *Examine the following paragraph that summarizes three letters from Reading One. Discuss the questions that follow with a partner.*

These three letters, written by American women military officers during the Gulf War, dealt with the women's pride in their jobs, their thoughts of home, and the frustrations of life in the armed forces. In two of the letters, the women officers described commanding both men and women in weather forecasting units and aerial intelligence services. All three women expressed their concerns about home: leaving children in a husband's care, planning a wedding, hiding the dangers of war so that a husband wouldn't worry. The women also wrote of fear and sadness, but they were cheered by the support of their families and thoughts of home.

a. Look back at Reading One. Which three letters does this text summarize?

b. Is there a main idea sentence in the summary? Underline it.

c. Does the summary use the exact words from the letters, or new words?

d. Compared to the three letters, how long is the summary?

Preparing and Writing a Summary

A **summary** contains the essential information from a text or article. In a general way, writing a summary can help you check if you have understood or remembered the main ideas of any reading passage. More specifically, summarizing information from textbooks and coursework is an essential tool in studying for examinations in American universities. Being able to write a summary is also a necessary skill when gathering information for research papers. Finally, summarizing facts and opinions is important for business presentations, work meetings, and conferences.

The list that follows outlines the steps for writing a summary.

1. Identify the main ideas.

2. Decide what you are going to leave out. Include only the most essential details.

3. Reorganize the ideas in a way that makes your points clear. You do not have to follow the order of the original text.

4. At the beginning, include a sentence stating the subject matter of the summary, where the original text came from, and/or the original author's name.

5. Use your own words. Do not copy from the text unless you use direct quotes and quotation marks, or indirect speech.

6. State only the author's opinions and not your own.

7. Make sure your verb tenses are appropriate and consistent when you use reported speech.

8. Make the summary short, no more than 25 percent of the original text and, in many cases, much less.

9. Be sure to edit your work. Polish it to make the language flow smoothly.

2 *Write a sentence summarizing the paragraphs that follow. Remember to use your own words. Compare your sentences with those of a partner.*

1. "I saw torched bunkers, vehicles, shells from ammunition. It was truly unreal. The Iraqi soldiers were barely living from day to day on beans and rice. You could tell that they weren't expecting such an early ground war because they left their boots behind. You could also tell that an Allied tank not only shot at the bunker but ran right over the top of it. That is the price these soldiers had to pay. The thoughts that ran through me almost made me cry." (*Letter 5*)

_____

_____

2. "My most dreadful moment was collecting two dead Iraqi soldiers and putting them in body bags. Normally this wouldn't have been my mission. A crew who did this line of work was not available, so my unit asked for volunteers. I turned white as a ghost when I was asked to volunteer. But I felt someone should care for them properly instead of just letting them rot away as soldiers missing in action. At least their families would know their whereabouts. If I had died in this war, I would have wanted people to take care of my body. Despite the fact that they were the enemy, they *were* still human beings fighting this crazy war, who were just as frightened as all of us." (*Letter 7*)

_____

_____

3. "They have just opened the sports complex so we can get a little recreation. The females can only go from 1300 to 1500 hours. We have to enter through the back door; the front door is for males. We're not allowed to drive civilian cars, only military vehicles, so to get anywhere they have public transportation for our use." (*Letter 6*)

_____

_____

4. "I honestly don't believe I'll continue my career in the Army, not because of the war but because the Army is tough and if you don't get tough with it and become strong, you are lost. I've learned to respect others, to survive in whatever conditions arise."

"For those women who think that the service is for them, please think seriously about it. It's not a picnic. Getting up at 3 A.M. to move is scary and deep down you know you have to go on and get it over with. I feel truly thankful to have made it through this war safely." (*Letter 5*)

"My biggest fear is being captured. We were told that if captured, we would be raped, tortured and murdered. I could only say that they would have to murder me. I can't give up my ground to anyone." (*Letter 4*)

"It's kind of lonely. . . . We work eight hours a day, seven days a week. Before, it was twelve hours a day, but they worried about our getting burned out. The stress level in this place is very high." (*Letter 6*)

_____

_____

❸ *Look back at letters 4 to 9 in Reading One. Write a summary of the information on one of the following themes from these letters: being female in the military, the attitude toward the enemy, patriotism.*

ON YOUR OWN

A. WRITING TOPICS

Choose one of the writing topics below. For the essay questions (2–5), remember to provide a thesis statement and sufficient explanations, examples, and support to develop your main idea. Use the vocabulary and grammar you have studied in this unit when you write.

1. Find a magazine or newspaper article about women in the military in a country other than the United States.

    or

    Find an article about the history of the military. (You can use an excerpt from the encyclopedia or other reference materials.) Write a summary of the article. Give a copy of the article to your teacher along with your finished summary.

2. Women of all ages are increasingly active in business, professional, and military life. Some people, both men and women, react to this trend by saying, "A woman's place is in the home." Do you agree or disagree? Explain your answer in a short essay.

3. Do you think letters from men who are soldiers would be similar to or different from the letters written by the women soldiers in this unit? Explain your answer in an essay and refer to the readings.

4. Do you believe that military service should be required as a way to develop good citizens? If you believe that it should, would you require it for men only or for both men and women? Write an essay explaining your opinion and refer to the experience of a country you know about.

5. Do you think a person has the right to refuse military service for religious or moral reasons? For political reasons? Write an essay to explain your view.

B. FIELDWORK

PREPARATION

Choose a country not represented by any of the students in the class, and research the policies in that country toward women in the army. Before starting your research, brainstorm with a partner for questions that you believe would be worth investigating.

Here are some questions you may want to consider:

1. Are women allowed to serve in the military in this country? In what capacity? Can women do combat duty? What is the percentage of women soldiers?

2. Does this country have compulsory (required) military service, or do citizens volunteer for the military? Are women drafted?

3. Are there provisions for *conscientious objectors*—people who, because of religious or moral beliefs, refuse to engage in physical combat? Is some sort of alternative service to the country possible? Can women participate?

4. Does this country have professional military preparatory schools? Can women enroll?

5. Can women become officers? Can they command men as well as women?

6. Can women soldiers be married? Can they be mothers?

7. Does one's military service have an effect on one's future career in this country? Is there a lot of respect for the military in this country?

RESEARCH ACTIVITY

After you have prepared a list of questions, go to the library or do an Internet search. When you do your research, be sure to take detailed notes about the information you find and the sources you use.

SHARING YOUR FINDINGS

Write a summary of your findings to share with the class. Follow the guidelines for writing summaries in Section 6B of this unit.

THE CELLIST OF SARAJEVO

1 APPROACHING THE TOPIC

A. PREDICTING

Look at the photo above and the title of this unit. What do you think this unit will be about? Write down your thoughts for a few minutes, and discuss your ideas with a partner.

B. SHARING INFORMATION

Work in a small group. Ask each other the following questions and explain your answers.

1. What kind of music do you enjoy? Jazz? Rock'n'roll? Classical? Folk?

2. What creative things do you like to do? Play a musical instrument? Paint? Write? Dance? Design or decorate? Sew? Something else?

3. Do you enjoy going to the movies, the theater, concerts, museums?

2 PREPARING TO READ

A. BACKGROUND

Read this information, and then discuss the questions that follow with a partner.

Whether we are professional artists or not, the creative arts play an important role in our lives. Through the attention we pay to colors, materials, shapes, and sounds when we select our clothes and decorate our homes, our creative instincts are continually at work as we express our identity and make our mark in the world.

It is also through creativity—through the language of music, for example—that people reach out and connect with each other. Music allows people to share emotions and feelings that are common to all of us. It is also a comfort in or a refuge from a world that is sometimes cruel and hard to understand.

One of the most difficult realities that people must face is the destruction and cruelty of war. In recent times, the suffering of the city of Sarajevo in the former republic of Yugoslavia has inspired artists and others to come to its aid. Sarajevo, once a prosperous, tolerant city where people of many backgrounds lived together in peace, is now a city torn apart by war and ethnic rivalry. Sarajevo has come to represent the struggle of the human spirit to maintain its dignity in the face of hatred and destruction. The first reading in this unit, which combines the beauty of music with the sounds of war, grew out of this struggle.

1. What role does music play in your life?

2. Has it been a source of comfort or help through a difficult period?

3. In addition to comfort, what other emotions does music evoke?

B. VOCABULARY FOR COMPREHENSION

1 *Work in pairs and help each other guess the meaning of the underlined words from the context of the sentences. Then write a synonym or your own definition of the word. Use your dictionaries if necessary. The first one has been done for you.*

1. Despite his <u>unassuming</u> presence, the young composer was, in fact, a great musical genius.
   <u>modest</u>

2. The children's <u>anticipation</u> was seen in their excited faces as they waited for the concert to begin.

   _____

3. The music had a <u>haunting</u> quality because its sad and wistful tones made the audience think of their unhappy past.

   _____

4. Handel's *Messiah*, Beethoven's Fifth Symphony, and Tchaikovsky's *1812 Overture* are all important parts of an orchestra's <u>repertoire</u> in Western music.

   _____

5. Much of the classical music of the nineteenth century reflected the <u>furor</u> and violence of revolutionary times.

   _____

6. The band played so loudly that the people held their hands to their ears waiting for the sound to <u>subside</u>.

_____

7. The folk music made the people feel so happy and <u>exuberant</u> that they became very hopeful about the future.

_____

8. In the past, many composers have <u>defied</u> the standards of society to produce new music.

_____

9. Despite our poor, <u>croaking</u> voices, we filled the room with joyous song.

_____

10. Because of the joy and beauty it brings, this musical composition will be <u>cherished</u> by its listeners for years to come.

_____

11. When people are depressed, listening to music <u>soothes</u> their pain.

_____

② *Match the words on the left with the synonyms on the right. The first one has been done for you.*

_c_ 1. unassuming	a. decline
_____ 2. anticipation	b. unforgettable
_____ 3. haunting	c. modest
_____ 4. repertoire	d. enthusiastic
_____ 5. furor	e. comfort
_____ 6. subside	f. program
_____ 7. exuberant	g. hoarse
_____ 8. defy	h. expectation
_____ 9. croaking	i. angry disturbance
_____ 10. cherish	j. oppose
_____ 11. soothe	k. treasure

READING ONE: The Cellist of Sarajevo

A. INTRODUCING THE TOPIC

Read the following quotation from Georges Braque and answer the question. Then read Paul Sullivan's article and keep Braque's statement in mind as you read "The Cellist of Sarajevo."

The French painter Georges Braque (1882–1963) said that "Art is a wound that becomes light." What do you think this statement means? Write a few sentences in response, and discuss your ideas with a partner.

_____

_____

_____

By Paul Sullivan (from *Reader's Digest*)

The Cellist of Sarajevo

1   As a pianist, I was invited to perform with cellist Eugene Friesen at the International Cello Festival in Manchester, England. Every two years a group of the world's greatest cellists and others devoted to that unassuming instrument—bow makers,[1] collectors, historians—gather for a week of workshops, master classes,[2] seminars, recitals and parties. Each evening, the 600 or so participants assemble for a concert.

2   The opening-night performance at the Royal Northern College of Music consisted of works for unaccompanied cello. There on the stage in the magnificent concert hall was a solitary chair. No piano, no music stand, no conductor's podium.[3] This was to be music in its purest, most intense form. The atmosphere was supercharged with anticipation and concentration. The world-famous cellist Yo-Yo Ma was one of the performers that April night in 1994, and there was a moving story behind the musical composition he would play.

3   On May 27, 1992, in Sarajevo, one of the few bakeries that still had a supply of flour was making and distributing bread to the

---

[1] *bow makers:* people who make the flexible stick used to produce sound by players of the cello and other stringed instruments
[2] *master class:* form of teaching in which a celebrated musician instructs a group of pupils in front of other pupils or a paying audience
[3] *podium:* elevated platform

starving, war-shattered people. At 4 P.M. a long line stretched into the street. Suddenly, a mortar shell fell directly into the middle of the line, killing 22 people and splattering flesh, blood, bone and rubble.

4   Not far away lived a thirty-five-year-old musician named Vedran Smailovic. Before the war he had been a cellist with the Sarajevo Opera, a distinguished career to which he patiently longed to return. But when he saw the carnage from the massacre outside his window, he was pushed past his capacity to absorb and endure any more. Anguished, he resolved to do the thing he did best: make music. Public music, daring music, music on a battlefield.

5   For each of the next 22 days, at 4 P.M., Smailovic put on his full, formal concert attire,[4] took up his cello and walked out of his apartment into the midst of the battle raging around him. Placing a plastic chair beside the crater that the shell had made, he played in memory of the dead Albinoni's *Adagio in G minor*, one of the most mournful and haunting pieces in the classical repertoire. He played to the abandoned streets, smashed trucks and burning buildings, and to the terrified people who hid in the cellars while the bombs dropped and bullets flew. With masonry exploding around him, he made his unimaginably courageous stand for human dignity, for those lost to war, for civilization, for compassion and for peace. Though the shellings went on, he was never hurt.

6   After newspapers picked up the story of this extraordinary man, an English composer, David Wilde, was so moved that he, too, decided to make music. He wrote a composition for unaccompanied cello, "The Cellist of Sarajevo," into which he poured his feelings of outrage, love and brotherhood with Vedran Smailovic. It was "The Cellist of Sarajevo" that Yo-Yo Ma was to play that evening.

7   Ma came out on stage, bowed to the audience and sat down quietly on the chair. The music began, stealing out into the hushed hall and creating a shadowy, empty universe, ominous and haunting. Slowly it grew into an agonized, screaming, slashing furor, gripping us all before subsiding at last into a hollow death rattle and, finally, back to silence.

8   When he had finished, Ma remained bent over his cello, his bow resting on the strings. No one in the hall moved or made a sound for a long time. It was as though we had just witnessed that horrifying massacre ourselves. Finally, Ma looked out across the audience and stretched out his hand, beckoning someone to come to the stage. An indescribable electric shock swept over us as we realized who it was: Vedran Smailovic, the cellist of Sarajevo!

9   Smailovic rose from his seat and walked down the aisle as Ma left the stage to meet him. They flung their arms around each other in an exuberant embrace. Everyone in the hall erupted in a chaotic, emotional frenzy—clapping, shouting and cheering. And in the center of it all stood these two men, hugging and crying unashamedly: Yo-Yo Ma, a suave, elegant prince of classical music, flawless in appearance and performance; and Vedran Smailovic, dressed in a stained and tattered leather motorcycle suit. His wild, long hair and huge mustache framed a face that looked old beyond his years, soaked with tears and creased with pain. We were all stripped down to our starkest, deepest humanity at encountering this man who shook his cello in the face of bombs, death and ruin, defying them all. It was the sword of Joan of Arc—the mightiest weapon of all.

10   Back in Maine a week later, I sat one evening playing the piano for the residents of a local nursing home. I couldn't help contrasting this concert with the splendors I had witnessed at the festival. Then I was struck by the profound similarities. With his music the cellist of Sarajevo had defied death and despair, and celebrated love and

---

[4] *concert attire:* a tuxedo or formal dark suit worn by musicians at a concert

life. And here we were, a chorus of croaking voices accompanied by a shopworn[5] piano, doing the same thing. There were no bombs and bullets, but there was real pain—dimming sight, crushing loneliness, all the scars we accumulate in our lives—and only cherished memories for comfort.

Yet still we sang and clapped.

11   It was then I realized that music is a gift we all share equally. Whether we create it or simply listen, it's a gift that can soothe, inspire and unite us, often when we need it most—and expect it least.

---

[5] *shopworn:* not in the best condition after years of use

Vedran Smailovoc and his sister Violetta Smailovic in the finale of a concert at the Statue of Liberty, New York.

B. READING FOR MAIN IDEAS

Work with a partner. Read the statements and decide which three represent the main ideas of Reading One. Then discuss the reasons for your choices.

1. Involving yourself in what you do best will always help you to emerge victorious from the most difficult situations.

2. Music can help solve political problems.

3. Music can give people the strength they need to soothe both physical and emotional pain.

4. Music can make people sympathize with the suffering of others.

5. Destroying things is not the only way to win a war.

6. Art creates a community of people.

C. READING FOR DETAILS

Work with a partner. Number the eight episodes in the order in which they appear in "The Cellist of Sarajevo." Two have been done for you.

___6___ Yo-Yo Ma plays a cello concert of David Wilde's work at the Royal Northern College of Music in Manchester, England.

___1___ Vedran Smailovic plays the cello with the Sarajevo Opera in the 1980s.

_____ The author plays the piano in a nursing home.

_____ David Wilde reads a newspaper article about Smailovic playing the cello in the midst of bombs; Wilde writes a cello composition in Smailovic's honor.

_____ Smailovic plays the cello in the streets of Sarajevo.

_____ The author is invited to perform at the International Cello Festival in Manchester, England.

_____ On May 27, 1992, a breadline in Sarajevo is shelled.

_____ Smailovic is invited up on the stage and embraces Yo-Yo Ma.

D. READING BETWEEN THE LINES

Based on what you have read in "The Cellist of Sarajevo," answer the following questions about the motivations and feelings of the people in the story. When you are finished, compare your answers with those of another student.

1. Why did Vedran Smailovic play the cello in the streets of Sarajevo for exactly twenty-two days and always at 4 P.M. every day?

_____

_____

2. Why did Yo-Yo Ma choose to play the cello piece entitled "The Cellist of Sarajevo"?

_____

_____

3. Why did Vedran Smailovic agree to make a personal appearance at the festival?

_____

_____

4. Why did Yo-Yo Ma and Vedran Smailovic embrace each other and cry?

_____

_____

5. What was the author's purpose in describing exactly how Yo-Yo Ma and Vedran Smailovic were dressed?

_____

_____

6. What connection does the author make between the nursing home and the situation in Sarajevo?

_____

_____

READING TWO: The Soloist

A. EXPANDING THE TOPIC

You are going to read an excerpt from the novel The Soloist _by Mark Salzman. It is about a man who was a famous concert cellist when he was a child and a young man; he lost his "musical ear" because of the great nervous pressure of playing concerts. He became an unassuming music teacher for many years until, all of a sudden, his gift returned to him. Before you read, consider the following questions and discuss them with a partner._

1. Have you ever been able to do something very well (for example, a sports activity, playing an instrument, dancing) and then lost this ability, because something happened to you or because you changed in some way?

2. How do you think people feel when they lose the ability to do something they really love doing?

3. What can they do about it, if anything?

The Soloist

BY MARK SALZMAN

1   An idea came to me, and I turned off the lights in the studio. In the darkness, I put the cello's spike into a loose spot on the carpet, tightened the bow and drew it across the open strings. I took off my shirt and tried it again; it was the first time in my life I'd felt the instrument against my bare chest. I could feel the vibration of the strings travel through the body of the instrument to my own body. I'd never thought about that; music scholars always talk about the resonating[1] properties of various instruments, but surely the performer's own body must have some effect on the sound. As I dug into the notes I imagined that my own chest and lungs were extensions of the sound box; I seemed to be able to alter the sound by the way I sat, and by varying the muscular tension in my upper body.

2   After improvising for a while, I started playing the D minor Bach suite, still in the darkness. Strangely freed of the task of finding the right phrasing,[2] the right intonation, the right bowing, I heard the music through my skin. For the first time I didn't think about how it would sound to anyone else, and slowly, joyfully, gratefully, I started to hear again. The notes sang out, first like a trickle, then like a fountain of cool water bubbling up from a hole in the middle of a desert. After an hour or so I looked up, and in the darkness saw the outline of the cat sitting on the floor in front of me, cleaning her paws and purring loudly. I had an audience again, humble as it was.

3   So that's what I do now with my cello. At least once a day I find time to tune it, close my eyes and listen. It's probably not going to lead to the kind of comeback[3] I'd fantasized about for so long—years of playing badly have left scars on my technique, and, practically

---

[1] *resonating:* making a deep, rich sound that vibrates the material of the instrument or the body
[2] *phrasing:* a way of linking the notes to each other in order to bring out the melody of the music
[3] *comeback:* starting a career again and returning to the heights of fame or celebrity

speaking, classical musicians returning from obscurity are almost impossible to promote[4]—but I might eventually try giving a recital if I feel up to it. Or better yet, I may play for Dr. Polk if our date at the concert goes well. Occasionally I feel a stab of longing, and I wish I could give just one more concert on a great stage before my lights blink off,[5] but that longing passes more quickly now. I take solace in the fact that, unlike the way I felt before, I can enjoy playing for myself now. I feel relaxed and expansive when I play, as if I could stretch out my arms and reach from one end of the apartment to the other. A feeling of completeness and dignity surrounds me and lifts me up.

---

[4] *promote:* to get bookings or jobs for a client
[5] *before my lights blink off:* before I die

Working with a partner, read the following situations and decide how they may be similar to or different from the experience described in The Soloist. *Each situation may have both similarities and differences, or just similarities, or just differences. Explain your decisions in writing. The first one has been done for you.*

1. The great composer Ludwig van Beethoven lost his hearing in mid-career. He was then unable to hear speech, music, or any sound, but he went on to write some of the greatest music in the Western classical repertoire.

   Similarities: Both of these men lost a part of themselves. They lost abilities that meant a lot to them.

   Differences: Unlike the cellist in "The Soloist," Beethoven lost his physical ability to hear any sound at all. Beethoven's deafness was total and not the result of nervous anxiety. Furthermore, Beethoven continued to compose great music, whereas the cellist was forced to give up playing concerts and become a teacher.

2. A successful painter becomes disillusioned with the rich people who buy his paintings but don't understand the meaning of his art. He goes off to a small town to teach and paint just for himself and his cherished friends.

   Similarities: _____

   _____

   Differences: _____

   _____

3. A famous novelist develops "writer's block" and can't write any more. Every time she sits down at the computer, she gets hot and dizzy and can't continue. Many months later, she discovers that if she stops using the computer and holds a pencil until it seems to become an extension of her hand, her dizziness subsides and she can start to write novels again.

Similarities: _____

_____

Differences: _____

_____

4. A famous actor develops such severe nervousness before each performance that he has to abandon acting forever. He becomes an insurance salesman.

Similarities: _____

_____

Differences: _____

_____

B. LINKING READINGS ONE AND TWO

Work in pairs. Each student should choose one of the interview situations described below. Write three questions that you would like to ask the person you have chosen to interview. Interview your partner. Then have your partner interview you. Answer the questions in the way you think the person in the reading would answer them.

1. Interview Vedran Smailovic about his decision to play the cello in the midst of bombs and bullets.

2. Interview Mark Salzman's cellist in "The Soloist" and ask him how he feels about the loss of his musical ability and its partial return after many years.

3. Interview Paul Sullivan, and ask him why he plays the piano for senior citizens in a nursing home.

_____ **Responds to Questions**

Question: _____

_____

_____

_____

Answer:_____

_____

_____

_____

Question: _____

_____

_____

_____

Answer:_____

_____

_____

_____

Question: _____

_____

_____

_____

Answer:_____

_____

_____

_____

_____ **Responds to Questions**

Question: _____

_____

_____

_____

Answer:_____

_____

_____

_____

Question: _____

_____

_____

_____

Answer:_____

_____

_____

_____

Question: _____

_____

_____

_____

Answer:_____

_____

_____

_____

5 REVIEWING LANGUAGE

A. EXPLORING LANGUAGE

1 *Work in a small group. Decide whether each adjective listed in the chart below expresses the feeling of happiness, sadness, or anger. Some express more than one feeling. Put a checkmark (✓) in the appropriate columns. Two words have been done for you.*

	Happiness	Sadness	Anger
1. agonized		✓	
2. cheering			
3. emotional			
4. exuberant			
5. haunting			
6. mournful			
7. moving	✓	✓	
8. ominous			
9. raging			
10. screaming			
11. slashing			
12. solitary			

2 *Write a short paragraph summarizing what Vedran Smailovic did for twenty-two days in Sarajevo. Use at least five of the adjectives from the chart.*

B. WORKING WITH WORDS:
Adjective Suffixes

In the following sentences, both *moved* and *moving* are adjectives.

- The man was <u>moved</u> when he heard the cellist's story.
- The <u>moving</u> story brought tears to the man's eyes.

The adjective *moved* modifies the noun *man*. The *-ed* suffix shows that the noun it modifies has been affected by something else. In this case, the man was moved by the story. The *-ed* adjective reminds us of the passive voice. It reflects a reaction ("to be moved by").

The adjective *moving* modifies the noun *story*. The *-ing* suffix shows that the noun it modifies has an effect on something else. In this case, "the story moves the man." The *-ing* adjective reminds us of the active voice. The *-ing* adjective reflects an action ("the moving story" = "the story that moves us").

Complete the paragraph that follows by filling in the blanks with the correct adjective.

The audience was settling into their seats, happy because the warm

summer evening in Boston had had a _____ effect on them.
1. (relaxed/relaxing)

But when the refugees came on stage to tell their stories of war and pain

and suffering, the audience was _____ The refugees told of
2. (horrified/horrifying)

_____ brutal soldiers and _____ panicked
3. (terrified/terrifying)   4. (terrified/terrifying)

people running for their lives. The audience was _____ by
5. (inspired/inspiring)

tales of bravery and compassion, but this _____ story of
6. (haunted/haunting)

senseless violence remained in their minds for a long time.

SKILLS FOR EXPRESSION

A. GRAMMAR: Reporting Ideas and Facts with Passives

1 *Working with a partner, examine the following sentences and discuss the questions that follow.*

◆ <u>Many people say</u> that music is an international language.

◆ <u>Music is said to be</u> an international language.

◆ <u>It is said</u> that music is an international language.

a. Which sentences are in the active voice and which are in the passive voice?

b. In the second and third sentences, who says music is an international language?

c. Is there a difference in meaning among the three sentences?

FOCUS ON GRAMMAR

See reporting ideas and facts with passives in *Focus on Grammar, Advanced.*

Using the Passive Voice

To Shift Focus

Using the passive voice shifts the reader's focus to *the thing being done* or *the process being described,* rather than to the specific agent. For this reason, in academic writing and scientific description, the passive voice is often used.*

◆ *Active:* A **craftsman dried** and **varnished** the wood for the cello.

◆ *Passive:* The **wood** for the cello **was dried** and **varnished.**

Using the passive voice relieves the writer of a certain amount of direct responsibility for what is said. For this reason, it is often used in reporting the news when the source of the news is not clear or cannot be told.

◆ *Active:* An **observer said** that the soldiers came from Sarajevo.

◆ *Passive:* **It was said** that the soldiers came from Sarajevo.

---

* NOTE: If there is no specific reason to use the passive, the active voice is generally preferred in English.

To Report Ideas and Facts

The passive voice creates a distance between the writer and the idea being communicated. That *impersonal* distance is the reason why the passive is preferred for reporting the ideas of others. The writer is reporting on something without adding his or her personal views, creating a sense of objectivity and impartiality.

- *Impersonal distance:* **Music is said to be** an international language.

- *Greater impersonal distance:* **It is said** that music is an international language.

GRAMMAR TIP: Because the writer is not interested in identifying the specific agent responsible for this statement, he or she uses the passive voice without *by* or an agent. In this example, "music is said to be an international language" has become a universal truth and it is not necessary to identify the agent ("by many people," or "by great musicians," or "by experts," and so on).

Structures Commonly Used

Two structures can be used to form the passive:

Subject + passive form of the verb + *to be*	**Music is said to be** an international language.
The agreement of the subject (noun) and verb must be carefully considered. If the subject of the sentence is plural, the verb must be plural.	**Musical *compositions are* said to be** included in the box found in the composer's attic.

The second structure uses the impersonal pronoun *it* and *that* followed by an independent clause.

It + **passive form of the verb +** *that*	*It* **is said that** *music* is an international language.

Verbs Commonly Used

The verbs ***think, consider, regard, say, allege, believe, claim, know,*** and ***suggest*** are commonly used to report facts, ideas, and beliefs.

2 *The sentences below are in the active voice. First, read each sentence and rewrite it in the passive voice. Examine both versions of the sentence and decide which is more effective. Then give a reason for your decision. The first one has been done for you.*

1. Many people say that music and art are essential parts of every child's education.

   It is said that music and art are essential parts of every child's

   education.

   This sentence is more effective in the impersonal passive voice

   because the agent ("many people") is very vague.

2. The government decided to give money to the school creative arts program.

   _____

   _____

   _____

   _____

3. The orchestra will have to dismiss many musicians beginning next week.

   _____

   _____

   _____

   _____

4. Sigmund Freud, the father of psychoanalysis, claimed that the imagination is the link to our innermost feelings.

   _____

   _____

   _____

   _____

5. Many teachers believe that an education in the arts develops sensitivity.

   _____

   _____

   _____

   _____

3 *Work with a partner. Read the following passage about how the arts are being used to help children. Look at the underlined sentences. Decide whether or not these sentences would be more effective if they were changed into the impersonal passive. (Remember that the passive voice is preferred only in specific cases. Most lively writing will use the active voice.) Then, on a separate piece of paper, rewrite the sentences that you think should be changed.*

(1) People say that the creative arts have a healing effect on children. (2) We know that administrators at the Illinois Department of Children's Services are active supporters of this method. Last year they offered classes in art, theater, dance, and music to help children deal with their inner feelings. (3) The program was so successful that it quickly expanded.

(4) Several hundred children participated in the arts program this year. Children in the Illinois program show an awareness of how the arts are related to feelings. According to their teachers, some children associate a specific color with a particular emotional state: red with anger, orange with happiness, and so on.

(5) Teachers, administrators, and others in the program say that many children are learning how to relieve their tensions by drawing pictures about fighting instead of actually fighting. (6) They also claim that some of the children, noting that Leonardo Da Vinci and Michelangelo expressed both exuberant and mournful feelings in their art, are convinced there is a definite connection between these great artists and themselves. These insights are wonderful moments in building a child's emotional world.

B. STYLE: Using Descriptive Language

1 *Working with a partner, examine this paragraph from Paul Sullivan's "The Cellist of Sarajevo," and discuss the questions that follow.*

For each of the next twenty-two days, at 4 P.M., Smailovic put on his full, formal concert attire, took up his cello and walked out of his apartment into the midst of the battle raging around him. Placing a plastic chair beside the crater that the shell had made, he played in memory of the dead Albinoni's Adagio in G minor, one of the most mournful and haunting pieces in the classical repertoire. He played to the abandoned streets, smashed trucks and burning buildings, and to the terrified people who hid in the cellars while the bombs dropped and bullets flew. With masonry exploding around him, he made his unimaginably courageous stand for human dignity, for those lost to war, for civilization, for compassion and for peace. Though the shellings went on, he was never hurt.

   a. Why is this brief summary less interesting and effective than the whole paragraph?

   ◆ Despite the bombs, a man named Smailovic played the cello in the streets of Sarajevo in memory of the dead.

   b. Give examples of how the author makes a great effort to describe actions, places, and objects very carefully.

   c. Do you see examples of repeating patterns in his language?

   d. Study the sentence structure in the paragraph. How many sentences start in the same way?

THE USE OF DESCRIPTIVE LANGUAGE

Good writers use **descriptive language** when they want to give us the complete picture and to involve us fully in the story that they are telling. Writing without descriptive language just reports facts. This is good when the writer's primary goal is simply to communicate the facts of a situation. But if the goal is to go beyond the facts to move, inspire, and persuade the reader, the writer must use powerful descriptive language. Three ways the writer can create powerful descriptive language are to use well-chosen adjectives, to develop internal rhythms in the sentence by using parallel structure, and to vary sentence structure.

Adjectives

Adjectives can be used to describe feelings, to relate how any of the five senses—sight, smell, taste, hearing, and touch—were stimulated throughout an experience, and to report simple facts. They can also be used to reflect the writer's values and judgment.

Adjective phrases can also be used in descriptive writing. Adjective phrases begin with present participles ("-*ing*" forms of verbs) or with prepositions (*for, with, like,* and so on) and modify a noun just as adjectives do.

   ◆ Example: "[Smailovic walked] into the midst of the battle *raging* <u>around him</u>."

Adjective clauses are also found in descriptive writing. They begin with *that, who, which* (adverb clauses beginning with *while, although, though*).

   ◆ Example: "He played . . . to the terrified people *who* <u>hid in the cellars</u> . . ."

Parallel Structure

Powerful descriptive passages have a certain music-like quality that is achieved when paragraphs have good internal sentence structure. Musical sentence rhythms are created by using **parallel structure**—by repeating patterns or sequences of action verbs, adjective, nouns, adverbs, prepositional phrases, or adjective-noun pairs in one sentence. By threading sequences of images together—as a film editor does with the frames of a film—the writer is able to paint a complete picture and draw the reader into the world he is describing.

♦ Example: ". . . <u>for</u> human dignity, <u>for</u> those lost to war, <u>for</u> civilization . . ."

Varied Sentence Structure

Varied sentence structure also contributes to good descriptive writing. The repetition of word patterns can be effective within the sentences themselves, but the repetition of the same grammatical sentence structure is not effective. Good writing should never have all the sentences in a paragraph starting in the same way. When this happens, the writing is very boring. Sentences should be both long and short, both simple and complex.

2 *Go back to the paragraph at the beginning of this section (see pages 223–224) and do the following activities.*

1. Circle all the adjectives, adjective phrases and clauses, and identify the purpose each one serves. Do they make facts more precise; communicate sights, sounds, or smells; tell about feelings; or communicate the author's value judgments?

2. In that same paragraph, underline all the parallel structures that give a certain music-like quality to the language.

3. Which sentence is the only one in the paragraph that begins with a subject-verb pattern? Why do you think this is the only sentence that starts in this way?

3 *Work in a small group. Using the techniques you have just learned, analyze the descriptive language in the following paragraph from Mark Salzman's The Soloist.*

1. Underline the adjectives and adjective phrases.

2. Circle the repetitive patterns and parallel structures.

3. Discuss the variety of sentence structures in the passage.

After improvising for a while, I started playing the D minor Bach suite, still in the darkness. Strangely freed of the task of finding the right phrasing, the right intonation, the right bowing, I heard the music through my skin. For the first time I didn't think about how it would sound to anyone else, and slowly, joyfully, gratefully, I started to hear again. The notes sang out, first like a trickle, then like a fountain of cool water bubbling up from a hole in the middle of a desert. After an hour or so I looked up, and in the darkness saw the outline of the cat sitting on the floor in front of me, cleaning her paws and purring loudly. I had an audience again, humble as it was.

4 *Write a paragraph in which you describe your own feelings in response to a specific work of art. Do you feel like Paul Sullivan did when he heard the cello concert? Or like the narrator in Mark Salzman's book when he played the cello in the dark?*

1. Think of a particular piece of music, a poem, or a work of art that you love.

2. Introduce the work of art and write a descriptive paragraph about your feelings, emotions, and reactions when you experience it.

3. Pay attention to the adjectives you use, to parallel structure, to sentence variety.

ON YOUR OWN

A. WRITING TOPICS

Choose one question and write a well-organized response. Use what you have learned about descriptive language to make your writing lively and effective. Use vocabulary from the readings and the passive voice when appropriate.

1. Choose a painting, a photograph, a piece of music, or any other nonverbal work of art (not a work of literature or poetry). Explain why you have chosen it, and write a paragraph describing your observations about it, your emotional and intellectual reactions to it, and your conclusions and recommendations to others who may want to see and/or hear it in the future.

2. Choose one of the following quotes and write an essay explaining what it means to you. Use examples from your own life experiences or your reading to explain your understanding. Say whether you agree or disagree with the quote.

"Art is a wound that becomes light."

Georges Braque

"Art is a human activity having for its purpose the transmission to others of the highest and best feelings to which men have risen."

Count Leo Tolstoy

3. Do you think that art and music should be an important part of the academic program in elementary and secondary schools? Should every child be required to learn to play an instrument and work on studio art? Why or why not? Discuss the advantages and disadvantages of making music and art a part of the academic curriculum for each child.

4. Choose one of the traditional arts of your culture: quilt-making, pottery-making, beadwork or weaving, making mosaics, practicing traditional dances, songs, or theater. Describe this traditional handiwork, craft, or art and tell what kinds of material it used and what it meant in the culture. What is the meaning of this art for people today?

B. FIELDWORK

PREPARATION

The character in "The Soloist" was haunted by the loss of his musical ear and the exuberant feeling of accomplishment that he used to have when he gave concerts to audiences that cherished his flawless performances. We leave him on a positive note as he seems to have rediscovered his musical gift. He now anticipates the possibility of playing for new audiences, either on the concert stage or in the privacy of his own home.

Work with a partner. Interview a musician to find out how he feels about the instrument he plays and how he feels when he is playing this instrument. Interview a professional musician, if possible. If not, you can interview someone for whom music is a serious hobby, or a rock guitarist who plays in a student band—someone who plays an instrument all the time even though he is not a professional.

Before conducting the interview, brainstorm with your partner to come up with questions you may want to use in the interview. In addition to your own questions, you may want to ask about this information:

1. What was his first experience with the instrument?

2. At what age did he first take lessons?

3. How does he feel about the instrument?

4. What feelings does he have when he plays for an audience and when he plays for himself?

5. Which does he enjoy more—playing with other musicians or playing alone?

RESEARCH ACTIVITY

To find a musician, you may want to consider the following possibilities:

1. Ask friends to introduce you to a professional musician or someone who plays an instrument.

2. Consult the orchestras or the music schools in your area.

3. Contact the host of a local radio program who interviews musicians on the air.

Talk with your partner and consider what other resources may be available to you.

SHARING YOUR FINDINGS

After you have conducted the interview, work together and write a summary of your findings. Use descriptive language as you explain how the person you interviewed feels when he plays his instrument, either in public or at home.

THE RIGHT TO READ

1 APPROACHING THE TOPIC

A. PREDICTING

Why is free speech important in a democracy? What would daily life be like without the freedom to speak your thoughts or read what you want? How important is freedom of speech? Discuss your views with a partner.

B. SHARING INFORMATION

Below are six free speech issues that have developed in the United States. In the space provided, write a sentence explaining whether you think this type of speech should be permitted or not. Then compare your answers in a small group. When you have finished your discussion, look in the Answer Key to discover how these issues have been dealt with in the United States.

1. Should publishing a book that some people consider disrespectful to a particular religion be allowed?

_____

_____

2. Should burning the national flag because you disagree with your country's policies be allowed?

_____

_____

3. Should people be allowed to distribute pornography (disturbing sexual pictures and language)?

_____

_____

4. Should encouraging young men to refuse military service in wartime because you don't agree with war in general or a particular war be allowed?

_____

_____

5. Should making rude comments about the U.S. president, making fun of him, and being disrespectful in the press be allowed?

_____

_____

6. Should selling rap music with obscene lyrics and lyrics that are disrespectful of the police be allowed?

_____

_____

2 PREPARING TO READ

A. BACKGROUND

Read this information and examine the chart below with a partner. Then discuss the questions that follow on page 232.

Because a free exchange of ideas is essential to preserving a democratic society, the First Amendment to the U.S. Constitution states that "Congress shall make no law . . . abridging [diminishing] the freedom of speech, or the press." But do Americans always respect this right?

Free speech has often been attacked in the United States by those who have opposed the expression of ideas they didn't like. The chart below measures the American people's support for the expression of three unpopular ideas: atheism (not believing in any god), communism, and racism. People were asked: If an atheist/Communist/racist wanted to make a speech in your community, should he or she be allowed to do so? Should he be allowed to teach in the local college? If she writes a book, should the book be permitted in the local public library?

The question of censorship in public libraries and school libraries is at the heart of the readings in this unit. School programs and public libraries can choose whatever books they want to use. These programs are under the financial and political control of the individual states and local communities. In some communities, there are bitter disputes about the kinds of books children read in school and the kinds of books they read in the free local library. Today these disputes represent important free speech issues.

PERCENTAGE OF AMERICANS IN VARIOUS YEARS WHO WOULD . . .*

		Permit the Speech	Let Them Teach	Keep Book in Library
Atheists	1954	37%	12%	35%
	1974	62%	42%	60%
	1988	70%	45%	64%
Communists	1954	27%	6%	27%
	1974	58%	42%	59%
	1988	66%	48%	59%
Racists	1976	61%	41%	60%
	1988	61%	42%	62%

*From *Scholastic Update*, 9/21/90

1. In 1988, 70 percent of the people who answered the survey said they would allow an atheist to speak in their community. Do you agree with this point of view and the other results of the 1988 survey?

2. Why do you think attitudes toward atheists and Communists have changed so much in recent years?

3. How do you explain the results involving racism?

B. VOCABULARY FOR COMPREHENSION

Read the following sentences. Match the underlined word(s) with a synonym from the columns below. Write the appropriate letter in the blank space next to each sentence number. Compare your answers with those of a partner.

a. censored	**e.** filed suit	**i.** renowned
b. conducive	**f.** inhibit	**j.** under the guise of
c. curse	**g.** profane	**k.** upheld
d. extensive	**h.** purported	**l.** vulgarity

_____ 1. Some of the most <u>famous and well-known</u> lawyers in America specialize in constitutional law, the study of which laws are allowed by the Constitution.

_____ 2. In the first half of this century, many books, such as *Lady Chatterley's Lover* by D. H. Lawrence and *Ulysses* by James Joyce, were <u>banned</u> in the United States and couldn't be sold in bookstores.

_____ 3. These books were prohibited because they were <u>claimed</u> to be too sexual and immoral. American attitudes have changed today, and these books have earned the respect of serious scholars.

_____ 4. Most parents and schools forbid young children to use <u>swear</u> words and other bad language.

_____ 5. <u>Hiding behind</u> First Amendment rights, some people today sell pornographic material that makes many Americans angry.

_____ 6. In recent years, the courts have <u>supported</u> efforts to restrict or eliminate pornography and violence as it relates to children.

_____ 7. Some Americans are also concerned about language that is <u>treating the name of God with contempt</u>, because such language goes against their religious beliefs.

_____ 8. Some parents are afraid that their children are learning <u>rude and disrespectful speech and behavior</u> from American culture, which is too free.

_____ 9. In the 1950s, civil rights organizations, whose members were both black and white, <u>went to court</u> to obtain equal treatment under the law for all Americans.

_____ 10. When the Supreme Court ended legal separation of the races in schools in the 1954 decision _Brown v. Board of Education_, it created a situation <u>favorable</u> to future struggles for racial equality in other areas of social life.

_____ 11. After <u>considerable</u> study of the question, most Americans would agree that the Bill of Rights is a necessary part of our fundamental liberties.

_____ 12. If we pass laws to <u>restrict</u> the public expression of opinions we disagree with, we are limiting our own freedom and hurting democracy.

READING ONE: "Book Banning Must Be Stopped"

A. INTRODUCING THE TOPIC

You are going to read an essay by Marcia Cohen entitled "Book Banning Must Be Stopped." It was written when the author was nineteen years old and a sophomore (second-year student) at Brown University and it appeared in Seventeen Magazine. _Before you read, do the activity that follows._

Judging from the title, the author, and the information given above, write three questions that you think this essay might answer.

1. _____

_____

2. _____

_____

3. _____

_____

By Marcia Cohen (from *Seventeen Magazine*)

Book Banning Must Be Stopped

1   "I can't wait to go home and relax," my friend Marianne declared as she stuffed assorted articles of clothing into her overnight bag. After taking three midterm exams that week, Marianne planned a quiet evening at home. "Marcia, you're an English major," she said, looking up from her bag. "Can you think of a good book for me to read?" "How about *Native Son* or *To Kill a Mockingbird*?" I said. "Or did you ever read *Flowers for Algernon* or *Ordinary People*?"[1] The four books I recommended have something in common. Although good by my standards, each has been attacked as dangerous by certain people or groups in communities across the United States. Along with other works by renowned authors, such as Alice Walker, John Steinbeck, Kurt Vonnegut, and Mark Twain,[2] these books— four of my all-time favorites—have been challenged, censored, banned, burned or removed from American schools and libraries in recent years.

2   Censorship of textbooks and other books in school libraries appears to be increasing in all parts of the country. People for the American Way, a Washington-based lobby group that recently conducted its fourth annual study of censorship, reports that incidents of censorship have increased 35 percent in the past year. In the past four years these incidents have more than doubled. Last July, the American Library Association published a list of more than five hundred books that have been banned, challenged, or removed from schools and public libraries around the country, ranging from *Harriet the Spy*, by Louise Fitzhugh (considered "dangerous" because it "teaches children to lie, spy, back-talk,[3] and curse"), to *The Merchant of Venice*, by William Shakespeare (purportedly anti-Semitic).

3   Often under the guise of upholding community values, censors attack books for profane or obscene language or for scenes of sex and violence. Apparently they believe that by shielding us, they will discourage us from adopting undesirable attitudes, speech, and behavior. The censors may mean well; however, I don't think teenagers encounter many words or details in books that they have not already been exposed to in real life. Besides, I am no more apt to swear after reading *Go Ask Alice* than I am to

---

[1] *Native Son* by Richard Wright: a book about growing up black in America; it contains violent scenes; *To Kill a Mockingbird* by Harper Lee: a coming-of-age story set in the American South; *Flowers for Algernon* by Daniel Keyes: a book about a mentally retarded man; *Ordinary People* by Judith Guest: a story of an unhappy family

[2] *Alice Walker*: contemporary African-American writer; wrote *The Color Purple*; *John Steinbeck* (1902–1968): American novelist; wrote *Grapes of Wrath* about very poor farm workers in California in the 1930s who fight back against injustice; *Kurt Vonnegut*: contemporary American writer; wrote *Slaughterhouse Five* about the senseless horrors of war and becoming a prisoner of war in World War II Germany; *Mark Twain*: nineteenth-century American writer; wrote *The Adventures of Huckleberry Finn* discussed further in Section 6

[3] *back-talk*: to "talk back" to your parents means to be rude and disobedient

speak in blank verse[4] after reading *Macbeth*.

4   Instead of zeroing in on certain passages or words they find offensive, these censors should focus on understanding the value of the work as a whole. For example, J. D. Salinger's *Catcher in the Rye*, which contains numerous four-letter words,[5] has been a recent target of criticism. In recent years, the novel has been challenged, banned, or removed in school districts in states including Washington, Ohio, Florida, and Michigan. Perhaps by examining this work as a whole, the censors would realize its real literary value. Through his protagonist's use of strong language in a clearly unnatural "tough kid" style, Salinger depicts the struggles of a vulnerable boy who hides behind a facade as he grows up in a world that frightens and confuses him. In this work, vulgar language emphasizes Salinger's message and serves a definite purpose.

5   Even more disturbing to me than attacks on so-called dirty books are those against books that express *ideas* with which censors—who are often political, social, or religious extremists—disagree.

6   In Alabama, the state textbook committee rejected thirty-seven textbooks after various conservative groups had objected that the books failed to reflect certain "religious and social philosophies." In Oregon, environmentalists wanted to remove a social studies book because they believed it contained "pro-industry propaganda."[6] And last July a group of fundamentalist Christian parents in Church Hill, Tennessee, filed suit against the county's public schools. The group argued that a series of schoolbooks preached "secular humanism,"[7] a doctrine that they said places man above God. In a ruling conducive to still more censorship, the judge upheld the parents' right to keep their children out of the reading classes.

7   This kind of censorship alarms me because it resonates with intolerance. Why must our access to reading materials be denied simply because they violate some group's aesthetic, moral, religious, or political views? Why should one group be allowed to impose its views on an entire classroom, school, or state? By submitting to the demands of one group, don't we limit the freedom of another?

8   Education should teach us to be tolerant and respectful of differences. These virtues cannot be taught in a classroom that bans books with "unacceptable" ideas.

9   As students, we read for many reasons. We read to explore life in certain historical periods, cultures, and regions. We read to examine problems of human justice, to explore basic issues of race, class, sex, and age. By encountering many different and conflicting ideas and beliefs, we learn to think critically, to ask intelligent questions, and to form our own opinions.

10   Educators, I think, should not tell us *what* to think but should teach us how to think. Rather than flatly stating whether a certain book has value, instructors and school officials should encourage us to read extensively and to decide for ourselves. By encouraging lively debates in the classroom, teachers can help us to clarify what we believe and why.

11   Book censorship, by inhibiting a free and open exchange of ideas, squelches[8] the vitality of our classrooms and threatens our freedom to learn. In addition, I cannot help but wonder about its implications. When our right to read is restricted, how safe can our other rights be?

---

[4] *blank verse:* a type of poetry that doesn't rhyme
[5] *four-letter words:* words that deal with bodily functions and are not used in public
[6] *"pro-industry propaganda":* information from industrialists that is one-sided or that misrepresents the views of the opposite side, that is, the environmentalists
[7] *secular humanism:* a philosophy that seeks to encourage moral behavior without religion; these ideas are opposed by many fundamentalist Christians because they believe that people must follow the literal meaning of the Bible
[8] *squelch:* to suppress, or stamp on

B. READING FOR MAIN IDEAS

Fill in the blanks in this chart. On the left are the ideas Marcia Cohen disagrees with. On the right are her own views. Use your own words to fill in the blanks. Compare your answers with those of another student.

Pro-censorship Views

1. Some books will influence teenagers to use bad words and to behave badly.

   (Paragraphs 3, 4)

2. Censorship is necessary because without it children will be exposed to points of view that conflict with their communities' political, social, religious, and moral beliefs.

   (Paragraphs 6–11)

Marcia Cohen's Answers

1a. Teenagers have already heard bad words and decided whether they wanted to use them or not.

1b. Censors do not consider the artistic value

_____

_____

_____

2a. When you give in to some people's

   demands, you _____

_____

_____

2b. Through education, we should learn to be

_____

_____

_____

2c. Students need to learn how_____

_____

_____

_____

2d. Teachers should teach their students _____

_____

_____

_____

2e. Book censorship not only threatens our

freedom _____, but also puts our

_____in danger.

C. READING FOR DETAILS

Read the following quotes from Marcia Cohen's essay. Then circle the correct response. Compare answers with another student.

1. "Besides, I am no more apt to swear after reading *Go Ask Alice* than I am to speak in blank verse after reading *Macbeth*." This sentence means that:

    a. the author is going to speak in blank verse now

    b. the author is going to use bad language now

    c. the author is not going to speak in blank verse or use bad language

2. "In a ruling conducive to still more censorship, the judge upheld the parents' right to keep their children out of the reading classes." This sentence means that:

    a. the judge decided to limit censorship

    b. the judge's ruling agreed with the parents

    c. Marcia Cohen agreed with the judge

3. "As students, we read for many reasons." What are not some of the reasons mentioned in the reading?

    a. to explore other cultures and past civilizations

    b. to examine important social questions

    c. to find entertainment and a release for our imagination

4. "Even more disturbing to me . . . are [attacks] . . . against books that express *ideas* with which censors . . . disagree." Which example of people trying to get books banned was mentioned in the reading?

    a. a group of environmentalists who didn't like a book that took the business point of view

    b. a group of religious fundamentalists objecting to Darwin's theory of evolution

    c. a group of mothers objecting to dirty words found in a school library book

5. "Censorship . . . threatens our freedom to learn." What explanation of this statement was not provided in the reading?

    a. censorship means that some authors would have to go to prison

    b. censorship makes it impossible to have a free exchange of ideas

    c. censorship means that someone else would have to do our thinking for us

D. READING BETWEEN THE LINES

Decide how you think Marcia Cohen would respond to the following statements. Answer by writing in the spaces provided, and give the paragraph number from the reading to support your opinion. Then discuss your answers with a partner. The first one has been done for you.

1. "Reading the Communist Manifesto is too dangerous."

   Marcia <u>would disagree. She would say that young people must be</u> <u>allowed to explore different ideas and beliefs, even if these ideas are</u> <u>unpopular, and that teachers should help young people learn to think</u> <u>critically and to ask questions.</u>

   Paragraph: <u>9</u>

2. "Asking students to read books both for and against the Vietnam War is a good way to learn."

   Marcia _____

   _____

   _____

   Paragraph: _____

3. "I don't want my science class to read about Darwin's theory of evolution because it goes against my personal religious beliefs in God's creation."

   Marcia _____

   _____

   _____

   Paragraph: _____

4. "All these men exchanging pornographic stories on the Internet . . . it's just disgusting and it ought to be stopped."

   Marcia _____

   _____

   _____

   Paragraph: _____

5. "Films should not be cut [edited] to eliminate violent or sexual content."

Marcia _____

_____

_____

Paragraph: _____

6. "If we tell our children the truth about how our country treated Native Americans and slaves, our children will be ashamed of their heritage."

Marcia _____

_____

_____

Paragraph: _____

7. "The university administrators should dismiss professors who have extreme political opinions."

Marcia _____

_____

_____

Paragraph: _____

4 READING TWO: Some Books That Have Been Banned from School Libraries

A. EXPANDING THE TOPIC

In Reading Two, you will learn more about books currently banned from some libraries and school districts in the United States. Before you read, discuss the following question with a partner.

Do you think certain books should be banned from local or school libraries, or do you think libraries should be free to choose the books they want?

Some Books That Have Been Banned from School Libraries

1. To Kill a Mockingbird, by Harper Lee

Through the eyes of two white children, nine-year-old Scout and her brother Jem, the reader follows the story of their lawyer father's defense of a black man falsely accused of raping a white girl in a southern town in the 1950s. Scout's family is rejected by the other white people in the town even though her father is only doing his duty, and Scout learns the meaning of conscience and human dignity. Some people do not approve of this book because it is about segregation[1] and a period in history that Americans are not proud of, and because it deals with rape and shows some adults getting drunk and violent.

"What did her father say, Tom? You must tell the jury what he said."
Tom Robinson shut his eyes tight. "He says you goddam whore, I'll kill ya."
"Tom, did you rape Mayella Ewell?"
"I did not suh."[2]

2. Ordinary People, by Judith Guest

Ordinary People is the story of a family that doesn't communicate. One son accidentally drowns, and his brother, Conrad, tries to kill himself out of guilt. When he is released from a mental hospital, Conrad returns home to try to improve his relationship with his parents. His father reaches out to him but his mother cannot, and the family breaks up. In the end, Conrad finally meets a girl he likes who has recovered from the terrible life she led in the past. Some parents do not like the book's themes of suicide and breakdown of the family.

"I started hanging around. You know, with kids my parents were afraid of. They were wild, I guess. Only not really, they were just

---

[1] *segregation:* from the late nineteenth century to the 1950s and 1960s in the southern United States, the races were separated in all aspects of daily life: separate schools, separate cars on trains, taxis, water fountains, toilets, etc., giving inferior treatment to black Americans
[2] *suh:* sir

stupid. And I was stupid. And I started doing a lot of stupid things with them." She sighs, her voice tired and flat. "Nothing interesting. Nothing even unusual, just the same old stuff. We smoked, we took pills, we junked around. Sometimes we needed money and kids stole stuff. I had enough money. My dad felt so bad about me by then he was keeping me well supplied, but I would go with them and steal, just for kicks.[3] And then one time we got caught."

3. Harriet the Spy, by Louise Fitzhugh

Harriet the Spy is about a lonely twelve-year-old girl who wants to learn about the world. She spies on people and writes everything she learns and all her thoughts about her friends and neighbors in a diary. When her friends find her diary and read the nasty things she's written about them, they decide to teach Harriet a lesson. Harriet may not be a very nice little girl, but she is funny and smart and, in the end, she becomes a better person. Some people object to this book because they feel it teaches children to spy (Harriet even sneaks into people's homes) and curse (Harriet uses some mild bad language).

Sport walked over and Harriet's heart went into her sneakers. "FINKS!"[4] Harriet felt rather hysterical. She didn't know what the word meant, but since her father said it all the time, she knew it was bad.

4. The Catcher in the Rye, by J. D. Salinger

This is a book about Holden Caulfield. Ever since Holden's younger brother died, he has been having trouble doing what is expected of him. After getting thrown out of three private schools, sixteen-year-old Holden is deeply depressed and runs away to New York to try to find the meaning of life. He hates snobs and superficial people and calls them all "phony."[5] But since most people and most things in the world are phony to him, some parents are concerned about what they see as the antisocial message of this book as well as the four-letter words.

We horsed around a bit in the cab on the way over to the theatre. At first she didn't want to, because she had her lipstick on and all, but I was being seductive as hell and she didn't have any alternative. Twice, when the goddam cab stopped short in traffic, I damn near fell off the seat. Those damn drivers never even look where they're going, I swear they don't. Then, just to show you how crazy I am, when we

---

[3] *just for kicks:* just for fun
[4] *finks:* (slang) stupid people
[5] *a phony:* an insincere person; a false person

were coming out of this big clinch, I told her I loved her and all. It was a lie, of course, but the thing is, I meant it when I said it. I'm crazy, I swear to God I am . . .

Anyway, I'm sort of glad they've got the atomic bomb invented. If there's ever another war, I'm going to sit right the hell on top of it. I'll volunteer for it, I swear to God I will.

5. Heather Has Two Mommies, by Leslea Newman

This is a book about a lesbian couple who are raising a three-year-old daughter. The book explains that many children in America today are growing up in nontraditional families. According to this book, even though families do not always have a mother and a father, they can still be loving and caring. Some people do not want children to read this book because they fear it undermines their religious values and the traditional idea of the family.

A long time ago, before Heather was born, Mama Jane and Mama Kate were very good friends. After they were friends for a long long time, Kate and Jane realized that they were very much in love with each other. They decided they wanted to live together and be a family together.

6. The Grapes of Wrath, by John Steinbeck

The Grapes of Wrath was first published in 1939. It is the story of the Joad family, pushed off their land in Oklahoma by the banks and big agricultural interests. As unwilling migrants, they travel to California with many others and go from farm to farm, working for so little money that they can hardly eat. In a land of plenty, they are starving. Some people don't like this book because it shows American injustice to the poor, because it shows people so desperate that they do sad and terrible things, because much of the dialogue is written in a dialect of substandard English, and because it shows how the have-nots fight back and try to form workers' unions.

Ma said, "How'm I gonna know 'bout you? They might kill ya an' I wouldn't know." . . .

"I'll be ever'where—wherever you look. Wherever they's a fight so hungry people can eat, I'll be there. Wherever they's a cop beatin' up a guy, I'll be there. If Casey knowed, why, I'll be in the way guys yell when they're mad an'—I'll be in the way kids laugh when they're hungry and they know supper's ready. An' when our folks eat the stuff they raise an' live in the houses they build—why, I'll be there."

Work in pairs. Try to imagine what the six authors would say to defend the value of their works. Student A should write the authors' defenses of books 1, 2, and 3, and Student B should write the counterarguments. Then switch roles for books 4, 5, and 6.

Student A	Student B

1. **To Kill a Mockingbird**

Harper Lee

Author's Defense: *Counterargument:*

_____ _____

_____ _____

_____ _____

_____ _____

_____ _____

2. **Ordinary People**

Judith Guest

Author's Defense: *Counterargument:*

_____ _____

_____ _____

_____ _____

_____ _____

_____ _____

3. **Harriet the Spy**

Louise Fitzhugh

Author's Defense: *Counterargument:*

_____ _____

_____ _____

_____ _____

_____ _____

_____ _____

Student B	Student A

4. The Catcher in the Rye
J. D. Salinger

Author's Defense: *Counterargument:*

_____   _____

_____   _____

_____   _____

_____   _____

5. Heather Has Two Mommies
Leslea Newman

Author's Defense: *Counterargument:*

_____   _____

_____   _____

_____   _____

_____   _____

6. The Grapes of Wrath
John Steinbeck

Author's Defense: *Counterargument:*

_____   _____

_____   _____

_____   _____

_____   _____

B. LINKING READINGS ONE AND TWO

It is your turn to write what you think about banning books in schools and libraries. On a separate sheet of paper, write your opinion about the issues raised in Readings One and Two. Then form small groups and take turns reading your opinions to each other. Discuss your agreements and disagreements and answer the following questions.

1. How many people in the group agreed with you? _____

2. How many disagreed? _____

3. Among those who agreed with you, were there any arguments and ideas you hadn't thought of?

_____

_____

_____

_____

4. Among those who disagreed, were there any arguments that convinced you to change your mind?

_____

_____

_____

_____

5 REVIEWING LANGUAGE

A. EXPLORING LANGUAGE: Word Forms

Working in groups, fill in the chart on page 246 with other forms of the words from the readings. Use the dictionary if necessary. ("X" indicates that no word belongs in that space either because no such word exists or because it is not commonly used.)

Noun	Verb	Adjective	Adverb
1. access			
2. X		conducive	X
3.	confuse		
4.	expose		X
5.	inhibit		
6.		offensive	
7.		profane	
8.	remove		X
9.	shield	X	X
10.	X	vulnerable	

B. WORKING WITH WORDS

The letter on pages 247–248 was written by a parent to the principal of the high school her children are attending. In the letter, the parent explains why she is not happy that a particular book has been included in the school's curriculum. Complete the letter by placing the correct words from this list in the blanks.

access	inhibiting	remove
conducive	offensive	shield
confused	profanities	vulnerable
exposed		

Dear Mr. Anderson:

I have decided to write to you today because I have learned that the novel *Ordinary People* is going to be read this year in all 10th grade English classes. I am very upset about this decision and would like you to (1) _____ this book from the proposed curriculum. Let me explain why I believe this should be done.

First of all, *Ordinary People* is (2) _____ to me because it gives teenagers the message that it is normal or "ordinary" these days to have sex with one another. Moreover, the teenagers in the book use language that is full of (3) _____ .

In my opinion, there is no reason why children should have (4) _____ to such reading material. I say this because vulgar language is definitely bad for children. My children, like all children their age, are too young and (5) _____ to be (6) _____ to such obscene language and behavior. Without the proper guidance, they may end up speaking and behaving that way.

Another reason why I object to the book is that *Ordinary People* also communicates the message that "ordinary" families are falling apart these days. I find this viewpoint to be particularly alarming because it is totally contrary to the image that I want my children to have of the family. I am trying to teach my children family values so that they will have the greatest respect for family life and the kind of security it provides. If they learn things in school that conflict with what they see in their life at home, they will be very (7) _____ .

I can only say that as a parent, I am very much aware of the fact that parents need to (8) _____ their children from any references to the ugly realities of life. It is for this reason that I do not want to send my children to school to learn about the difficulties only a minority of people experience. Instead, I want their school lessons to reflect the morally healthy lifestyles that the majority of the people in their community lead. I uphold this view because I truly believe that a certain unity needs to exist between the home and the school. And if this kind of unity is not achieved, our schools will be guilty of (9) _____ rather than encouraging our children's growth. Furthermore, once this happens, the potential value of their education will be undermined, and we will have no hope of ever producing good and loyal citizens for American democracy.

I do hope you will consider my request. Deep in my heart, I know that the inclusion of *Ordinary People* in the school's curriculum is not (10) _____ to the kind of education my children deserve to receive.

Thank you for your kind attention to this matter.

Sincerely,

Elizabeth Jones

Elizabeth Jones

SKILLS FOR EXPRESSION

A. GRAMMAR: Review of Verb Tenses

❶ *Examine the following sentences with a partner. Indicate whether the underlined verbs refer to the past, present, or future. Then identify any operative words (words that are used to indicate the need for each tense, for example, **since**).*

1. The Constitution <u>has been functioning</u> as the supreme law of the United States since April 30, 1789, when George Washington <u>became</u> the first president.

2. Although the Constitution <u>was</u> officially <u>approved</u> on June 21, 1788, it <u>had been written</u> by the Founding Fathers almost a year before, in the summer of 1787, at the Constitutional Convention.

3. The people <u>were</u> afraid that the rights <u>they had enjoyed</u> up to then would be taken away by the new Constitution, which <u>spoke</u> only of the branches of government and <u>said</u> nothing about the rights of the individual.

4. People <u>were</u> therefore <u>protesting</u> quite angrily about the lack of guarantees for individual liberties when the Constitution <u>was</u> finally <u>approved</u> on June 21, 1788.

5. With the support of James Madison, the first ten amendments to the Constitution <u>were approved</u> in 1791.

6. These amendments—which <u>guarantee</u> freedom of worship, of speech, of the press, of assembly, and other rights such as the right to live safely within the privacy of one's home without fear of the police— <u>are known</u> as the Bill of Rights.

7. The Bill of Rights <u>has been</u> the basis of American democracy for more than 200 years now.

8. By the year 2091, when a great celebration will undoubtedly take place, the Bill of Rights <u>will have existed</u> for 300 years as the protector of our freedom.

FOCUS ON GRAMMAR

See verb tenses and time in *Focus on Grammar, Advanced.*

Verb Tenses

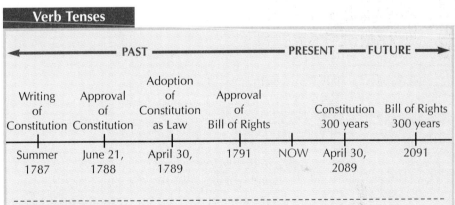

PAST				PRESENT	FUTURE
Writing of Constitution	Approval of Constitution	Adoption of Constitution as Law	Approval of Bill of Rights		Constitution 300 years	Bill of Rights 300 years
Summer 1787	June 21, 1788	April 30, 1789	1791	NOW	April 30, 2089	2091

Simple Past Tense

Use the **simple past tense** to refer to an action or state of being that happened only once on a specific date in the past, or to refer to a series of actions or states of being that occurred over a period of time in the past:

Specific Date in the Past

◆ The Constitution **was approved** on June 21, 1788.

◆ George Washington **became** the first president on April 30, 1789.

◆ The first ten amendments to the Constitution **were approved** in 1791.

Series of Actions That Occurred Over a Period of Time in the Past

◆ It **took** about four years for the Bill of Rights to become a reality.

◆ During that period, people **argued** that the Constitution did not guarantee their individual rights.

◆ People **were** afraid that their individual liberties would be taken away.

- -

Past Perfect Tense and Simple Past Tense

Use the **past perfect tense** when referring to two related past events, where one occurred before the other. Because we know that the Constitution "had been written by the Founding Fathers almost a year before" it was approved, we need to use the past perfect tense for the action that occurred first and the simple past for the second event:

simple past

◆ Although the Constitution **was** officially **approved** on June 21, 1788,

past perfect

it **had been written** by the Founding Fathers almost a year before in the summer of 1787, at the Constitutional Convention.

- -

Past Progressive Tense and Simple Past Tense

Use the **past progressive tense** in conjunction with the simple past tense when referring to an action that was taking place at the same time ("when") another action took place:

past progressive

◆ People **were** therefore **protesting** quite angrily about the lack of guarantees for individual liberties when the Constitution

simple past

◆ **was** finally **approved** on June 21, 1788.

- -

Past Perfect Progressive Tense and Simple Past Tense

Use the **past perfect progressive tense** in conjunction with the simple past tense when referring to an action that had already been taking place for a period of time when another action took place:

past perfect progressive

◆ People **had** already **been protesting** quite angrily *for almost a year* about the lack of guarantees for individual liberties *when* the

simple past

Constitution **was** finally **approved** on June 21, 1788.

Present Perfect Tense and Present Perfect Progressive Tense

The **present perfect tense** and the **present perfect progressive tense** are both a combination of the past tense and the present tense. We know that the Constitution began to function on April 30, 1789, in the past and that it still functions/is still functioning in the present. Use these tenses to show that an action or state of being that started in the past continues/is continuing in the present:

present perfect

◆ The Constitution **has functioned** officially as the supreme law of the United States since April 30, 1789.

present perfect

◆ The Bill of Rights **has been** the basis of American democracy *for* more than 200 years now.

present perfect progressive

◆ The Constitution **has been functioning** officially as the supreme law of the United States *since* April 30, 1789.

For the present perfect and past perfect progressive tenses, the operative words are *since* (followed by the specific date: *since April 30, 1789*) or *for* (followed by the length of the period of time: *for 300 years*).

- -

Future Perfect Tense and Future Perfect Progressive Tense

The future tense is used when we refer to how things will be in the future. Use the **future perfect tense** and the **future perfect progressive tense** to say "definite" things about the completion of events in the future. For instance, because the Constitution will have functioned/ will have been functioning as the official law of the land for 300 years by the specific date, April 30, 2089, we are making a statement about a "definite" fact of the future:

future perfect

◆ The Constitution **will have functioned** officially as the supreme law of the United States for 300 years by April 30, 2089.

◆ *By* 2091, when a great celebration will undoubtedly take

future perfect

place, the Bill of Rights **will have existed** *for* 300 years as the protector of our freedom.

<u>*future perfect progressive*</u>

◆ The Constitution **will have been functioning** officially as the supreme law of the United States for 300 years *by* April 30, 2089.

For the future perfect and future perfect progressive tenses, the operative words are *by* (followed by the specific date or *then: by April 30, 1789* or *by then*) and *for* (followed by the length of the period of time: *for 300 years*).

❷ *Work with a partner and use the timeline about Mark Twain and his masterpiece,* The Adventures of Huckleberry Finn, *to complete the following sentences. Fill in the blanks with the correct tenses of the verbs provided.*

M A R K   T W A I N

Nov. 30, 1835	Mark Twain is born.
Summer, 1875	He publishes *The Adventures of Tom Sawyer;* he begins to write *The Adventures of Huckleberry Finn.*
Dec. 10, 1884	He publishes *The Adventures of Huckleberry Finn* in England.
Feb. 18, 1885	He publishes *The Adventures of Huckleberry Finn* in the United States
1905	The New York Public Library says *The Adventures of Huckleberry Finn* should not be read by children because of the vulgar language used: "sweat" instead of "perspiration."
Apr. 21, 1910	Mark Twain dies.
Today	Many groups want *The Adventures of Huckleberry Finn* banned because of the hateful language used in referring to Jim, the runaway slave.
Feb. 18, 2085	People celebrate the 200th anniversary of the publication of *The Adventures of Huckleberry Finn* in the United States.

1. Since 1905, there _____ a controversy about the
(has been/is/had been)

appropriateness of *The Adventures of Huckleberry Finn* for young

readers.

2. Mark Twain _____ *The Adventures of*
(had published/published/publishes)

Huckleberry Finn when he _____ 49 years old.
(had been/is/was)

3. When *The Adventures of Huckleberry Finn*

_____ in the United States on February 18,
(were published/published/was published)

1885, *The Adventures of Tom Sawyer* _____ already
(have/has/had)

_____ a favorite of American readers.
(became/becomes/become)

4. When *The Adventures of Huckleberry Finn*

_____ in the United States, it
(is published/had published/was published)

_____ already _____in print in England for
(had/has/will have)   (be/been/is)

more than two months.

5. Readers _____ the book for at least twenty
(enjoyed/had enjoyed/were enjoying)

years when, in 1905, the New York Public Library upheld the view

that it was not appropriate for children because of the vulgar

language used.

6. When Mark Twain _____ , people _____
(dies/is dying/died)   (was/were/had)

still _____ the literary value of *The Adventures of*
(questioned/questioning/questions)

Huckleberry Finn.

7. When many groups try to ban the book today, they do so because they

_____ concerned about the hateful language used to
(had been/were/are)

describe Jim, the runaway slave.

8. By the year 2085, *The Adventures of Huckleberry Finn*

_____ by young readers for
(will be read/will have been read/had been read)

two centuries.

3 *Work with a partner. The following text is about the U.S. Supreme
Court, the highest court in the country, which decides how to interpret
the Constitution. Complete these paragraphs about free speech for
students by filling in the blanks with the correct tense of the verbs
provided. The verbs can be in the active or passive voice.*

HOW THE SUPREME COURT HAS CHANGED

In 1969, when school administrators _____ it difficult for
                                        1. (make)
students to demonstrate against the Vietnam War, the nine Justices of the
Supreme Court _____ that "students do not shed their rights
                    2. (rule)
to freedom of speech or expression at the schoolhouse gate." In other
words, students have the same right to free speech that adults have.

But by 1988, the Supreme Court _____ much more
                                      3. (become)
conservative. The new Justices _____ restrictions on
                                      4. (put)
students' First Amendment rights when they _____ a high
                                                 5. (support)
school principal who _____ student articles on teen
                          6. (remove)
pregnancy and divorce from a school newspaper. When this decision
_____ , some people were very shocked because students
   7. (make)
_____ their right to free speech for nineteen years!
   8. (enjoy)

Since 1988, there _____ a growing debate in the United
                       9. (be)
States about the free speech rights of students under eighteen years of
age. Some people are happy that the more conservative Supreme Court of
recent years has changed the 1969 ruling. They insist that high school
students _____ not mature enough to deal with such sensitive
            10. (be)
issues as pregnancy, drug addiction, and divorce. But others maintain
that if students are not allowed to present their views of sensitive issues
in school newspapers, they _____ to participate fully in a
                              11. (prepare—use "not")
democratic society's free exchange of ideas when they are no longer in
school. For these people, the 1988 ruling _____ a form of
                                                12. (legalize)
censorship. After all, "If you can't write it, you can't read it." Looking
to the future, they wonder by what point in time they _____
                                                         13. (succeed)
in convincing people that students have rights, too.

B. STYLE: Argumentative Essays

1 *Reread "Book Banning Must Be Stopped" by Marcia Cohen. Think about why her essay is successful in presenting its arguments. How does she organize her arguments to make them clear and forceful? What language does she use to argue for her point of view? Discuss these questions with a partner, and find examples from her essay that contribute to making it a strong one.*

INTRODUCTION AND THESIS STATEMENT

The aim of an **argumentative essay** is to convince the reader to agree with the author's point of view or opinion. An argumentative essay tries to be very persuasive by appealing to *reason* and *logic*.

An argumentative essay must introduce and explain the background to the issue or problem. But, in the thesis statement, the author must take a stand and present his or her point of view *strongly* and *clearly*. In addition, an argumentative essay usually suggests a course of action for the future, such as "we must stop banning books."

SUPPORTING YOUR VIEWS

In most good argumentative essays, the writer's point of view is obvious in the first paragraph. But an essay is not a mere opinion. The body of the essay should provide support or reasons for the author's point of view: factual details, explanations, examples, and even, in appropriate cases, anecdotes from personal experience.

REFUTING OPPOSING POINTS OF VIEW

Writing an argumentative essay is like taking one side in a debate, either for or against. The writer must not only show that his or her ideas are correct; he must also show that his opponent's views are wrong. Refuting an opponent's views involves showing why the opponent's arguments are incorrect. To be effective, an argumentative essay must contain a point-by-point **refutation** of the main arguments of the opposing view.

CONCESSION

If an opponent has a valid point or expresses an idea that is true, the writer must, in honesty, concede it. It is very rare that the arguments on one side are *all* bad and on the other *all* good. After admitting that the opposition may have a good point, the writer can go on to show that overall, his or her reasons are superior to the opponents' views. For example, supporters of book banning say that children must be guided and protected by their parents. Even someone who is against book banning can realize that parents do have a duty to guide their children. An opponent to book banning could write a **concession** like this:

◆ Although it is true that parents must guide their children's development, censorship is not the best way to accomplish this because it does not develop critical thinking skills.

Every argumentative essay should have at least one concession to show some understanding of the ideas of the opposite side. The concession should not appear in the conclusion, and it cannot be allowed to change the main idea or divert attention from the thesis staement of the essay.

CONCLUSION

The **conclusion** should follow logically from the arguments in the essay. It summarizes the main ideas and reaffirms the thesis. It may also offer suggestions for the future.

2 *Go back to Marcia Cohen's essay. In which paragraphs does she provide the reasons, explanations, and examples that support her views? Underline the passage that refutes the specific ideas of her opponents about a book. Do you find any concession in her essay?*

3 *Work in a small group. First, reread the letter on pages 247–248 in which a supporter of censorship gives reasons in favor of banning books. Come up with counterarguments to refute this point of view. Use the vocabulary from the readings.*

Then, write an outline for an essay defending the need for book banning. Go through Marcia Cohen's anticensorship essay and think of ways that you could refute each of her main arguments, which are outlined on page 257. List your refutations in the space provided, and make at least one concession.

ANTICENSORSHIP
(*Marcia Cohen's view*)

PRO-CENSORSHIP REFUTATION

a. Censors do not consider the artistic merit of the book as a whole but only focus on specific parts out of context.

_____
_____
_____

b. Censorship represents intolerance toward other people's ideas.

_____
_____

c. When some people don't like a book, they want to ban it and take it away from all of us. Censorship will take away our freedom to decide for ourselves.

_____
_____
_____

d. Teenagers should be allowed to make up their own minds about important issues. That is the best training for the citizens of a democracy.

_____
_____

CONCESSION

_____
_____
_____

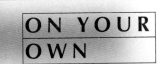

7 ON YOUR OWN

A. WRITING TOPICS

Choose one of the topics on page 258 and write a well-organized response agreeing or disagreeing with the opinion expressed. Be sure to support your point of view with explanations and examples. Include a refutation of the main ideas of your opponents and one concession. Use the vocabulary you studied in this unit, and make sure the verb tenses are appropriate.

1. *We all know that books burn—yet we have the greater knowledge that books cannot be killed by fire. People die but books never die. No man and no force can abolish memory.*

   Franklin Delano Roosevelt, 1942

   Explain the meaning of this quote. Do you agree or disagree with this statement?

2. *Opinion:* Citizens should love and respect their country whatever happens. This is especially true of the national flag. Burning the flag because you disagree with a government policy or a war effort is unpatriotic and disrespectful to soldiers and fellow citizens. Flag burning should be forbidden.

   Write an essay agreeing or disagreeing with this opinion statement.

3. The museum director in a small town has been arrested because the museum has shown an exhibit of photographs, some of which are considered pornographic. Conservatives in the town feel that a museum which families attend together is no place for "dirty pictures." The director claims that the photos are only one part of a larger exhibit by a renowned artist. He has placed the erotic pictures in a special section of the museum where only adults over eighteen years of age may enter.

   What do you think? Should the museum director be arrested for obscenity or not? Argue your case.

4. *Opinion:* Freedom only for the supporters of the government, only for the members of one party—however numerous they may be—is no freedom at all. Freedom is always and only freedom for the one who thinks differently.

   Explain the meaning of this statement. Do you agree or disagree with this definition of freedom of expression?

5. *We hold these truths to be self evident, that all men are created equal, endowed [given] by their Creator with certain inalienable rights, that among these are life, liberty and the pursuit of happiness. That to secure these rights, governments are instituted among men, deriving their just powers from the consent of the governed. Whenever any form of government becomes destructive of these ends, it is the right of the people to alter or abolish it. . . . When a long train of abuses . . . evinces [shows] a design to reduce them to absolute despotism, it is their right, it is their duty, to throw off such government.*

   The Declaration of Independence, 1776

This passage from the Declaration of Independence defends the need for revolution if a government destroys its people's natural rights. Do you agree or disagree? What are these natural rights, according to the Declaration? Does this passage offer a good basis for government? Can you give other examples of people demanding their rights?

B. FIELDWORK

PREPARATION

We have seen how important issues of free speech are in American life. You are going to do research on an important free speech issue of your choice. You may choose any issue that is currently being debated anywhere in the world, such as burning the national flag in protest of a government policy, allowing people to distribute pornography on the Internet, publishing a book that some people consider disrespectful to a particular religion, and so on. Before you begin:

1. Form a small group and discuss with the members of your group which free speech issues are most important to you. During the discussion, try to identify the one free speech issue that you would like to research.

2. You will need to consider the kinds of questions that will guide you in your research. You may want to consider the following:

   ◆ the existence of a formal document guaranteeing free speech rights in the area in question

   ◆ the reasons for the current struggle

   ◆ the background of the groups fighting for free speech rights

   ◆ the background of the groups resisting their demands

   ◆ other significant historical details

3. Brainstorm with the group to consider other aspects of the problem that might be important.

RESEARCH ACTIVITY

If you were not able to identify a free speech issue of interest to you during your group discussion, you will need to read newspapers, "surf" the Internet, or consult a local librarian for help. You may also want to write to the following international human rights organizations for information:

Amnesty International
322 Eighth Avenue
New York, New York 10001
U.S.A.
[http://www.iop.org/amnesty]

The International Committee of the Red Cross
19 Avenue de la Paix
CH-1202 Geneva, Switzerland
[http://www.icrc.org]

The United Nations Human Rights Commission
Center for Human Rights Office at Geneva
CH-1211 Geneva 10, Switzerland
[http://www.unhchr.ch]

Once you identify an issue that you would like to study, use all of the above resources—newspapers, the Internet, the library, international organizations, and so on—to help complete your research.

SHARING YOUR FINDINGS

Write a report. Explain all aspects of the issue you studied to your group. Be sure to focus on the opposing views and to give your own viewpoint as well.

ANSWER KEY

UNIT 1 ◆ ADDICTION

2B. VOCABULARY FOR COMPREHENSION

1. genetic / inherited
2. demanding / strong
3. crushed / desolate
4. dejection / gloom
5. debatable / disputable
6. filled with tears / unable to speak
7. dry / abstinent
8. supplier / giver

3B. READING FOR MAIN IDEAS

1. The effects of drinking cut short Mantle's baseball career. He went out drinking with his teammates and didn't do his rehab work. He might have become an even greater athlete if he hadn't been addicted to alcohol.

   —Alcoholism led to Mantle's neglect of his family. He said he was not as good a father to his sons as his father was to him.

   —Drinking was an important part of his friendships with his teammates.

2. Mickey Mantle felt his father was vital to his success as a baseball player. But he died without seeing that success. Mantle felt lost without his father's love and encouragement and began to drink to escape the pain of his father's early death.

3C. READING FOR DETAILS

1935: Mickey Mantle's father began teaching him baseball.

1950: Mantle joined the New York Yankees baseball team.

1951: Mickey Mantle's father died at age 39.

1968: Mickey Mantle left baseball forever.

1994: Mantle was cured of alcoholism at the Betty Ford Center in California.

1995: Mickey Mantle and his family started a campaign for organ donor awareness.

3D. READING BETWEEN THE LINES

Suggested answers

1. a (Mantle's father always took a swig of whiskey after work: This shows a certain dependency on alcohol), c.
2. a, b, d
3. a, b, c
4. a, b, c, d

1. Mantle had an inherited weakness to alcohol in his family. He was also part of a time and a culture that encouraged men to socialize around alcohol. In addition, he deadened the pain of his father's premature death by drinking.

2. If he had told his father he loved him, he might have been able to cope with his father's death more effectively. His father was not a very communicative person and Mickey Mantle also had a tendency to run away from his feelings, especially by drinking.

3. Mantle regretted not spending more time with his family and those who loved and needed him. He felt he never worked hard enough for his success. Despite the fact that he was greatly loved by his many fans, Mantle was a man who lived with great self-doubt.

4. Answers may vary.

5A. EXPLORING LANGUAGE

1. management / manage / manageable / manageably
2. devastation / devastate / devastating, devastated / devastatingly
3. priority / prioritize
4. avoidance / avoid / avoidable / avoidably
5. toughness / toughen / tough / toughly
6. strength / strengthen / strong / strongly
7. survival / survive / surviving
8. denial / deny / deniable / deniably

9. determination / determine /determined
10. celebration / celebrate / celebrated

5B. WORKING WITH WORDS

1. devastated
2. managed
3. celebrated
4. strong
5. priority
6. survival
7. determined
8. deny
9. tough
10. avoided

6A. GRAMMAR

2. If Mickey Mantle's father hadn't trained his son to play baseball from the age of four, Mickey wouldn't have become a champion.

3. If Mickey Mantle hadn't centered his social life on alcohol, he might not have neglected his wife and children.

4. If Mickey Mantle had thought more about his old age, he would/might have taken better care of himself.

5. If Mickey Mantle's father hadn't died in 1951, he would have seen Mickey Mantle become a champion.

6. If Mantle hadn't gone to the Betty Ford Center the year before he died, he couldn't / might not have reconciled with his family at the end of his life.

Suggested answers

2. If his father hadn't died so young, Mickey Mantle probably would not have become an alcoholic.

3. If Mickey Mantle hadn't been an alcoholic, he might have been able to have a better relationship with his sons.

   If Mickey Mantle had been a dedicated father like Mutt, one of his sons might have developed into a great baseball player.

4. If Mantle hadn't been addicted to alcohol, he would have lived longer and better.

6B. STYLE

1. He was tough and expected to be obeyed.

2. He believed in hard work and discipline and in spending quality time with his son.

3. No. Mantle said that as a "natural," he never worked hard at anything at all: "Truth is, after I'd had a knee operation, the doctors would give me rehab work to do, but I wouldn't do it. I'd be out drinking. . . . Everything had always come naturally to me. I didn't work hard at it."

Mantle did not think of himself as a good father: "One of the things I really messed up, besides baseball, was being a father. I wasn't a good family man. I was always out, running around with my friends."

1. The sentence would have been a dull one because it only gives the facts. In the autobiography, we are given a full "picture" of what occurred. We know what kind of workday the father had.

   We see both father and son practicing pitching balls "in the backyard." We know that the mother's dinner had to wait until the father had given Mantle full instructions from the "right and left sides of the plate."

2. "dog tired," "long," "at the mine." The expression "dog tired" reveals the kind of brute force the father had to exert each day in order to get his job done. The adjective "long" tells us that the father had already worked quite a lot before he came home to "pitch batting practice" with his son. The phrase "at the mine" tells us where the father worked.

3. "I won't do it no more, Dad." (correct grammar: "I won't do it <u>any</u> more, Dad.") He brings us back to the past and lets us "hear" him speaking to his father like a child.

4

1. love unexpressed: "I loved my father, although I couldn't tell him that, just like he couldn't tell me."

2. The narrator tried very hard to please his father in every way possible. He probably did this not only to tell his father that he loved him, but also to earn his father's love.

3. It makes us feel closer to the narrator because we all want to have the courage to tell others that we love them and to be told that we are loved. In general, we all know how **weak** and **vulnerable** we feel when we are incapable of expressing our emotions.

7B. FIELDWORK

1. He might not have been scheduled for a transplant as soon as he was.

2. People who just became ill have priority over those who have been sick for a long time.

UNIT 2 ◆
BRIDGE ACROSS THE GENERATIONS

2A. BACKGROUND

1. . . . [because] Social Security pensions and Medicare health benefits are successful government programs that help senior citizens take care of themselves.

2. . . . [because] they no longer live with or near their extended families.

3. . . . [to] improve the local tax base and help strengthen the ties between the generations.

4. Answers may vary.

2B. VOCABULARY FOR COMPREHENSION

1. d	6. e
2. g	7. f
3. a	8. b
4. i	9. c
5. h	

3B. READING FOR MAIN IDEAS

2a. The teachers were afraid the seniors would either dominate the classes or not say a word. They were worried that the seniors wouldn't like the teachers.

2b. All the older students contributed well to the classes and really liked their teachers.

3a. The seniors didn't know very much about the town's educational programs and were hesitant about paying taxes for them.

3b. They enjoyed learning about new teaching methods and working with young people.

4a. Some teenagers thought that seniors just sat around doing nothing.

4b. The teens learned that senior citizens had the same abilities and desire to succeed as they did.

3C. READING FOR DETAILS

1. F	4. T
2. F	5. T
3. F	6. F

3D. READING BETWEEN THE LINES

Schools in the 1920s: 1, 2, 4, 7, 9, 10

Schools in the 1990s: 3, 5, 6, 8, 11

4A. EXPANDING THE TOPIC

Suggested answers
1. a, c
2. b, c
3. c
4. a, d
5. a, d

5A. EXPLORING VOCABULARY

1. b	4. b, c
2. a, c	5. b, c
3. a, b	

5B. WORKING WITH WORDS

1. reticent	6. incurred
2. vice versa	7. dispel
3. enroll	8. compassion
4. apprehensive	9. mobility
5. demeaning	10. contempt

6A. GRAMMAR

1. Why the Wilton school officials invited
2. Whoever reviews
3. what it is
4. What educators hoped
5. what senior citizens were
6. how their tax dollars were being spent
7. what it means
8. how teenagers feel

9. how their older friends look at
10. what it means
11. What one is
12. how one looks
13. why there is
14. That many other communities have created

Answers will vary.

6B. STYLE

1. This is not a good introductory paragraph because the first sentence is not a "general" statement that stimulates interest in the topic and the thesis statement is not specific enough.

2. This is a good introductory paragraph. It goes from the general to the specific and ends with a thesis statement that announces what the writer will discuss in the body of the essay.

3

1. This is not a thesis statement. It is a fact.

2. This is a thesis statement. The writer will discuss how "dispelling labels" can contribute to the growth of democracy.

3. This is not a thesis statement. It is a fact.

4. This is a thesis statement. The writer will prove how "reading literature" can be "a lifelong process of learning" in the body of the essay.

5. This is a thesis statement. The writer will discuss how the "mobile society" has caused a gap to exist between age groups.

6. This is not a thesis statement. It is a fact.

7. This is a thesis statement. The writer will show in the body of the essay how "bringing the young and old together in the classroom is beneficial to both generations."

4

1c. This is the best thesis statement because it connects with the subject of the paragraph and gives the reader a clear indication of what ideas the author is going to develop in the essay.

Choice (a) is not good because the subject of the paragraph is geographic mobility as it relates to family values, not geographic mobility as it relates to the American dream.

Choice (b) is not good because there is no specific indication of which problems the author is going to discuss in the essay and the

economic growth of the country as a whole is not the subject of the paragraph.

2a. This is the best thesis statement because it connects with the subject of the paragraph, which is avoiding preconceived notions about age, and gives a clear indication of the author's solution, which is re-education.

Choice (b) is not good because there is no specific indication of which problems the author is going to discuss in the essay.

Choice (c) is not good. Although stereotyping is a subject of the paragraph, the author's intentions are too vague.

UNIT 3 ◆
THE ROAD TO SUCCESS

2B. VOCABULARY FOR COMPREHENSION

1. c   6. e
2. g   7. j
3. a   8. b
4. h   9. d
5. i   10. f

3B. READING FOR MAIN IDEAS

Suggested answers

Part II. Katie's journey away from home gives her time to clarify her thoughts about her values, her family, and her future plans.

Part III. Katie's successful performance gives her the courage to continue to follow her dream.

3C. READING FOR DETAILS

1. a   5. a
2. c   6. b
3. c   7. a
4. b   8. c

3D. READING BETWEEN THE LINES

Answers will vary.

4A. EXPANDING THE TOPIC

Suggested answers

1. STAY FOCUSED. "Say 'No way!' to nifty distractions."

2. SELF-ESTEEM. "Give your best to the world without being a braggart."
SATISFACTION. "Take humble pride in all of your accomplishments."

3. CURIOSITY. "You talk, talk and talk some more to people to find out what makes them tick. You soak up information like a sunbather taking in sunshine. Take good advice."

4. ERRORS. "Never accept failure as a permanent state."

5. CHILD DRIVE. "You pay attention to inner urges that speak to you about what work you love to do."
SET GOALS. "Choose commitment."

6. ENERGY. "You maximize your energy by eating, sleeping, exercising and working in recognition of your own special rhythms."

5A. EXPLORING LANGUAGE

1. a blue-eyed boy
2. a three-cornered hat
3. a thin-lipped woman
4. a broken-hearted girl
5. a ten-year-old law
6. a ten-pound weight
7. a five-year plan

2.
1. "an oh-so-easy, wait-a-minute time-step"
2. "my knock-down, drag-out"
3. "could-you-just-die"
4. "great big Broadway-baby finish"

5B. WORKING WITH WORDS

1. take it out of you
2. the better part
3. shabby
4. to the nines
5. Reluctantly
6. miss a beat
7. picked up the pace
8. For want of
9. hold the curtain
10. backed
11. the long haul

6A. GRAMMAR

1. I
2. I
3. N: Dennis O'Grady, who is quoted in this unit, is a popular writer on motivational thinking.
4. I
5. N: A college speaker, whose exact name I've now forgotten, helped us to understand the power of positive thinking.

6. N: A modern idea, which I do not share at all, is that success can only be measured in financial terms.
7. I
8. I

3
2. A young man who entered the restaurant hungry left it with a full belly.
3. Katie, whose brother had just died, was off to find a new place in the world.
4. Katie was thinking about the mother whose son had just thrown his hat out the window of the bus.
5. Katie waited two hours at the diner, where she had an excellent view of the people lining up for the theater.
6. Tap dancing is an American dance form that was popularized by Hollywood movies.

6B. STYLE

2

Suggested answer

A person who is successful in public life does not necessarily have a happy private life.

3

Answers will vary.

UNIT 4 ◆
WATER, WATER EVERYWHERE . . .

2A. BACKGROUND

1
1. Lake Itasca
2. Gulf of Mexico
3. Cairo, Illinois

2
a. St. Louis
b. Hardin
c. Ste. Genevieve
d. Valmeyer
e. Hannibal
f. Des Moines

2B. VOCABULARY FOR COMPREHENSION

1. b
2. a
3. a
4. b
5. c
6. c
7. b
8. a
9. c
10. a

3B. READING FOR MAIN IDEAS
CAUSES

2. Levees were built to protect riverside cities.

3. In the summer of 1993, it rained more than anyone had ever before believed possible.

5. After the floodwaters receded, the evidence of all the flood damage was visible.

3C. READING FOR DETAILS
EFFECTS

1b. The reconstituted river lost its bordering flood-plain and the wetlands that would have held water when the river overflowed.

2a. There was less rich silt, more erosion, and the land no longer had the potential to absorb water.

3a. 80

3b. There was a debate about whether or not levees should be rebuilt.

4a. 50

4b. more than 10 billion dollars' worth

5a. The federal government offered disaster relief and authorized 5.7 billion dollars in aid.

5b. Private citizens volunteered to help flood victims repair the damage.

3D. READING BETWEEN THE LINES

1. f   4. e
2. d   5. c
3. b   6. a

4A. EXPANDING THE TOPIC

Available fresh water would be just over a teaspoon, less than one half of 1 percent of the total. About 97 percent of the water on our planet is seawater. Another 2 percent is locked up in ice caps and glaciers. The rest is under the earth's surface, too difficult and expensive to extract.

3, 4, 1, 5, 2

5A. EXPLORING LANGUAGE

1. *Water vehicles:*   barge, trawler, tugboat
2. *Bodies of water:*   bed, channel, river, tributary

3. *Water movement:*   bubble, cresting, floodwater, overflow, swelling, trickle, washout
4. *Flood residue:*   debris, scum, silt, sogginess

5B. WORKING WITH WORDS

1. tributaries   5. debris
2. swelling   6. silt
3. overflowed   7. channel
4. floodwaters

6A. GRAMMAR

a. Because
b. consequently
c. such . . . that

Suggested answers

1. Because the Mississippi was closed to shipping above St. Louis for two months, millions of tons of grain, fertilizer, and coal were delivered late.

   The Mississippi was closed to shipping above St. Louis for two months; consequently, millions of tons of grain, fertilizer, and coal were delivered late.

2. People at first thought that the Flood of '93 was a bad dream since there was a one in a hundred chance of a similar flood happening in any given year.

   There was a one in a hundred chance of a similar flood happening in any given year, so people at first thought that the Flood of '93 was a bad dream.

3. Since the floodwaters were being squeezed tightly by levee walls, the water ran faster and faster, stressing the levees downstream.

   The floodwaters were being squeezed tightly by levee walls; therefore, the water ran faster and faster, stressing the levees downstream.

4. The foundation of the house needed to be repainted because four feet of water had filled the first floor.

   Four feet of water had filled the first floor; consequently, the foundation of the house needed to be repainted.

3

1. The Mississippi River raged with such fury in 1993 that the river destroyed everything that came in its path.

2. The water had become so cloudy that people were now certain that the levee was losing its foundation.

3. The soil of the levees was so fertile and the property was so cheap that people moved onto the land reclaimed by the levees.

4. The floodwaters had been channeled so tightly that the water ran faster and deeper, stressing levees downstream.

4

1. such	5. that	9. therefore
2. that	6. consequently	10. such
3. Because / Since	7. so	11. that
4. so	8. since / because	

6B. STYLE

1

a. *Thesis statement:* "For if all the oceans should die—by which I mean that all life in the sea would finally cease—this would signal the end not only for marine life, but for all other animals and plants of this earth, including man."

b. *Causes:* trawlers, landfill, sticky gobs of oil, plastic refuse, poisonous effluents

c. *Effects:* decaying bodies and stench, a greenhouse effect, melting ice caps and world-wide flooding, drought, famine, disease, chaos, anoxia, death

d. There is more focus on the effects.

2

1. the sea is a cesspool → decaying bodies → stench

2. dead seas won't act as a buffer → too much carbon dioxide creating a greenhouse effect → the polar ice caps would melt → flooding of coastal cities → people moving inland

3. no rain → global drought and famine

4. the end of sea algae and land vegetation → anoxia and the end of human life

3
Correct order of sentences: 3, 4, 1, 2, 6, 7, 5

UNIT 5 ◆
WHAT IS LOST IN TRANSLATION?

2B. VOCABULARY FOR COMPREHENSION

2. attacked, pressured

3. abandon, leave behind

4. affectionate, emotional

5. restriction, moderation

6. express, release

7. unemotional, uncomplaining

8. hinder, advise against

3B. READING FOR MAIN IDEAS

	Reading One	Reading Two
1.	no	no
2.	yes	no
3.	yes	yes
4.	no	no
5.	yes	no

no = not supported by the reading
yes = supported by the reading

3C. READING FOR DETAILS
Suggested answers

1

Polish Ways

2. People can make many gestures while talking.

3. In Poland, people can stand quite close to each other while speaking.

4. In Poland, people can touch each other to show casual friendliness.

5. People say more exactly what they are thinking, even if it is sharply critical of the person they're talking to.

Canadian Ways

2. Canadians do not use their hands very much while speaking.

3. In Canada, people leave a lot of room between themselves and the person they are talking to.

4. In Canada, touching people is often seen as an aggressive act.

5. People must tone down their sharpness to be polite.

Chinese Things

2. The Chinese flag was not as pretty as the American flag.

3. In Chinese school, you had to copy ideographs with an old-fashioned and awkward pen.

4. Her grandmother's Chinese seemed loud, quick, and unbeautiful, without rhythm or organization, common.

5. When she spoke Chinese, she thought other people would think she was mad and speaking gibberish.

American Things

2. The American flag was prettier than the Chinese flag.

3. In American school, Elizabeth liked learning about multiplication, the planets and interesting books to read.

4. Americans' speech seemed gentle and refined.

5. When she spoke English, she felt that people treated her better.

3D. READING BETWEEN THE LINES
Suggested answers

1. B	5. N
2. Ev	6. Ev
3. Ev	7. B
4. El	8. B

4A. EXPANDING THE TOPIC
Answers will vary.

5A. EXPLORING VOCABULARY

2. friendliness	5. atrocities
3. embarrassment	6. storminess
4. loyalty	7. ferociousness

5B. WORKING WITH WORDS

1. fabric	8. come to terms with their roots
2. fragile	9. perpetually
3. atrocities	10. hygienic [twice]
4. asylum	11. blend in
5. beleaguered	12. loose
6. cluster	13. giving vent to
7. trapped	14. storminess

6A. GRAMMAR
2
Answers will vary.

UNIT 6 ◆
THE LANDSCAPE OF FAITH

2B. VOCABULARY FOR COMPREHENSION

2. i	6. c
3. h	7. f
4. b	8. g
5. a	9. d

3B. READING FOR MAIN IDEAS
Suggested answers

1. To the Dalai Lama, death is not to be feared. Life must have a meaning in usefulness to others.

2. The Dalai Lama feels that despite some local wars, world war has become unlikely. The public's attitude toward war and violence is very negative in many parts of the world.

3. If the Tibetan people of their own free will decide that the role of the Dalai Lama is no longer meaningful to them, there will be no more Dalai Lamas.

4. The world will disappear and come again and disappear and be reborn again in an endless cycle.

3C. READING FOR DETAILS
The Role of the Dalai Lama in the Future: 1, 6

The Dalai Lama's Attitude toward War: 3, 4, 10

The Dalai Lama's Philosophy of Death: 8, 11

The Future of the Earth: 5

(2, 7, 9 were eliminated)

5A. EXPLORING VOCABULARY

Names of Religions:	Buddhism, Christianity, Confucianism, Hinduism, Islam, Judaism
Places of Worship:	church, mosque, shrine, synagogue, temple
Religious Leaders:	bishop, clergy, monk, priest, rabbi, theologian
Religious Practices:	ordinances, prayer, rituals, worship

5B. WORKING WITH WORDS

1. b	6. c
2. c	7. b
3. a	8. b
4. a	9. c
5. a	10. c

6A. GRAMMAR

2

3. Count
4. Non-Count
5. Count

3

1. The	6. the	11. X	16. the	21. a	26. the
2. the	7. a	12. X	17. the	22. a	
3. a	8. the	13. the	18. the	23. X	
4. This	9. the	14. a	19. The	24. a	
5. the	10. the	15. a	20. the	25. X	

UNIT 7 ◆
MANAGING A CAREER

2B. VOCABULARY FOR COMPREHENSION

2. b	6. c
3. a	7. c
4. c	8. b
5. a	9. c

3C. READING FOR DETAILS

1. b	6. c
2. c	7. b
3. a	8. a
4. c	9. a
5. b	

3D. READING BETWEEN THE LINES

Suggested answers

Advantages of Temping for Employers

4. The company pays no benefits to workers other than an hourly wage.

For Employees

2. Temps learn new skills on the job while earning money.

3. Temps can have a more flexible work schedule and more independence.

Disadvantages of Temping for Employers (your ideas)

1. There is a lack of continuity on the job.

2. Customer or client relationships can suffer.

3. Morale problems can develop.

For Employees

1. Employees have no job security.

2. They are paid less than other employees who may be doing the same job.

3. They have no health benefits if they or a family member gets sick; they have no retirement fund.

4A. EXPANDING THE TOPIC

1

1. no	4. no
2. yes	5. no
3. yes	

Why? Explanations will vary.

5A. EXPLORING LANGUAGE

1. trainer	5. employer
2. interviewer	6. payees
3. employee	7. trainee
4. hirees	

5B. WORKING WITH WORDS

1. b	5. k	9. e
2. j	6. d	10. g
3. l	7. a or c	11. h
4. a or c	8. i	12. f

6A. GRAMMAR

2

Expressions with Infinitives: have the ability to lead, want the opportunity to build, invite you to join

Expressions with Gerunds: will include supervising and providing, will involve designing and putting into operation, have experience working, be comfortable communicating, are committed to achieving, are challenged by the idea of creating

4

1. supervising	6. designing
2. to take on	7. putting
3. to grow	8. being
4. to work	9. hearing
5. responding	10. to learn

UNIT 8 ◆
WHEN THE SOLDIER IS A WOMAN...

3B. READING FOR MAIN IDEAS

1. F
2. F
3. F
4. F
5. T

4A. EXPANDING THE TOPIC

1

1. c, d
2. a, b
3. a, b, c
4. a, b, c, d

2

Suggested answers

1. The United Nations encouraged the women to form cooperatives and build local businesses in order to help the country recover from the devastation of war. Cooperatives are a good way to build capital by pooling the abilities and earning power of several people. The UN probably also wished to encourage women in their efforts to become productive citizens.

2. The women learned skills and discipline in the army, and they learned to have confidence in their own abilities. They also had a taste of what it is like to be treated as an equal. Even if their options are quite limited in the present, the memory of their experiences may help them and the next generation of women to develop business skills and take a larger role in society.

5A. EXPLORING VOCABULARY

1

1. medical	5. technical
2. military	6. sexual
3. traditional	7. tribal
4. patriarchal	8. aerial

2

1. voluntary
2. recreational
3. vehicular
4. ministerial

5B. WORKING WITH WORDS

1

1. b	5. a
2. c	6. a
3. a	7. c
4. c	

6A. GRAMMAR

2

Suggested answers

1. At her interview today, she said that her unit, the 11th Air Defense Artillery Brigade, had been put on alert last night.

2. She admitted that she was scared but not of the war.

3. She explained that she didn't want to leave her family behind.

4. She told us that all she had been able to think about was her family.

5. She wondered if she would ever see them again.

6. She thought that this was one of the hardest things she would ever have to face.

7. She told us that the soldiers were strong. She added that they were there to fight if they had to, to keep the rest of the world, especially U.S. citizens, safe from harm.

3

Suggested answers

8. Mr. Martin said, "I was in the Army until June 1990."

9. He said, "I started taking care of the children at that time."

10. He said, "My son is learning to walk and run and he misses his mother."

11. He said, "We talk to her on the phone every two weeks."

UNIT 9 ◆
THE CELLIST OF SARAJEVO

2B. VOCABULARY FOR COMPREHENSION

2

2. h	7. d
3. b	8. j
4. f	9. g
5. i	10. k
6. a	11. e

3B. READING FOR MAIN IDEAS

3, 4, 6

3C. READING FOR DETAILS

6, 1, 8, 4, 3, 5, 2, 7

5A. EXPLORING LANGUAGE

agonized: sadness
cheering: happiness
emotional: happiness, sadness, anger
exuberant: happiness
haunting: sadness
mournful: sadness
moving: happiness, sadness
ominous: sadness, anger
raging: anger
screaming: sadness, anger
slashing: sadness, anger
solitary: happiness, sadness

5B. WORKING WITH WORDS

1. relaxing
2. horrified
3. terrifying
4. terrified
5. inspired
6. haunting

6A. GRAMMAR

Suggested answers

2. It was decided to give money to the school creative arts program.

   This sentence is better in the active voice because it expresses a specific fact and not a general truth. Furthermore, it is important to know that the money is coming from the government and not from private donors or businesses or charities.

3. It is said that many musicians will be dismissed.

   This sentence is better in the impersonal passive because this format distances the writer from any direct responsibility and because there is no official source for this statement.

4. It is claimed that the imagination is the link to our innermost feelings.

   Imagination is believed to be the link to our innermost feelings.

This sentence is better in the active voice because it is a belief attributed to a specific and very important person. Putting the sentence in the passive is possible but weakens its overall meaning by leaving out the agent.

5. It is believed that an education in the arts develops sensitivity.

   An education in the arts is believed to develop sensitivity.

   This sentence can be in the impersonal passive because it is not necessary to identify the agent. This general thought could be a universal truth.

Suggested answers

1. *"The creative arts are said to have a healing effect on children."* Best choice

   "It is said that the creative arts have a healing effect on children." Another possibility

   This topic sentence should be in the impersonal passive because it is reporting an idea; the focus of the sentence should be on "the creative arts" and their effects, not on the vague agent, "people."

2. *"Administrators at the Illinois Department of Children's Services are known to be active supporters of this method."*

   This sentence should be in the impersonal passive because "we know" is a very unclear formulation; who is "we" in this sentence? The focus should shift to concentrate on reporting the ideas of the Children's Services' workers.

3. This sentence should stay as it is.

4. This sentence should stay as it is.

5. This sentence could stay as it is, but it could also be changed: *"Many children are said to be learning how to relieve their tensions by drawing pictures about fighting instead of actually fighting."*

   The impersonal passive would leave out "teachers, administrators, and others in the program" because it is generally understood that teachers, administrators, and others would be the people who would naturally comment on the program.

6. If the previous sentence is left in the active voice, this one should be in the active voice, too. If the sentence is changed to the impersonal passive, this one should be changed, too.

"It is also claimed that some of the children . . . are convinced there is a definite connection between these great artists and themselves."

6B. STYLE

Suggested answers

1. The descriptive language of this paragraph falls under four categories: facts, sights, sounds, and the author's value judgments.

   Facts: that the shell had made, dead, hurt

   Sights: full, formal, raging around him, placing a plastic chair beside the crater, abandoned, smashed, burning, terrified, who hid in the cellars, while the bombs dropped and bullets flew, with masonry exploding around him

   Sounds: raging around him, burning, terrified, while the bombs dropped and bullets flew, with masonry exploding around him

   Author's Value Judgments: mournful, haunting, unimaginably courageous, for human dignity, for those lost to war, for civilization, for compassion and for peace

2. put on . . . took up . . . walked out . . ., abandoned streets, smashed trucks, and burning buildings, and to the terrified people; for human dignity, for those lost to war, for civilization, for compassion and for peace

3. "He played to the abandoned streets, smashed trucks and burning buildings, and to the terrified people who hid in the cellars while the bombs dropped and bullets flew."

   This sentence is the most important sentence of the paragraph because it summarizes the full drama of Smailovic's heroic action, which was repeated for twenty-two days in the midst of the dangers described.

3

1. *Adjectives:* freed, right, first, cool, humble
   Adjective phrases: after improvising for a while, in the darkness, freed of the task, through my skin, like a trickle, like a fountain of cool water, bubbling up, from a hole, in the middle of a desert, sitting on the floor, in front of me, cleaning her paws and purring loudly

2. the right phrasing, the right intonation, the right bowing

   slowly, joyfully, gratefully

   like a trickle, . . . like a fountain

   sitting, . . . cleaning, . . . , purring

3. Only two sentences start with a subject-verb pattern:

   "The notes sang out, first like a trickle, then like a fountain of cool water bubbling up from a hole in the middle of a desert."

   "I had an audience again, humble as it was."

   They are important sentences of the paragraph because in each instance they give the simple facts, the conclusions or results of aspects of the process of rediscovering his musical ear, which the narrator describes in the other sentences.

UNIT 10 ◆
THE RIGHT TO READ

1B. SHARING INFORMATION

The question is not whether most Americans agree or disagree with flag burning, pornography, and so on, but whether such expression is protected under the Constitution's guarantee of free speech. Examples of speech that are *not* protected by the First Amendment include libel (destroying a private person's reputation in writing), slander (destroying such a reputation in speech), and inciting to riot. Even in these cases, however, there is no "prior restraint," meaning that the government cannot forbid the publication of a book or article. The authors assume the responsibility and suffer the consequences if their work is prosecuted in the courts after the fact.

1. In the United States, there are no laws against blasphemy (insulting a religion), and according to the separation of religion and the state written into the First Amendment, people can think and write what they choose about God.

2. Citizens have burned the American flag as a protest against war—for example, during the Vietnam War and the Gulf War. The Supreme

Court ruled that flag burning is allowed as free speech protest.

3. In 1996 a federal court ruled that the Internet, "the never-ending, world-wide conversation" and "the most participatory form of mass speech yet developed," deserves "the highest protection from government intrusion." In other words, there should be no censorship on the Internet. There is not even any government regulation of the Internet, as there is for television. However, any kind of pornography involving children on the Internet and everywhere else is illegal and is prosecuted. Parents can obtain special software to block inappropriate Internet material for their children.

4. Threats to free speech have existed in America in times of war (during the Civil War, President Lincoln barred mail and newspapers sympathetic to the enemy; Socialists were jailed for encouraging resistance to World War I). During the cold war in the late 1940s and 1950s, people were jailed or lost their jobs for being Communists. During the Vietnam War, however, many people encouraged opposition to the war and were not arrested.

5. The press and public in the United States are free to criticize the president as they choose.

6. In the 1973 case *Miller v. California*, the Supreme Court declared that a work must be "patently offensive" (obviously disgusting) and lack all artistic, literary, political, or scientific value to be declared legally obscene. Because a definition of *obscenity* is difficult to arrive at, it is very difficult to get juries to prosecute such a crime. In addition, many (if not most) Americans dislike the idea of censorship. In 1985 the Parents Music Resource Center began encouraging the use of warning labels placed on musical recordings whose material is considered inappropriate for children under age eighteen.

2B. VOCABULARY FOR COMPREHENSION

1. i	5. j	9. e
2. a	6. k	10. b
3. h	7. g	11. d
4. c	8. l	12. f

3B. READING FOR MAIN IDEAS

Suggested answers

Marcia Cohen's Answers

1b. Censors do not consider the artistic value of a work that has bad words in it. They do not realize that an author's use of vulgar language may serve a definite purpose.

2a. When you give in to some people's demands, you limit other people's freedom and teach intolerance.

2b. Through education, we should learn to be tolerant and respectful of differences. We cannot learn to be that way if books with unwanted ideas are banned.

2c. Students need to learn how to think critically, to ask intelligent questions, and to form their own opinions.

2d. Teachers should teach their students how to think and not what to think. Therefore, class discussions about ideas reflecting many different points of view should be encouraged.

2e. Book censorship not only threatens our freedom to learn, but also puts our other rights in danger.

3C. READING FOR DETAILS

1. c
2. b
3. c
4. a
5. a

5A. EXPLORING LANGUAGE

1. access, access, accessible, accessibly
2. X, conduct, conducive, X
3. confusion, confuse, confused, confusedly
4. exposure, expose, exposed, X
5. inhibition, inhibit, inhibited/inhibiting, inhibitedly
6. offense, offend, offensive, offensively
7. profanity, profane, profane, profanely
8. removal, remove, removed/removable, X
9. shield, shield, X, X
10. vulnerability, X, vulnerable, vulnerably

5B. WORKING WITH WORDS

1. remove
2. offensive
3. profanities
4. access
5. vulnerable
6. exposed
7. confused
8. shield
9. inhibiting
10. conducive

6A. GRAMMAR

1. has been
2. published, was
3. was published, had . . . become
4. was published, had . . . been
5. had enjoyed
6. died, were . . . questioning
7. are
8. will have been read

❸

1. made
2. ruled
3. had become
4. put
5. supported
6. had removed
7. was made
8. had enjoyed
9. has been
10. are
11. will not be prepared
12. legalizes
13. will have succeeded

6B. STYLE

❷

Support in paragraph 4: <u>"Perhaps by examining this work as a whole . . . emphasizes Salinger's message and serves a definite purpose."</u>

Concession in paragraph 3: "The censors may mean well;"